Writing is the only way I can think of to form something new from a man who's already gone, writes Kelly O'Dell Stanley. What a gift to the reader as she excavates her relationship with her father in authentic and transparent prose. Such a positive story of love and loss that is relatable to everyone. The story is centered and creative; solid, yet surprising. Bravo. Bravo.

Gwynn Wills, Amherst Writers and Artists Workshop Facilitator;
Founder, Calliope Writers Group

Kelly O'Dell Stanley's *The Artist* evokes all the adoration and tension of growing up with a well-known artist for a father. When her mother, then father, famed watercolorist Rob O'Dell, die she weighs their impact on her identity. How did they shape her upbringing and her gifts? The same Midwestern humbleness and excellence that characterized her father and his art shines through her writing, drawing us all into the place, family, and self-discovery we too easily overlook in rural America and ourselves.

Maria Reynolds-Weir, writer

How do you tell the story of a loved one's life? In *The Artist*, Kelly O'Dell Stanley's writing—an antidote to grief—combines her incandescent voice with her father's notable watercolors to create a masterpiece of its own design. What does it mean to be an artist? Value your unique perspective, use your gifts. In this stunning book, both O'Dells model just that.

Melissa Fraterrigo, author of *Glory Days*

Kelly O'Dell Stanley paints her words with a vibrant palette of grief, identity, unwavering love, and the power art has to mix it all together to find one's true colors. Written with resiliency and vulnerability, *The Artist* is a story for all of the dreamers who seek the courage to answer one of life's most formidable questions: "What if?"

J.R. Jamison, award-winning author of *Hillbilly Queer: A Memoir*

In moments like little paintings, Kelly O'Dell Stanley's *The Artist, Ladoga, Indiana* brings her father Rob O'Dell alive, capturing not only what made him the gifted painter he was but his influence on her own journey as an artist.

Barbara Shoup, *An American Tune*

Kelly O'Dell Stanley writes the way her father painted, working with genuine affection for her subjects, paying attention to the smallest, most important details, and revealing as truthfully as possible the life she has seen, heard, lived, and felt.

There's wonder in the ways she brings his paintings to life in words as masterful as his brushstrokes.

And while O'Dell Stanley honestly captures the pain of losing her father, *The Artist* is also a book of faith and resurrection: faith that we find our true selves when we deeply love another; and resurrection in the ways we live on in the lives of those we love and who loved us."

Steve Charles, former editor of *Wabash Magazine,* Editor of The New Platypus Review, and author of the forthcoming memoir *The Generous Year*

In 2024, collectors continue to inquire if we have any art by Rob O'Dell. They ask by name, and they ask by style. "Do you have any work by the man who created the scenes with the white snow and white sky?" Rob was the master of negative space and the king of small details. Rob's work was and is timeless, identifiable, and completely unique. When is a rural scene not just another rural scene? When it's an O'Dell!

Juli Petter, J Petter Galleries

Rob was a friend and mentor to many. In his easy manner he was always willing to share his unique skills with like-minded people. Personally, he was my role model and inspiration when I was a fledgling artist considering painting as a more serious endeavor.

Jerry Smith, Dolphin Fellow of the American Watercolor Society

As a daughter who lost her father the same year as Kelly O'Dell Stanley, I read *The Artist* with a lump in my throat. Written with love and warmth, *The Artist* is a remarkable memoir and celebration of a daughter's love for her father and a respect for his artistic talent. In honest prose, often flowing into poetry, Kelly brings a mixture of tender and hard moments, joy and loss, what it means to carry the O'Dell name and her father's legacy, and how it shapes her own creative journey and discovery.

Jama Kehoe Bigger, author of *Then Came a Miracle*,
former director of Midwest Writers Workshop

The Artist, Ladoga, Indiana is a true story of two artists, father and daughter, and their different paths to the same address, where a studio continues to connect them after the father's death. It tells how a daughter dealt with grief: what she lost, what she kept, and what she became while rebuilding a life.

Lisa Wheeler, writer

An authentic portrait of family, grief, and self-searching. This touching memoir will inspire you to take a scenic drive in the country, hug your loved ones, and perhaps even pick up a paintbrush.

Sherry Stanfa-Stanley
Author of *Finding My Badass Self: A Year of Truths and Dares*

LADOGA, INDIANA

a memoir by
KELLY O'DELL STANLEY

For Daddy O, the best dad
a girl could ever have,
and for all those
whose lives he touched.

To view some of the paintings
described in these pages, visit
robodellart.com/the-artist-book/

being an artist
IS LIKE BEING
yourself
FOR A LIVING.

—Emily McDowell

ONCE UPON A MOMENT

10″ x 14″

Description: Close-up
of rusted bucket hanging
upside down over a
weathered fence post

A Hallmark envelope the color of a cloudless summer sky
appeared in our mailbox. The big loopy cursive nearly filled the
rectangle but contained only four words, "*The Artist, Ladoga,
Indiana*," with a stamp. The St. Louis postmark had us baffled
until Dad sliced the envelope open with his pocketknife. Jim
and Jeannine, longtime friends of my parents, sent the card as
an experiment: Would it make its way to him with only those
identifying words? They were amused by the quaintness of our
rural, small town, and simultaneously aware of my dad's far-
reaching fame.

Naturally, the woman at the post office took one glance and
dropped it in the slot for Rural Route 2, Box 129, and the mail
carrier didn't bat an eye as he slammed closed the flimsy metal
door of the mailbox at the end of our driveway. It's not like
there was more than one artist in Ladoga, and this was before
the days of the very-detailed 911 addresses, so it wasn't really all
that difficult to figure out that this letter was intended for Rob
O'Dell.

But it *was* pretty funny.

We all have our things we're known for, and when Dad died, we knew exactly what his thing was. Of course we would display his paintings at his funeral. There was no better way to remind those who loved him of who he was, to more eloquently and simply honor the way he made this world a more beautiful place.

It wasn't until later that I thought, *Who does that? Who else is so defined by what they do, what they make, that it makes sense to be honored in that way?*

Artists are different kinds of creatures. What we create shows the world who we are. We must be supremely confident in our ability to see/make/produce/form/create—and eternally battle a profound insecurity that whispers, *What if other people don't see what I see? What if I fail? What if my friends have been lying to me about my talent and the world discovers that I am an imposter? What will I do if this doesn't work out? Maybe I shouldn't even try.*

I suspect that the fear of being found out—of the world noticing all the ways we are ordinary and unspectacular—is always there, whether you're an artist or not. But the spark that drives *me* to create, the same spark that inspired my dad's work (and life), burns just a tiny bit stronger than the fear. Sometimes it burns so bright and hot I wonder if my soul will literally combust. At other times, it sustains and nourishes me. Occasionally it splutters and wanes, threatening to go out completely. But a nagging insistence deep inside tells me that it cannot be ignored. No one else in the world can do or say just the same thing in quite the same way. If I don't do what I'm called to do, the world will miss out on something important.

And, dare I say, irreplaceable.

I'll never be the same kind of talent as my dad. No one else was exactly like him. It isn't because of what he painted or how he rendered the shapes. It wasn't only a matter of advanced techniques and a lifetime of practice. It was about what he said to people through his art. That they are seen. Known. Valued, in spite of the imperfections.

So that day, as mourners filed through the church whispering their condolences, hugging and shaking hands and reconnecting with lost acquaintances, I stood at the front of the church and felt surrounded by love. Dad's watercolors encircled the room, as integral to the murmured conversations as the actual words people spoke. They connected people to each other. They reminded people how remarkable Dad was.

At his celebration of life, those paintings gave us a gift: Dad, tangible and present again. His watercolors ensured that even when he was gone, some part of him would remain. They said, *Don't worry. You may feel lonely, but you are also beautiful. And you are never alone.*

Even when, like me, they've been left behind.

vignette

Watercolor is, as its name implies, a wet medium. You can't apply the pigment without adding water, and a good watercolorist takes advantage of the inherent properties of the paints. One of my dad's techniques involved sprinkling ordinary table salt onto paper where the paint was damp. As the salt crystals soaked up the water, they'd also absorb some of the pigment. When the paint was fully dry, he would gently brush off the dried salt, leaving behind a delicate lacy white pattern—in one painting, the effect looks like the tops of weeds lining a roadside, in another, a sprinkling of delicate wildflowers, or perhaps dappled sunlight filtering through the trees on a sunny day.

This technique doesn't work if the paint is too wet. Or if it's too dry. Over time, Dad learned just the right moment to apply the salt for maximum effect—so that it leaves the desired mark.

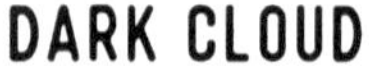

DARK CLOUD

22" x 29"

Description: Trees along a
fencerow, seemingly bracing
for the onslaught against a
dramatic gray sky

A cluster of barns, stately but rickety, huddle together against the falling snow.

A row of birds, mere dots from this distance, line the sagging roofline before taking to the air again.

Meadows of dancing wildflowers—fuchsia and yellow and pure white—shimmy in the spring breeze.

Strong, vibrant, blazing orange and gold trees line a fencerow, a backdrop much too spectacular for the dilapidated wooden gate propped precariously in the foreground on concrete blocks.

In the quiet evenings, the sun drops below the horizon while laundry hangs stiffly on the line between the house and barn. Nothing stirs in the silence of the day's end.

I sort through stacks and stacks of unframed rectangles of watercolor paper, all with that peculiar stiffness of colored pigments hardened on textured, heavy paper that was taped flat to a drawing board to dry. The paint is thin, sheer, conforming to the topography of the paper on which it lies, but the residue of the salt crystals that created texture in the painted landscapes remains, leaving the sheets feeling gritty and crusty.

My dad, Rob O'Dell, has painted rural Midwestern landscapes for his entire 50-year career. When my sister was young, she told her teacher that her daddy painted barns, and the teacher pictured a man in white pants up on a very big ladder.

Dad was the other kind of barn painter.

He may not be a household name, but even putting aside my obvious bias, I can objectively say he is a talented and accomplished watercolorist, having won awards from the Hoosier Salon, Indiana Watercolor Society, and numerous art fairs and exhibitions, and selling work to collectors around the world. He's supported our family full-time, my whole life, with nothing but his art. He has a way of taking the monotony of Indiana farmland and rendering its quiet, ordinary beauty in a way that is extraordinary. He is amazing.

Was. Not *is*—*was*. I cannot make myself get the tense right. Because maybe if I don't give in to the rules of grammar, if I stubbornly and persistently refuse to accept the *was* and hold tightly to the *is*, he won't really be gone.

Alone in my dad's studio, in the quiet of the echoing space with soggy tissues tucked into my pocket, I reverently set each piece aside. The flat file drawers are full of forgotten pieces, interspersed with scraps of mat board, copies of old prints with damaged corners, and artwork by others that Dad traded for through the years.

The remnants of his life's work, which once felt ordinary and commonplace to me because I've witnessed it all my life, now seem so fragile and precarious. No more Indiana barns, no more hollyhocks, no more trees or sagging fences or faded Coca-Cola signs or rusted buckets upside down on wooden posts. No more of Dad's ordinary, everyday paintings that I had seen so many times that I stopped appreciating their nuances.

I slowly excavate the contents of each drawer, holding my breath and hoping for the profound discovery that will change everything. The one that will make it feel like Dad is still here, that will unlock something long lost and left behind. That will explain why he kept an unfinished drawing, or why he cut a landscape in half and started a new painting on the back of it, or why he chose to stash a beautifully rendered painting in a drawer instead of framing it.

Lord, can you please just let Dad speak to me? One more time? Something, anything.

A noisy farm truck passes outside the plate glass windows fronting the turn-of-the-century, small-town-downtown building that served as my dad's studio. I grab a pencil to knock away a cobweb hanging from the light poised above his painting table, and as I lower myself into his chair, it rolls backward on the hardwood floor. My gaze traces the white enamel trays of brushes, ranging from his "49-er," a cheap hardware store favorite, to a delicate, tapered natural sable brush, or a one-inch-wide, flat wash brush that lists for $83.99. I pull out my phone to document this holy tableau he left behind. These brushes, as familiar as his hands, were carefully rinsed, the bristles gently smoothed back into shape, laid down just so in preparation for the next day's work. These sponges smoothly spread water across the page before splashes of pigment bloomed into a sky. That particular shade of brown, dried in the middle of the tray, was the last color he ever mixed.

Dad's only been gone a few days, but the air in this place feels dusty and stale. Still, I don't disturb his things. Maybe then he'll come back.

My heart is both full to overflowing and wrung out. My soul, hushed and expectant. If the definition of "holy" is "set apart," then this moment in this space is surely a sanctified one.

I glance again at the large painting I pulled out of the flat files. Although I flipped past it at first—just another tree—it keeps drawing me back.

A lone tree, ancient and regal. Bare winter branches with peeling bark, crooked and broken limbs stretched wide toward the sky. Oh, that sky. Threatening and oppressive, the dense gray clouds are barely restraining the imminent downpour. The sky feels so heavy that I can sense the atmospheric pressure pushing down on me, feel the humidity in the air. Strong and beautiful in its vulnerability, the tree is laid bare before the elements. It stands tall and majestic, remaining upright in the face of the storm.

Just as Dad coaxed that dense, oppressive feeling from the sky with the perfect combination of brushstrokes and colors and water and pigment, this painting is coaxing out my grief. The sycamore doesn't know what I've so recently learned: The storm isn't coming. For me, it has already passed.

And yet, against all odds, there it stands.

I stomp my foot and cry, "Dammit, dammit, dammit." Then burst into tears again.

vignette

Solitary objects such as a chair, a plow, or a bucket become a completed composition. The artist's precise ability to produce the colors and texture of wood make[s] them pleasing to view. Titles seem to be important also. A large wooden bucket entitled "Saturday Night" allows the viewer to imagine illusions beyond the simple object presented.

Compositions within compositions are produced by the artist painting a scene viewed through windows of a building. The effect is again one of loneliness because the artist creates the illusion of distance, by separating the observer from the scene.

—Mary Pat Hough, a review of Rob O'Dell's first one-man show at Welna Galleries,
Chicago Tribune, October 19, 1968

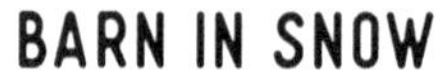

BARN IN SNOW

20" x 30"

Description: Aged brown
barn and rickety snow fence
in a sea of white

Not long after Dad died, my sister's husband, Doug, sent a group text to my sister and me. It read:

Trivia contest:

1 pt for guessing where I am

1 pt for guessing the artist

3 points for guessing the classic title

It was followed by a snapshot of a large painting hanging on a white wall. A bold, dramatic, weathered barn filled the right two-thirds of the paper. The edge of the snow-covered roofline (white against a white sky) was defined by the bare branches of a tree peeking out from behind it. An old snow fence meandered across the paper in a somewhat wobbly manner, leading to an old wooden gate that was propped open by a concrete block. Minimal color—grays, browns, black, and white.

I recognized our local library, so I felt slightly confident in guessing the location, but the artist was a no-brainer. Definitely my dad. So I replied (in a hurry, trying to beat my sister), choosing the most obvious of Dad's old standby titles for my answer: **Library. Robert Vernon. Friday Flurries.**

Doug often referred to my dad by his middle name, Vernon, just as we called Doug by his middle name, Eugene.

Doug replied: **Kelly has 2 points. Nice try on the title.**

Damn. Since *Friday Flurries* was one of Dad's favorite titles—and there are probably a hundred different paintings of his out there with that title—I thought maybe I'd luck out.

I tried again. ***Winter Whites?***

Doug answered, **A little too fancy! The title reminds me of my dogs named Browny and Blacky.**

Ahh. Got it. ***Barn in Snow?***

I laughed when Doug replied, **Ding ding!!! Classic.**

As creative as my dad was, he wasn't a word person. Don't get me wrong—he could be creative *with* words (and, in particular, the way he would spell them), but he wasn't opposed to using the same titles again and again. If it worked once, it would work the next two or three dozen times. He felt no shame about that.

On the other hand, he had a gift for simply saying what he meant and leaving pretension out of it. Maybe that's just who Dad was, or maybe it was the result of not being raised in an academic environment. Dad always joked that he graduated 36th in a class of 35 in a one-room schoolhouse. He was probably exaggerating, but I've seen the report cards—lots of C's and D's, with A's in art and physical education.

After high school, Dad joined the Army and Mom went to Indiana University School of Nursing. Shortly after they were married, they moved to the Rogers Park neighborhood in Chicago. Mom worked as an X-ray technician to help put Dad through art school. Although he studied commercial art, he discovered he really loved to paint—but he had to be practical and make a living. After graduating from the American Academy of Art, he was hired to do Sears catalog layouts, in part because he was so good at doing pen and ink product illustrations. Dad told a reporter in 1985, "I worked 60 hours a week on a drawing board, with the two-martini lunch and everything. I couldn't hack it."[1]

On his own time, he explored watercolor techniques he'd learned from his favorite teacher at the Academy, Irving Shapiro. Before long, he began exhibiting his work at art fairs on weekends.

Dad liked to tell the story of an interview he had while in art school. "Ann's father had suggested I contact a certain president of an advertising firm. I took my three pencil sketches and one watercolor of cocker spaniel puppies, which I had copied from a post card. I didn't have a folio to carry them in so I wrapped them in plastic wrap. By the time I got to his office the wrapping was loose, the pictures had rubbed together and smudged and were in pretty bad shape. I told him I'd be willing to do anything, scrub floors, wash windows, anything. Needless to say I didn't get the job." Dad saw the man at one of his shows many years later and asked him how he kept from laughing out loud during the interview. "He said it hadn't been easy but he realized I was so sincere that he just held it back."[2]

While he was working, Mom would take me for walks around the neighborhood in my baby buggy. We'd return covered in soot and sweat, because it wasn't easy for my tiny 100-pound mother to lug her exuberantly chubby, redheaded baby (and late-'60s-style oversized stroller) up and down three flights of stairs. My parents liked the neighborhood—well, except for the multiple stabbings they viewed through the windows of our brownstone walk-up.

Dad continued to sell out at his weekend art fairs, and they began to wonder: Could he make a living as an artist? Was that even possible? Was it worth trying? Maybe, but only if the cost of living was low and the place they lived was safe.

"I was insatiable. After work, I'd come home and paint," Dad told me in 2014 on the way home from an art show. He didn't know I had activated the Voice Record app on the phone sitting in my lap. His work was being noticed and he had discovered something he loved. On top of that, he had a lovely wife and a darling baby girl. (His words, not mine.)

One of Mom and Dad's favorite weekend getaways early in their marriage was to visit Mom's grandparents, Glenn (known as "Lop" to his friends and "Boppy" to us) and Anna ("Mamaw") Walsh. They lived in a quaint little town of about a thousand people. Ladoga was quiet and pretty and right on the railway line, a straight shot from Chicago. In 1968, when I was 11 months old, my great-grandparents offered to let Mom and Dad move into a deserted farmhouse five miles east of Ladoga—for free—if they'd do the work needed to make it livable. It had been built by George Otterman, my mom's great-grandfather, in the late 1800s.

The price was right. Dad was hopeful. Mom wanted a change. It was now or never.

Dad's boss, Barney Donnelley, was a frustrated artist himself, and he offered Dad the gifts of security ("Your job will be here waiting if you want to come back") and belief ("I don't think you'll need to come back"). "I'll always have a job for you," he told Dad. "But now's the time to see if you can ride this success any further."

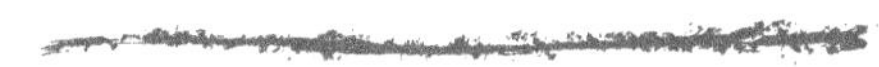

More than ten years after Dad and I talked while driving home from the 2014 art fair, long after both Mom and Dad were gone, I found a letter Mom had written to her parents when I was just a few months old.

> We've made a hard decision after several years of thinking, and six months of serious planning. We're moving to the farm in June. We're both awfully unhappy in Chicago. We've had dreams of living in the country since we've been married and circumstances have just snowballed until we're heading for permanence in a life we don't want. We've had great philosophical discussions about whether the purpose of life is to do what is expected or to try to do what will make you happy. I suppose it seems irresponsible to try to buck the system and do what you want. … Our final decision is that we must try it for a year. We know if we hold off any longer it'll be too late and we'll never know.

Mom went on to say that if Dad didn't make enough from his art, he could do carpentry work, paint, drive a tractor or truck. But hopefully that wouldn't be necessary because of all the additional paintings he could do and time and proximity to market his work across Indiana and Illinois. Welna, his Chicago gallery, had agreed to continue carrying his work.

Mom wrote:

> It can be done—we know of several people that have made it and don't have nearly the potential Bob does. … I have so much faith in him and in us. His art is at a turning point, and I feel with proper concentration and enough time, he can make it as an artist.

She closed the letter with this:

> Don't think of us as failures. We merely think that we have the means to live the life that we want, and must find out if it is possible before we get too stuck in the mud to pursue a goal like this. … We don't ever seem to do the things you'd

have us do, and it makes me awfully sorry, but we have to live with ourselves first. ... And we'll know much more what our capabilities are, and whether it's true that you can get what you're willing to work for.

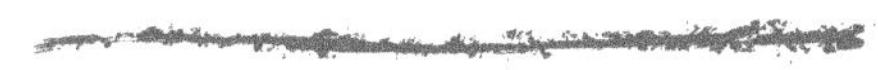

I'd known they had taken a big risk to try to make a living solely on Dad's art, but when I heard the story growing up, Mom and Dad conveniently left out the part about defying their parents. Oh, how I wish I could ask them about it now.

That day in 2014 as I recorded Dad, though, I didn't know any of that.

"What a chance we took," Dad said. "We had a new car and didn't owe anyone anything."

The three of us moved in with Mom's grandparents while Mom and Dad started cleaning out the decrepit farmhouse. Mom discovered journals in the attic written by her great-grandfather, George Otterman, detailing how he'd built the barns and house. Years later, she got the property certified as a Hoosier Homestead Farm, a designation awarded to land that had remained in the same family for over 100 years.

It was a safe place for Mom to build a life with her little family. No one locked their doors. People shouted, "The keys is in it," when you needed to move their cars. In this community, she could get away from the suburban country-club lifestyle she grew up in, where people evaluated houses by hanging-feet of closet space and drove only luxury vehicles. Status had never mattered to her. She just really loved being in this place they'd transformed into a home, reading library books on the front porch swing, making homemade soups ... pretty much whatever she wanted. She played Bunco with friends one night a month, volunteered with the PTO when my sister and I were in school, even took some pottery classes and photography workshops and briefly partnered with a friend to open a home decor store in town. Eventually she volunteered with the EMTs, and when I was 16, she went back to school to complete her nursing degree.

Incidentally, Dad never did any other jobs. He started selling enough art right away to support us and restore the house.

On weekends, my family traveled to about 15 art fairs a year. Dad's biggest following was in his and Mom's shared hometown of Decatur, Illinois. Before I was born, when Dad was still in art school and painting on the side, his parents had told him about Arts in the Park, a new downtown art festival. He went, the first time he'd publicly displayed his work—and it was the site of his first-ever sale.

"I sold a painting for $40 that year and thought I was rich," he said in an interview on the 50th anniversary of that same art fair. "I immediately wanted to do more and more. I knew that's what I wanted to do for the rest of my life."

Arts in the Park was home to his greatest-ever single weekend of sales, too. Maybe not in dollars sold, but in the currency artists so often lack—affirmation. In the early 1970s, he arrived at the park early to set up his booth, and as he unpacked, he began to attract a crowd of onlookers.

"I was unloading the truck, and by the time I finished unloading, we had sold every single painting we brought," he said. "I never even got a chance to show the work. It's never happened to me anywhere else, not even close."

Still, though, there were many years when people met him at the curb, helping him unload the back of his vehicle in order to have first dibs on the newest Rob O'Dell paintings. At other early art fairs, he sometimes sold out on the first day of a weekend-long show, and then painted all night long so he could sell more the next day.

Dad's parents were proud of him, but they never imagined

that anyone could make a living from their art. They had minimal education—my grandpa completed sixth grade, spent a few years in the Navy, and then had his own cabinet shop in the back of the house. My grandma, who'd completed eighth grade, worked in a school cafeteria. Dad was the third of six kids they raised. Art wasn't practical enough to be on their radar.

But my mom's parents had education, money, and large, affluent social circles. Willie ("Dot") was head of radiology at the local hospital, and "Mah," my grandma, had been trained as a nurse and did lots of social and volunteer work—like running the Medical Auxiliary and hosting luncheons. My mom had a younger brother, Mike, who served in Vietnam, never married, and lived at home until he died in the late '70s of brain cancer.

I've found letters from both Mah and Dot written to my parents, very harshly explaining all the reasons they should not get engaged. They needed to wait and see if they were really right for each other. Although Bob, as he was known then, was "a very polite young man" whose parents had raised him well, they weren't sold on the match. But once it was clear that Bob and Annie were staying together, Mah and Dot recognized Dad's talent (and perhaps lack of other career options). Since of course they wanted him to be able to provide a good life for my mom, and they were all about the value of education, they encouraged Dad to go to art school after the Army. (Apparently their encouragement didn't extend to his moving to rural Indiana, turning his back on commercial art and city living a few years later). Still, though, once the decision was made, my grandparents made sure their doctor friends saw Dad's work, and they leapt at the chance to buy Dad's early paintings—they saw them as investments. From there, the word spread.

Two years into what was becoming a successful career gamble, my sister, Kerry, came along. I was chubby with bright orange hair, but Kerry was slim and delicate, like Mom. A little curly-haired blonde who carried her Raggedy Ann doll everywhere.

We grew up having Mom and Dad both at home. Mom cooked a hot breakfast most days, and after Dad was done eating, he started painting. When we first moved into the farmhouse, Dad's studio was in the enclosed back porch, but apparently his children were chatterboxes who spent too much time hanging on the folding gate separating him from the rest of the house, so he decided to move a little farther away.

The building that became his studio started its life as a "summer kitchen," just outside the back door opposite a milk house. In the 1940s, someone moved it to its present location about 200 feet behind the house, next to the barn, and for the next 20 years it served as a granary. When Kerry and I proved to be so talkative, Mom and Dad emptied out the little building, ran electricity to it, and installed an oil stove and a large picture window with good morning light, by which Dad set up his drafting table. A few years later, with the tiny building bursting at the seams from paintings stacked against every wall, Dad added a second room to provide gallery space. He worked out there until 1990, when he bought the building in downtown Ladoga (four miles from their house).

Because there had once been a separate summer kitchen outside, the original kitchen in the house was tiny. Knowing that people gather where the food is, my parents tore down walls and expanded it to a 20-foot-square room. Two large picture windows butted up next to each other in one corner, clad in macramé window hangings and custom-made stained glass panels of leaves in greens and golds and browns. The built-in window seats beneath were filled with the types of kitchen gadgets most people then didn't have space to store—ice cream maker, electric skillet, ice bucket. Since the old farmhouse was drafty, we eventually added a wood-burning stove, which relocated the table to the center of the room.

I remember sitting around that table, a chunky wooden antique that was smack-dab in the center of the room. The wooden base was painted barn red with a round butcher-block top. Each of us had our own spots. Until Kerry was in middle school, she sat in a wooden antique chair with a raised seat. We called it the high chair, but it wasn't meant for kids. Still, though, she was small and didn't mind the boost. I sat next to her, with my back to the TV, which was tuned to the 5 p.m. news and every IU basketball game ever played (particularly during the Bob Knight years). Everyone in my family was a huge sports fan—except me. I'd rather be reading, but I wasn't allowed to do that during supper. Mom was next to me, with her back to the stove and countertops on which she prepared all the food. We ate things like meatloaf made with Lipton's onion soup mix, green bean casserole, and Rice-A-Roni. Beefy tomato-noodle soup. Beef and noodles. Sausage patties with fried potatoes and bread and gravy. Yum. Dad had the best view of the games on TV. Sometimes he'd yell at the screen, but his temper was nothing compared to Bobby Knight's. No chairs were ever thrown, but boy did my parents love IU basketball, even in the team's losing years.

We played solitaire on that table—Yahtzee, Sorry, Uno, Boggle—and on holidays we'd break out the ice bucket full of change to play Tripoli on a cardboard game board Dad had drawn for us.

When Dad had a show coming up and a bunch of paintings to name, we'd sit around the table and brainstorm. Once in a while Dad came up with some deeply philosophical or cleverly creative classics (*Friday Flurries, On the Crest, Waiting, Sentry, Vantage Point, Three Times a Lady* [for a painting featuring three squares of purple irises]), but usually they were merely literal, names you could take at face value (*Autumn Trees, Montgomery*

County Barn, Parke County Bridge).

I remember our excitement when we discovered a prolific photographer one state over who shot the same subject matter as Dad painted. His catalog of images was like an encyclopedia of titles we could, *ahem*, borrow. And his titles were lovely and poetic. Dad kept a folder of handwritten, dog-eared sheets of assorted notepaper with lists of titles in his, Mom's, Kerry's, and my handwriting. Sometimes he'd put a check mark next to it when he used it, but there were never any guarantees that it hadn't been used. After all, he painted the same subject matter for 50 years.

My whole childhood, I stood around while people came up to Dad at shows, openings, or just on the street. "Do you remember me? I bought a barn from you, probably 15 years ago. It had a lot of white in it, and there was a fence that was falling down, and a trash can, and some snow. I think it was called [*insert classic title here—Friday Flurries / Barn in Winter / Summer Sunshine / Silent Snow / Snow Fence*]."

Dad would nod his head, his natural charm shining through, and give his patron a smile that made each one believe their specific painting was special to him. Unique. We would turn away to hide our laughs (and Mom's eye-rolling)—because of course Dad didn't remember that one specific barn he painted years ago.

Or so we believed. Looking back now, I think he probably remembered a lot more of them than we gave him credit for. Still, he painted around 200 pieces a year, many of them featuring images of barns in snow, and quite a few of them were named exactly as you might expect.

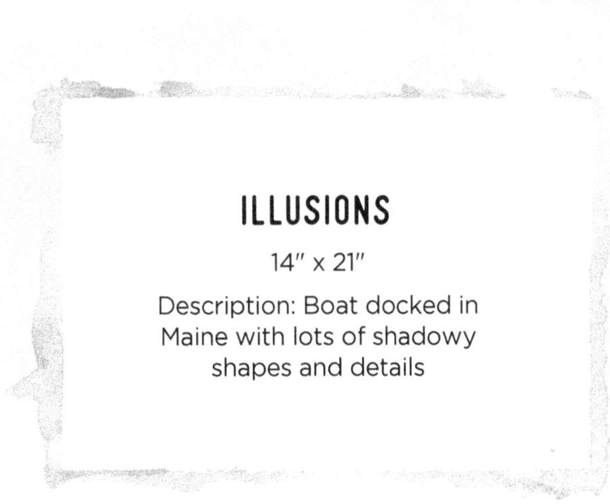

At one of my dad's early art shows, someone in the family overheard my Grandpa O'Dell (my dad's dad) talking to one of the patrons. Grandpa was a funny man with hard muscles and a Navy tattoo on his forearm. His armpits were too "delicate" for deodorant, so whenever he came in for a hug we braced ourselves and held our breath. He was sweet and gentle—but not the most tactful.

As he and this potential customer stood together looking at the paintings, he is reported to have said, "Well, if you seen one of Bob's paintings, you seen 'em all."

Most people don't notice the nuances, the small details that set Dad's paintings apart. They see nothing more than a barn, or a tree, or a pretty sky. In the '80s, Dad did some experimental works in which he explored this concept. One painting consists of three rows of identically shaped barns—viewed straight-on, with an open door in the front and center of each. There's no background—the barns are on a stark white illustration board, eight shapes stacked top to bottom, three across, twenty-four in all. Very graphic, quite simple.

Think Andy Warhol, but with barns instead of Marilyn.

Twenty-four of the same thing. Until you look closely. One barn has a weathered red circle painted beside the door. Each building has the same overall silhouette, with essentially the same door opening and coloration—he traced a hand-drawn template of the overall shape to begin—but the paint is applied differently on each, wiped on with small rectangular pieces of mat board, leaving different patterns of darker and lighter grays and browns for the barn siding. If you pay close attention, you'll see that the light and shadows cast in the open doorways reveal different things. Some of the barns have missing boards, but the gaps are in different locations each time.

Dad enjoyed playing with variations on the same theme, exploring the endless variations made possible through nuance and the capriciousness of watercolor—because no matter how many barns he painted, each was unique to him. He could model his paintings on the same photo of a specific barn a dozen times over, but every time he'd add something different—the fence would extend at a different angle, or the fields would slope down in a different direction, or this time he might add a tree or a silo or a defunct shed behind it. The barn might be in the upper-right corner of one painting and the lower-left of another. One might have birds lined up on the sagging roofline. Another might have an old 7-Up sign leaning against the fence, or a truck resting in the shadows of the open doorway, or a bucket overturned on the fence post. Dad might leave out trees that grew in inconvenient spots, or he might not. He sprinkled in fencerows and abandoned machinery, lean-tos and burn barrels full of branches, signs and barbed wire. There might be trees casting shadows in the morning light, or laundry hanging on a clothesline, or a tiny barn barely visible in the dark tree line. Infinite possibility built upon the same base.

I confess, after a lifetime of being around Dad's art, I started to feel like Grandpa did: If I'd seen one, I'd seen them all. Each painting was nicely done—but in the end, it was just another barn, or tree, or creek. It was a running joke. I'd stop by the studio, or Dad would bring a painting to my house to show me something he was excited about, and I'd say, "Ooh, I really like *this* one!" or, "Nice! Even better than usual."

After all, Dad already knew he was good at what he did. But he needed what most artists need: affirmation. He made me believe that my opinion mattered to him—and he knew I thought he was an amazing artist, even if I didn't love every painting. We didn't need fancy words to let each other know—or even any words at all. We just knew.

vignette

My father's paintings are the past, but they're also the present. The beauty in them lies in the fact that he portrays what any of us in rural America might see today. Yet there is a nostalgia to the image, too, a sense of remembrance. Of times past. Buildings are weathered and worn. Trees are sometimes broken, but sometimes alive in their full glory. The lack of people in the images makes the paintings appear timeless, quiet. You have a voyeuristic sense that you're witnessing something intimate or personal. You're in someone else's private space, but not for nefarious reasons. You're there to see. To not overlook what is before you, but to look into the past and be present.

ANNIE'S GARDEN

21″ x 14″

Description: Inspired by the flowerbeds beside my parent's house, this painting features two regal hollyhock stalks, pink and deep red, standing tall above small purple flowers and yellow and white daisies. The green background is a splashy wash of watery greens with a few defined leaves and lots of texture.

Mom died six years before Dad did, so when he got sick, I thought I'd handle it better. But here's the thing I didn't realize about grief—it's a cumulative, layered thing. One loss heaped upon another upon another. It doesn't get easier, it just continues to build. Over and over again until we die.

Not to be melodramatic or anything. Then again, I am my mother's daughter. And I still wasn't at peace about losing her.

My mom had been fatalistic, always sure that somehow the worst would happen to her. She seemed to feel rather vindicated when they told her she had terminal cancer. She'd anticipated it for years.

Her dad was head of radiology at a Catholic hospital in Decatur, Illinois. He and another doctor "pioneered the use of radioactive isotopes in the state of Illinois" in the 1940s (whatever that means). I memorized that description from an article I once read about him. In other words, they were early adopters of X-ray technology, using it for all sorts of novel purposes, such as radiating tonsils and checking the fit of one's shoes. My mom worked as an X-ray technician for several years, before they took the precautions they take today. She knew she'd had more exposure than was probably good.

I guess she was right.

Mom and Dad had different interests and often spent time separately, but one thing they both enjoyed was going out to dinner on a Sunday evening. Just a couple of months after she'd retired, she and Dad drove 45 minutes to have dinner at Olive Garden. (Around here, you have to drive that far to get "Italian" food that isn't pizza.) That night, in the bathroom, Mom leaned forward to wash her hands. The overhead lighting cast a strange shadow on her upper chest, and, touching it, she felt a hard lump, but no tenderness. Convinced she was likely dying, she got in the next morning to see our family physician. Dr. Miller was a man she'd worked closely with in her role as a school nurse. A friend.

He concurred with her assessment. I hated it when she was right.

Dr. Miller immediately scheduled an X-ray, and before she'd completed the 25-minute drive back home, he called. The radiologist found something; could she come for a biopsy immediately? The medical findings didn't warrant such urgency, but he knew how hard it would be for Mom to wait for answers. They first hypothesized that it was lymphoma, but various tests quickly pointed them to a different diagnosis: extensive-stage small cell lung cancer. With metastases in her liver and lungs.

Friday morning, less than one week after noticing the lump, she had her first chemo treatment.

I was so used to pooh-poohing Mom's negativity, I wasn't sure what to do when it actually was a horrible thing. She needed someone to acknowledge it as such, but Dad and I were determined to be positive. To not freak out unless we had to. Maybe it wouldn't be as bad as they thought. Maybe she'd have longer.

I really, really wanted to be right about that. The alternative was just not acceptable.

My grandmother, mom, and sister, though—all nurses—knew it was just a matter of time. An eternal cynic, my mom lived in the mental certainty that the worst possible thing would absolutely happen. If everything turned out okay, that would be fine, but hope was too powerful, and if she let it in, the disappointment would devastate her.

Even if she expected the worst, she never *accepted* it. Instead, she spent her last years completely ticked off. No wonder I had such a hard time coping with losing her. For Mom, there was no going peacefully into that good night; she raged against it. With chemo and radiation, she survived for three years from her initial diagnosis, a fate which was realized by only 4% of people with her type of cancer (according to my late-night, surreptitious *small-cell-lung-cancer-life-expectancy* Google searches that everyone told me not to do).

But Mom wasn't even happy about *that*. Still, while she suffered through the hassles and side effects of treatment and more scans and waiting for test results, she attended her grandkids' school programs and plays and sports events, drove Katie to voice lessons, started Bobby on guitar lessons, went to IU games, and wobbled her way through a trip to a Mexican resort with Kerry's family. For every family birthday, we gathered at Little Mexico, our family's favorite restaurant, and she continued her tradition of buying us quirky and thoughtful gifts up through her last Christmas. The gifts the year she was diagnosed were doozies: The grandkids all got custom-made neon signs spelling out their names, and I got an autographed Jim Morrison concert poster featuring his mug shot and fingerprints.

After Mom died, before we canceled her email account, I went through her sent emails, hoping for something to hold on to. But they broke my heart, filled with statements like, "Bob and the girls insist on treatment, so here I go again." You'd have thought we were torturing her.

If we'd known how she felt, I don't think we would have pushed her. It makes me sad that either she didn't feel able to tell us, or perhaps she expressed that but we didn't hear her.

When I talk about Mom, it's often heavily laced with frustration. She judged me and criticized me and bossed me around. She gave opinions I didn't want or ask for. She didn't seem to approve of anything I wanted to do, and she didn't understand me at all. Now, as a mom who's lived through three of my own kids' teen years, I know she understood me all too well. She wasn't weak; she was strong and rebellious and capable and smart. She was trying to protect me from my own bad decisions because she'd been there herself. After all, she married a man her parents didn't fully approve of, and the two of them defied their parents' expectations to leave the big city and a guaranteed income to move to a neglected farm in the country and try to survive on art. Being a rebel can have consequences— yet, as a fellow rebel, she was able to anticipate what I was thinking and head me off at the pass. I hated that.

Mom and I would scream at each other and storm out of the room in different directions. One time I was so angry I shouted, "You're a f—ing b—!" I have no excuse—except to say I was a horrible teenager, and she was my mom, and now I can't even remember what could have prompted that response, let alone justified it.

She ran out of the kitchen—probably to fume and/or cry in her room—while Dad remained at the kitchen table, where he was finishing his lunch. He was very still. Dad was always the calm one, talking slowly and calmly when my temper was out of control. That day, heart thumping, stomach churning, I could barely look at him. He didn't say a thing. He didn't have to. I could see the disappointment in his face. I knew I'd crossed a line. Dad had a temper, eventually, when pushed, but he didn't show it.

Well, hardly ever.

At book club a few years ago, Kerry's and my friends were talking about spanking, time-outs—how to discipline our kids. Someone asked, "Did *your* parents spank you?"

At the same time, we responded, "Once." We both remember one time Dad got really mad at me. I was probably 10 or 11. I have no memory of what I did (seems to be a recurring theme with me), but I think I smarted off to him. He jumped up and took two steps toward me, pulling back his arm like he was going to slap me. (He didn't.) I ran upstairs crying. It apparently terrified my sister, too.

And it never happened again.

So the extent of my childhood trauma is one incident where my father almost spanked me. Yeah, I'd say he was a peacemaker.

But he and Mom bickered constantly. They were very different, and it seems like Mom was always critical and Dad was always frustrated. Shortly before I left for college, I rode with Dad to Michigan to deliver paintings to a gallery. I took a deep breath and asked what I'd been wanting to know for a long time: "Why don't you guys just get a divorce? You fight all the time!"

He turned toward me in surprise. "I guess we never thought about it. We're not really fighting. It's just how we are."

After that, Dad and I didn't talk any more about it, but went about our usual post-gallery-delivery routine: Dinner at Red Lobster and a detour to buy me something at a mall before we went home.

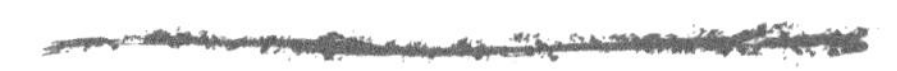

I read an article once that said to imagine this: You go to

clean out your fridge and you discover you have three unopened jars of pickles in your refrigerator. *Why do you have three? Who put them there? Who do you call to tell?* That's your pickle person. The one who wants to know the minutia of your life, the one you want to share those things with. My relationship with Mom always felt rocky, or at least a little turbulent, and now I'm sad to say I didn't always appreciate all the complex and amazing things she was. But she was always my "pickle person."

We talked about and shared books because we both loved to read. She'd drop off daffodils for Kerry and me at our houses, for no reason other than someone had had a fundraiser. She cut articles out of the paper for me to read and went with me to hear Philip Gulley, one of our favorite authors, read in a nearby town, long before I was writing myself. When that same author was the keynote speaker at a writing conference, she read about it in the paper and convinced me I should go. (And helped pay for it.)

I can't tell you how many times we discovered we'd both made our gross-to-everyone-else-but-us tuna casserole for lunch on the same dreary days, or were fixing the exact same meal for dinner, without having planned or discussed it.

When we had time, Mom and I would scour antique malls looking for a funny or quirky item for one of our houses. She bought me a cool set of green wooden mailboxes once because she knew I loved anything with little doors. I bought her saltshakers shaped like Depression-era housewives. Pale yellow dresses, white ruffled aprons, kerchiefs on heads, smudges of dirt on their cheeks. One of the pair is holding an iron; another, a watering can. "Dearie is wearie" is hand-lettered on their aprons. They made both of us laugh and were the beginning of several years of competing to find the ugliest or most absurd saltshakers possible.

When I had a new client, Mom wanted to know all about my

projects and would call me with random ideas—thematic names for a real estate developer's floor plans named after jockeys or racehorses, a color combination she noticed somewhere. She would ask me what I was going to wear to my meetings, who I was presenting to, and where it was (boardroom? office? one person or a whole team?) because she wanted to be able to picture exactly what I was doing. A month or so after Mom died, I had a client meeting in Indianapolis and then stopped at Target. As I walked back to my car, I burst into tears in the middle of the parking lot. With Mom gone, there was absolutely no one in the world who cared what I'd worn to my meeting. Not a single person in my life knew—or cared—that I'd stopped at Target. As great as my husband is, Tim is not one to care about those kinds of details.

Although one could say I had more freedom than ever before, I felt lost. Untethered. Mom was always right in the middle of my life—until she wasn't.

GIFTS OF HAPPINESS

14″ x 21″

Description: Detail of
daisies growing in a dirt
embankment

When Mom and Dad met, she was a 17-year-old country-club debutante, and he was a 19-year-old bad boy from the wrong side of the tracks. He wore blue jeans and white T-shirts with cigarettes rolled up in the sleeve, his red hair slicked back into a DA (also known as a ducktail). And he liked fast cars. He didn't make much working in his dad's cabinet shop, but he put everything he earned into his cars. Every year he'd trade up for the newest model—we have pics of him posing with his '57 Chevy, '58 Impala Convertible, '59 Corvette, and so on.

Nice cars or not, he didn't want to live like that forever. In an interview in 1973[3], Dad said, "My father was a cabinetmaker. My brothers were cabinetmakers. All I knew was I didn't want to become a cabinetmaker. In fact, I joined the Army so I wouldn't have to become a cabinetmaker!" He was stationed in Washington, DC, and he served 32 months in "The Old Guard," President Kennedy's Honor Guard. This is the group that guards the Tomb of the Unknown Soldier and marches in parades. One of the first ceremonies he participated in was the inauguration of President Kennedy.

Side note: My dad wasn't typically serious or formal, but once in a while when we were growing up, my sister and I would convince him to show us his moves. He would put on the shoes with the metal pieces that clicked when he snapped his heels together, then straighten his spine to his full 6'1" height and raise his chin, saluting and marching, pivoting abruptly as he turned sharp corners around the perimeter of our living room, face devoid of expression and movements precise.

While Dad was still in the Army, Mom began planning their upcoming September wedding. My grandmother sewed her ivory silk wedding gown with the tiniest waist and a big satin bow. The thing is, the wedding was still several months away, and Dad would be paid more from the military when he was married. So one weekend in April, Mom went to Washington, DC, and they had a secret justice of the peace ceremony, commemorated simply by three items pasted into a scrapbook: a church bulletin from Post Chapel at Fort Lesley J. McNair, a postcard of a drab motel, and a matchbook from the Zebra Room cocktail lounge, with no comments or other marks on the page. One year, when Kerry and I commented that it was weird that they never seemed to celebrate their anniversary, Mom let us in on their secret but swore us to silence.

Their parents would have been appalled, even all those years later. They always had certain expectations. Mom and Dad played along, had the official September wedding, and Mah and Dot were never the wiser.

But to get back to Dad's cars: As an adult, he drove practical vehicles. A big old 1976 station wagon with a rear-facing back seat and wood-paneled doors. A pickup truck with a cab on the back so he could transport his paintings in the wooden rack he built using dowel rods and covered in carpet squares for padding. (Think "old man" truck, not "manly off-roader.")

A chocolate brown mid-'80s minivan so we could take a
monthlong drive out West as a family to see the sights before I
left for college.

When Mom knew she was going to die, just a few months
after her diagnosis, she bought Dad a little silver Saturn Sky
convertible. She hated being in it herself—wearing a wig was
the bane of her cancerous existence, so she couldn't possibly ride
with the top down. But she also knew how he loved fast cars
and that the convertible would give him a little bit of joy which
might help soothe the ache of her being gone. Besides, gossip is
wicked in small towns. If he bought himself a flashy sports car
after she died, people would whisper about how recklessly he
spent the life insurance money. She could spare him by buying it
for him now.

Dad took several pictures of Mom leaning against the sleek
curves of that car, a pinup girl in her usual oversized, shapeless
corduroy shirt and khakis, wig slightly askew, forced smile
on her face. Dad drove the Sky whenever the weather was
nice, usually with his golf clubs upright and buckled into the
passenger seat, but never to take Mom to treatments because of
her *damn wig*.

Mom had a way of noticing what people needed before they
did. Not what they *wanted*, necessarily, but the perfect thing that
would make a difference in their life.

Shortly after she was diagnosed, she and I were running
errands. When we pulled into a parking lot beside our family
dentist's office, she said, "Now I'm going to tell you something
I haven't even told your dad—but you can't tell anybody. But
someone needs to know in case I die." Mom had retired just a
few months before her diagnosis. Before that, she worked at
my old high school as the school nurse, where she made friends
with a kid who hung out in the clinic with her to escape the
lunchroom. He was vibrant and interesting—but also awkward

and self-conscious, hiding his smile behind his hand because his teeth were so bad. She thought that if he had his teeth fixed, he might have the confidence to rise up beyond his circumstances. His family couldn't afford it, and she didn't want the awkwardness of his feeling indebted to her, so she created an imaginary dental fund, with the help of a local dentist, and declared him the recipient. She was afraid she'd die before the work was done and wanted to be sure they could finish it. She focused on one thing that might have held him back and did what she could to fix it. I wish I knew what happened to him—I only know the dentist's name but not the boy's—but it brought tears to my eyes to know how much she believed in others, even as she only believed in the worst-case scenarios for herself.

KAMPEN GOLF COURSE

14″ x 21″

Description: Rolling green and sand
trap of a new Purdue University
golf course. Painted at the request of
Purdue University to commemorate
the grand opening.

At 6:20 one morning, Dad called to say Mom had fallen and they were on their way to the ER. The hospital admitted her, although she had a do-not-resuscitate order and had at that point refused any further cancer treatment. Dr. Miller walked into her room, exasperated, saying, "Annie, why are you here? I thought you didn't want this."

The truth was that she *didn't* want it, but Dad, Kerry, and I didn't know what else to do. She was in a lot of pain. She had fallen and needed to be checked. We had to do something, right? What else *could* we do?

The social worker came and explained how hospice worked, and we *eenie-meenie-miney-moe*'d among the hospice brochures covered with pictures of angels and flowers and arranged for a hospital bed to be moved into the dining room.

We removed the large wooden dining table and placed the bed directly under the brass light fixture in the center of the room. On one wall sat Mom's large wooden antique desk, its cubbies overflowing with her address book, cards and notes from friends ("you'd think I was already dead with all the cards people are sending"), spare boxes of checks, and copies of the kids' school photos. In another corner sat a glass-fronted china cabinet filled with dishes from both grandmothers and with pitchers brought to the States from Irish ancestors. You had to walk through the dining room to get from the living room to the kitchen, and there were no doors—just wide openings connecting the rooms. The dining room was perpetually dark because of the shade of the ancient maple tree just outside the one large window. The wall to Mom's right led to the only bathroom on the main floor (because old houses are weird like that). Its old wooden door had colored stained glass inserts that you could see through if you really tried, and the door didn't completely latch, making visitors uncomfortable, but we were used to it.

Kerry, Dad, and I took turns keeping track of meds, reading instructions and calling hospice with questions, having no idea what to expect. One day, as I sat next to the bed, Mom bolted upright and looked at me in a panic. "What are we going to say?!"

"About what, Mom?"

"Get your dad. We need to talk about this."

I yelled for Dad, who was in the living room just around the corner, and he came rushing in. "What's wrong?"

"What are we going to say?" she repeated. "We can't say 'friends and family.'"

She was talking about the standard boilerplate language in obituaries: "She died surrounded by friends and family." Mom couldn't think of anything worse than us having to watch her go. Or maybe it wasn't about protecting us; she just didn't want anyone watching her.

Either way, we assured her we absolutely *wouldn't* be there for her. She settled back into sleep in moments.

We took turns sitting in the uncomfortable dining room chairs next to her bed. Kerry, the nurse, changed Mom's catheter bag. Friends came and went through the week, bringing food and wiping tears when they said their goodbyes to Mom. Dr. Miller had shared his top-secret personal cell phone number with us and called regularly for updates. One day he even came to the house. I still don't know how he timed it so perfectly, to come while she was still awake and alert, but it was one of her last coherent days. I thought he was just being nice, but he clearly knew precisely how close the end was. They talked about how she was feeling, other than the fact that she was dying. As he left, he said, "I love you, Ann," and walked out with tears streaming down his face.

Mostly the days were somewhat peaceful. Mom slept and we wandered around the house aimlessly, quietly ducking past her to go to the bathroom. But she still wasn't happy about what was happening to her, and that came screaming through in her treatment of my father.

As you might imagine, our house was full of art—whole walls covered with paintings done by Dad or his friends. Most of it was original, but we had a print hanging in the dining room, on the wall facing Mom's bed. In the 1990s, Dad had been commissioned to paint a golf course near the Purdue University campus that was designed by Pete Dye. Golf lovers tell us he's a big deal, but all we know is that Dad was hired to do the painting—and got to play on the course—and the golf course commemorated the opening by producing prints of it. Dad's copy was signed by Pete Dye himself during the celebration. He loved that thing and instead of his go-to plain walnut frame, he opted for a fancy gold one. The painting was fine, but golf courses didn't excite us in the same way they did him.

After a few days of lying in that bed looking at that wall, Mom suddenly pointed at the print and spat, "Take that damn thing off the wall."

Dad shuttled it away without saying a word.

A while later, her bald little head came back up as she looked at Dad. "You have on that damn shirt again." Dad was wearing his usual summer fare—a lightweight, striped knit golf shirt. She closed her eyes, exhaling another sour breath in relief at having said it. She repeated her complaints every day, no matter which shirt he had on. Never mind that she had bought them for him. As I've said, she was furious that she was dying. And her anger had to go someplace. She chose Dad.

Kerry, her husband, Doug, a couple of family friends, and I took turns sitting with her. We gave her more meds whenever she began wincing in pain. We watched the whites of her eyes grow yellow and listened as she made less and less sense, nodding when the hospice nurse whispered, "It's the toxins in her brain."

Since she wasn't being pleasant to Dad, he tended to stay just out of sight when she was awake. But as soon as her eyes would drift closed again, he'd walk through the room and kiss her forehead or grasp her hand for a moment.

While Mom was dying, I still had a life to lead, so one day I left for an appointment. Dad called. "Your mother wants to talk to you." His voice sounded funny and put me on alert. He handed her the phone.

"They'll be here to get me soon. The bus. That takes me to the place."

"What place, Mom?"

She cried, pleading. "The *place*." When I didn't know what to say, she gave a big sigh, her voice turning bitter. "They got to you, too, didn't they? You're in on it. You're all in on it."

Another afternoon, I sat beside the hospital bed in my usual chair, trying to think of something, anything, to write in my gratitude journal. Mom woke up and started talking about turtles, seemingly remembering a time right after her diagnosis when she rode with Tim and me to take our daughter Katie to a summer camp in St. Louis. The fields and rivers near Terre Haute, Indiana, were flooded, and we had to take tons of detours, and Tim kept saying, "Did you see that turtle? There's another one!" We thought he was seeing things and kept rolling our eyes at each other. Until finally we started seeing them, too—everywhere. They were scrambling, although maybe ambling would better describe their speed, to cross the highways to find dry ground.

Remembering the turtles made us both laugh. She leaned back against the elevated bed, eyes closed, hands clasped on her stomach, half smiling.

Sometimes I could follow her train of thought and sometimes I could not. "What's the name of that place where they have the celebrations?" she asked, talking about colored linens and whether we'd have enough dishes for all the people. After resting her eyes for a few minutes, she talked at great length about the canapé dishes we would use. I'd never heard her use that word before. And use it she did, dozens of times. *Canapé, canapé, canapé*, perhaps recalling the days of her parents entertaining the doctors and their wives. Then she said, "I know! We'll decoupage the canapé dishes. Oh wait, we can't because they're dead."

As my mind struggled to keep up, she commented, "I'm going to have pee wafting down my leg. My eyes are fluctuating. Come on, eyeballs."

She dozed a bit, then said, "Ooh, those guys are scary in their white T-shirts," nodding toward the corner of the room with an exaggerated shudder. "Why do they look like that?" she asked. Goosebumps broke out on my arms and I started praying, terrified. I kept this conversation a secret for years, wondering if it meant she was seeing demons and not angels, and what that meant for her eternal soul, until I realized that in the Bible, every time an angel appeared, people fell down in fear. Maybe "scary" wasn't such a bad thing after all.

She was asleep before I could answer her question. Either way, I knew it meant her time was nearing an end.

The next evening, several of us sat around the antique kitchen table in the center of Mom and Dad's large kitchen, where we could just see her hospital bed in the next room. I don't remember what donated meal we were eating—ham loaf? Taco soup? I was in "my" spot, facing away from the TV toward the dining room. I saw Kerry, beside me, carefully set down her fork.

"What's wrong?"

"I think she stopped breathing," she said as she pushed her chair away from the table.

We all rushed in and sat around the edges of Mom's bed. She took a breath in. We held our breath, too, and finally she let hers out.

And that was it.

Kerry held Mom's hand, saying, "You did it, Mom! You did it well!"

As fellow nurses, Kerry and Mom had had conversations about suffering and dying, specifically what would happen to her body and what the end would look like. Later, when I asked Kerry about her words in that moment, she said she had no idea what she meant. I think she was rejoicing with Mom that it was peaceful and fast. No gasping for air because her lungs weren't working. She'd faced her biggest fear, and Kerry was so happy for her.

I couldn't speak and I didn't want to touch Mom. I couldn't move. I had my arms wrapped around myself, hoping I could manage to not sob out loud. Dad, on the other side of the bed from me, looked from Kerry to Mom and then back to Kerry.

He had this look on his face, like a little kid, incredulous and flabbergasted. Hoping he'd somehow misunderstood.

"Is she gone? Is she really gone?"

Kerry said, "Yes, Dad, she's gone." Tears falling, he leaned forward and pressed a long kiss onto her still head.

ROCKY SHORE

8″ x 19″

Description: A moody early
painting (mid-1960s) showing
large boulders lining the edge
of a harbor, with seagulls
floating on the breeze

When someone you love dies, you think that's it, right? That
is the worst moment, and everything moving forward surely has
to be better, right? Nah. The hits just keep coming.

I was standing in the center of the sea of cafeteria tables at
the high school during school registration, moving from station
to station to register my kids—you know, pay the book fees, fill
out the health forms, order the yearbook. This was just before
they moved registration online, and the kids weren't required to
be present for it.

In my hands, I held a clipboard with the offending
paperwork. "Please draw a line through any incorrect
information," it said in bold. The so-called "incorrect
information" looked so innocent. Four words.

Emergency contact: Ann O'Dell.

Those seemingly innocuous words folded me physically in
half. I fought to steady my breathing, to not let the tears leave
my eyes. Nobody tells you about these things, about how you'll
be sucker punched at the most unexpected moments.

I looked around, wondering how other people were chatting

and walking and writing checks like nothing had happened. Because I had to somehow draw a line through my mom's name, admit she was gone and would never again be the go-to person for my kids. Since she was a school nurse in the neighboring school corporation, everyone knew Mom. People took extra-good care of her grandkids.

But now we don't belong to her anymore.

Drawing that line through the words felt like a sword through my gut. Losing her again.

But then, the million-dollar question: Who will replace her? Dad? I felt like it would be too much for him—the worry about whichever kid had a fever and had to leave school. He, too, was trying to adjust to this new world without my mom. It had only been a month.

With an unsteady hand, I scribbled in my sister's name and number. We still had Dad, technically, but it sure felt like we were on our own.

I didn't remove Mom's number from my phone, though. That seemed too permanent. As I write this, it's been almost 12 years and her contact is still in there. I really should get rid of it, though. One day my phone rang and it showed the caller: *Ann O'Dell.* I answered it, heart pounding, to hear some woman say, "Did you call me?"

"Uhh ... no. This is my mom's old number; it's kind of freaking me out. Who is this?"

"Oh, sorry. You must have butt-dialed me. I was just calling you back." Click.

Dammit.

About a year ago, Snapchat notified me that my contact Ann O'Dell had joined. *Add friend?* Uhh, no. I have no idea who has her old number, but I still can't bring myself to delete her contact. Just in case.

vignette

Next to Mom and Dad's house was a patch of hollyhocks. Ragged and shredded looking, yet somehow also tall and stately. Reds and pinks and whites swayed in the breeze, casting dramatic shadows onto the white siding. I steered clear of this patch of color because I was terrified of bees (a doctor once suggested that I might have an anaphylactic response), and the bees were everywhere. So my dad's hollyhock paintings, with their complete lack of stinging insects, are more beautiful to me than the reality.

Isn't that how memory works—we crop out the parts that are unpleasant and focus on the picture-perfect moments. As a general rule, Dad didn't narrow his subject matter to those bits of perfection to be found in the landscape around us. But when he painted these flowers, he focused on the color and shapes, the feeling of the sunlight and the breeze, and played with the shapes of the leaves and the negative space.

The final painting is not an accurate depiction of the actual scene. It's better.

And yet it's not a lie. It's also the truth of it.

NO PLACE

22" x 30"

Description: Dirt road meandering
through slightly rolling hills,
past a harvested cornfield,
large tree, and distant barn

Mom and Dad's house, a two-story white farmhouse with a
wide front porch, sits on four and a half acres with some trees
and a couple of barns and a garage. It was built by my great-
great-grandfather, the one whose name is in the front of the
antique books I store in boxes in the attic. His daughter is the
Anna who inspired my own daughter's name. The house that
he built is the one my parents moved into against their parents'
wishes, with one adorable red-haired toddler, where they labored
to make it into a lovely home.

This place is where I lay gingerly balanced in a rope
hammock at age ten, reading every Nancy Drew ever written,
and where I watched the Hardy Boys on Sunday nights in high
school. It's where Mom chronicled our mundane life with daily
notes on the kitchen table in thick, spiral-bound notebooks—*put
away laundry, I'll be home at 2.* It's where Dad walked across the
backyard to his studio building to paint every morning after
breakfast, and where we rang the old-fashioned dinner bell to
let him know supper was ready. It's where I mowed the grass
in a tube top, like no redhead should ever do—ever—my crispy

burnt skin ensuring I wouldn't be asked to mow again that year. The loop around the property on which I rode our three-wheeler is muscle memory—the slight rise in the front yard where there was once a brick walkway, how if you gather enough speed and hit the bump just right it'll loft you into the air. Just a little, but enough to make it worth doing—over and over and over again. Thankfully, I also knew where to duck so I wouldn't be decapitated by the clothesline. I know where the grass grows greener along the septic tank line, where the bees linger, and where the hollyhocks grow.

It's where I taped pages of elaborate, ornate alphabets to the large picture window at the end of the living room, grabbed handfuls of markers, and learned to draw beautiful typography by tracing. It's where I wandered through the backyard to watch Dad paint when I was bored, and where I was always bored.

It's where I lay late at night on the floor of my room, writing prayers in the wedge of light from the hallway. It's where I cried myself to sleep listening to Nazareth's "Love Hurts." And it's where Tim and I had our first Christmas together, where I learned to carve out space for "us" instead of "me."

It's where my cousin Kathy and I giggled upstairs, late into the night, when her family came to visit. It's where I had my first drink (way too young) and got to choose my first wallpaper (an ugly tan with little navy and rust-colored flowers on it). It's where I slammed doors and fought Mom and cut my thumb carving a linoleum block and made silk screens and took 4-H photos. It's the place I longed to escape from, where I wrote papers for scholarships that would take me away, into this wide world and out of small-town minds and hearts.

And it's where I returned with my kids to play Tripoli on a hand-drawn game board every Christmas. Where silver hooks jutted out from the brick fireplace mantle, holding the needlepointed stockings my mom and grandma made, filled to overflowing. Where my grandma fell asleep in her wheelchair after dinner, mouth wide open and head crooked back, snoring so loud my mom wanted to strangle her. It's where my kids pulled out the ice bucket full of loose change and rolled quarters and pennies, where they played Kings in the Corner and shrieked with laughter at Dad's nonsensical rhyme: "Kings in the corner, squirrels up a tree, Jacob's gotta pee, come with me." It's where Gran read them *But Not the Hippopotamus* before bedtime.

Every time I went into the bathroom, I looked at the laundry hamper built by my dad and grandpa. For decoration and ventilation, Dad had drilled a pattern of holes in the shape of a tulip, and my eyes went straight to the places where the two dots that he forgot to drill should have been (yet somehow he never completed).

I know the ten-degree rise in temperature when my head crests the curve of the stairwell, and the dusty smell of the attic—the fear of falling through gaps in the floorboards and the illicit pleasure of scavenging for forgotten treasure. I've memorized the view out my upstairs bedroom window, the only place we could watch for the school bus in the fall, because the fields of corn between us and the house before us on the route were so tall.

I know at what point the motion sensor light on the porch will come on, and just how far the spotlight illuminates the driveway before giving way to pitch darkness. I know which cookbook held the hundred-dollar bills Mom stashed for an emergency, and how cold the kitchen floor is on winter mornings, and how the sun slants across the field on the other side of our road in the evenings. I know how Mom sat on the porch swing that provided that view, reading the paper, settled and at home.

And how home was the only place she wanted to be when she died.

I remember my brother-in-law, Doug, sitting on the kitchen counter the night she passed, warning us not to watch them carry her body out, because he has never been able to erase the image of them carrying away his own dad. I remember how empty the dining room looked once they wheeled away the hospital bed and how none of us could ever forget it had been there.

I know how Dad wandered the house, sad and lost, for months after she died. All of this is forever imprinted in my mind. I was just starting to come to terms with losing Mom when Dad decided to sell the house. And that damn sneaky, slippery darkness dragged me right back into the thick of my grief.

FRONT PORCH

18″ x 24″

Description: Close-up of a
dilapidated house with unpainted
wooden siding and boarded-up,
broken windows under a sagging
roofline with lots of shadows

Sitting on the front porch, I am surrounded by muggy air, insects humming, pieces of grain floating in the breeze. As I sit in Mom's beloved porch swing, I take it all in. The fields across the street, the slightly rolling lawn Dad needs to mow, the bees buzzing as they move from one hollyhock blossom to the next.

It's wrong that Mom's not out here with us. It's wrong that she's no longer anywhere. Kerry sits beside me, and we coordinate our swinging motions as the swing creaks on its chains.

Rita and Judi, Mom's friends from high school, flew in for the memorial service. Most of the friends in their group married doctors, belonged to country clubs, and regularly upgraded to ever-larger houses. One of them, Jeannine, is the one who sent the letter addressed to "The Artist, Ladoga, Indiana," perhaps perplexed by her friend Annie's choices. As the story goes, Mom and Rita were together when they first saw my dad with a group of his friends. Mom called dibs on the redhead. (She got him.)

Mom didn't see these friends much except during a trip to St. Louis every year or so, or the occasional class reunion, which she agonized over because she'd "gotten fat" and had nothing to wear. She usually came home talking about their enormous houses, flashy clothes, and expensive cars, as she slipped on her favorite baggy gray sweats in the unfashionable beige-and-country-blue farmhouse she loved.

When Mom got really sick, though, those same friends came from Illinois and Texas to help. Rita, who had lost her husband to cancer eight years earlier, sent email updates to our extended circles so that Mom wouldn't have to—and then later, because Mom wasn't able to. Judi, who'd been fighting multiple myeloma for many years, was a little bulldog. Well, in looks, more like a chihuahua. Judi and Mom emailed weekly to commiserate about their f***ing cancers. She was a fierce and funny self-described princess who lived in Texas—and a force to be reckoned with. When she visited, Mom insisted on putting her in a hotel to save her the indignity of traipsing through the drafty, creaky old house to use their one full bath, illogically located off the dining room.

For Judi's and Rita's final visit to the house in Ladoga, Mom isn't here to worry about them.

Right now, Judi is delivering the funeral programs on disk to the printer and insisting he turn them around in time for the memorial service the next day. I have no doubt that she will make it happen.

As I slowly rock back and forth, I watch Dad and Rita standing just a few feet away.

"It's going to be so hard, Rob," Rita says. "Winter will be bad. Trust me on this."

He's never done well in winter anyway. To counter his seasonal affective disorder, he usually planned golf trips in the Southwest or jaunts to Vegas with his buddies, letting the sunshine rarely seen in Indiana that time of year boost his mood a bit. But now, without Mom, winter would be so much worse.

Dad and Rita walk down the concrete porch steps and circle around to the side of the house. Rita, outgoing and kind, athletic and vivacious, was still convincing him. "Rob, you should come visit. Let's make plans now so you have something to look forward to. We'll play golf. The sunshine will do you good."

As I listen, I imagine the two of them getting together. I look at her, not as my mom's 70-year-old friend, but as a woman. Objectively. She's trim, well-dressed, in sporty but quality clothing, with suntanned skin. Lines on her face from smiling all the time. I can see that she was once quite beautiful. She's still beautiful.

No, I think. Even if he liked her, he would never move to Florida. Dad's not like that. He wouldn't leave us.

But I just had a feeling.

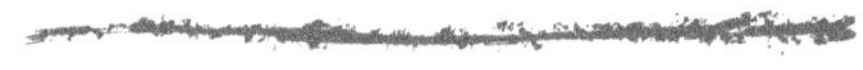

Nine months later, after Dad returned from his second trip to Florida to visit Rita, he invited me to have coffee at a local café.

"We're in love!" he declared. Trying not to look too happy about it, he couldn't help laughing.

"I'm not surprised at all," I told him—which surprised *him.*

Then I couldn't make eye contact because if I did, if I attempted to speak even one word, the dam would burst and I knew there'd be no coming back from it.

When my dear friend Terri's husband died, she explained an aspect of grief I'd never considered. As one-half of a couple, she was a particular person—but with the other half gone, everything changes. Even if she found someone new to love, she would never be that same person again. Though I was happy for my dad—really, I was—I mourned the loss of the man he used to be, the one who was the other half of my mom. The one who never would have dreamed of leaving the part of the country where his family was in order to go dancing on Wednesday nights at the Club, have dinner with friends, and wear loafers with no socks.

But that was his new life. When he called, he talked about buying a Lexus like Rita's (although he did keep the Saturn Sky convertible). He detailed his golf foursomes and his plans to fly home to attend the IU basketball game with Rita's son. He never used her first name with us. He referred to Rita as "She"—the capital *S* was implied. *She* wants this. *She* said that. *She* thinks I should do this.

I think he thought it would hurt us less if he didn't say her name.

Many evenings, instead of cooking supper, Kerry, Doug, and I sat around the coffee table drinking cabernet, trying to make sense of things.

"Has he always been like this?" one of us would ask.

"It's like he's a chameleon," someone else would say.

"Was he unhappy all along?" we would wonder together.

But no. He loved his life with Mom. He was content to putter around his studio and bring home a painting, hoping to wow Mom but often receiving only a tepid response, as was her way. He willingly slurped the homemade soups she fixed for dinner on cold days and watched TV while she read her latest library book in her Lands' End robe, a blue can of Cheez Balls beside her. He played golf at less-fancy courses and taught workshops and rode his ATV and ate bacon-and-egg sandwiches at the diner while shooting the shit with the local farmers. The relaxed pace, the assurance that he was doing what he loved, and the low-pressure schedule—it was just what he wanted.

While he had it, at least.

Honestly, I think that was part of the appeal. Rita didn't offer him a pale facsimile of his old life, but something entirely new—she was fun and vivacious and had friends who didn't know him as *Ann's husband*, not to mention she connected him to many who became enthusiastic new connoisseurs of his art.

Things were good in Florida, but he couldn't sleep at night worrying about who would mow the grass at the house up north and whether he lost any tree limbs in the recent storm. Neither Kerry nor I wanted to move our families into that place—we were content where we were—but it felt like adding insult to injury the way people practically threw offers at him the moment the house went on the market. It sold in a matter of days.

Another tether in my life broke loose, leaving me flapping wildly in the wind.

THE SEASONS CHANGE

10″ x 20″

Description: Vignette of a farmstead in late summer with the leaves on the trees beginning to turn colors

When I was in my early 20s, I cleaned out my cupboards and had a yard sale. I had this ugly little porcelain figurine of a cherub with an artist's easel. It had always been in my bedroom, but I never liked it, so I affixed a $2 price tag. A woman picked it up.

"Is this really two dollars?"

I replied yes as Mom said, a bit too loudly, "NO!"

Mom went on, "That is an antique. It's really valuable. It belonged to my Pap Smullen." Embarrassed, but determined not to make things worse with Mom, I told the lady, "Sorry. This isn't for sale." She sniffed, "Then don't put it out," and huffed her way down the driveway to her car.

That figurine now rests on a shelf in the antique hutch in my kitchen. It's as ugly as ever.

One day I searched online. It may be worth more than two dollars—but *valuable*? If I find just the right buyer on eBay, I might get $60. Marie Kondo would be disappointed in me for holding on to an item that spurs feelings of shame. But getting rid of it feels like a betrayal. It remains in the glass-fronted hutch built by "Boppy," my mom's other grandfather, because I don't want to let go of family history, even if I have no idea what that history is or whose faces are in the sepia photographs sitting in boxes in my attic.

I'm haunted by the stories I don't know. The lack of information renders the objects meaningless. No one alive can identify the faces in the crumbling photos upstairs. But letting go of them like they don't matter feels impossible. I fill every corner of my home with furniture and random things such as a carved wooden duck decoy that my grandparents kept on their living room table. I hold on to it all so tightly, grasping blindly for that missing connection.

I stuff mementoes into boxes, stacking them in teetering towers. Box upon box, much like the losses piled upon other losses—accumulating and stagnating until we die.

Apparently the cynic in my mother lives on in me.

Dad hired an auction company to box up the things we didn't want. The night of the big sale, I noticed that the custom ceramic mugs I bought for my parents one Christmas, with their names stamped into the clay, were on the sale tables.

I shoved them into my purse.

All of us smiled and greeted people as the auctioneer made his way through the room, selling boxes of dishes and old bicycles and Dad's mowing tractor. Bittersweet but bearable.

Until I saw what was up next. I grabbed Tim's arm. "Oh my God! That's the bassinet that everyone in my family has slept in! It wasn't supposed to be sold!"

One of my great-grandfathers built it, and my grandmother, mother, and uncle slept in it. When Kerry's and my kids were born, my grandmother made sure we took pictures of them sleeping in it, and now, their kids have slept in it. Five generations in all.

Tim very calmly said, "I've got this," and stood up. I tried to stop him; Mom taught me not to make a fuss in public. Once people realized the family was bidding, they stopped, and before long, Tim loaded it into our vehicle.

Sometimes, I guess objects do matter.

I don't feel embarrassed when I think about the bassinet, like I do with the cherub figurine; I find comfort in this small bit of continuation across the generations. Maybe my kids and grandkids will find security in the knowledge that they come from a long line of people who believed that family matters. A lot.

Still, though, my house fills with more than I need, the weight of what I don't know, the burden of holding on to all that I have.

Maybe eventually I will find ways to memorialize the people I have loved that don't clutter my home but instead overflow my heart.

And perhaps someday I'll even accept that I won't need my parents' house in order to feel like I have a home.

vignette

Working only in watercolor, a medium which best serves his talent, he has a reputation for honesty and truthfulness in his approach to the medium and his subjects. Rob O'Dell has observed the objects around him and distilled their contents so as to broaden one's sense of the commonplace.

—Brochure, The Folger Gallery, Carmel, Indiana, in the early 1980s

BETTER DAYS

20" x 28"

Description: Stark barn in snow
with missing boards in roof and
lots of negative space

In 2007, Tim and I were happy with our big old house on
a busy corner near downtown Crawfordsville. The preschool
our kids attended was diagonally across the street. On another
corner was the site of the "Strawberry Vegetable," which most
people called a "festival." (Our daughter Katie, at age three,
thought we were calling it a vegetable, and the name stuck.)
During this one weekend every June, people come from miles
away to eat breaded tenderloins, bloomin' onions, and elephant
ears—basically batter-dipped dough in a variety of forms.
Every June, Tim would put out orange traffic cones to keep
people from parking in our driveway and place a trash can
on the sidewalk for all the jumbo soda cups people somehow
managed to drop in front of our house. The girls always got
new strawberry-themed dresses to wear. And early on Saturday
morning, I would throw on clothes and run across the street to
help my dad set up his booth.

The vendors at the festival sold little pieces of rice with
people's names written on them, encased in a glass pendant;
hand-crocheted clothes for all manner of duck lawn ornaments;

some wire-wrapped jewelry; hand-thrown ceramics; and imported woven clothing. The usual small-town festival things, good and bad. There were two or three other local artists—professionals who were serious about their craft. And there was Dad, who had a prime location because he took part in this festival every year.

Dad and I had our routine down pat. We started with the wooden rack bungee-corded to the top of his truck or SUV, whatever he had at any given time. The rectangular panels with whitewashed, narrow wooden slats spaced a few inches apart were about four feet wide and seven feet tall, just short enough to fit under the collapsible white tent. Next we'd unload the paintings, largest first. He would hand them down to me, and I would arrange two similarly sized paintings back-to-back so that I could carry them by the hanging wires, my hands protected from their sharpness by little rectangles of foam rubber he kept for that purpose. We'd carry four paintings at a time until the 20 or 30 paintings he brought were leaning against the booth. Dad always knew how he wanted to hang them—again, largest first, then filling in the smaller ones around them. Sometimes he'd put a few summer scenes together or all the winter trees on one panel. Once in a while he'd stack three long horizontal paintings on top of each other. Dad cut up heavy wire coat hangers and bent them into hooks that fit over the wooden slats to hold the paintings. It was impossible to get them to hang straight from the wonky little shapes. It never looked totally orderly, but it was good enough.

Then I'd go home to get my kids ready, and people would line up to talk to Dad. I grew up hanging out at his booth at art fairs, but by the time I was an adult, he only did three festivals a year—this one because it was local, one on Memorial Day weekend in Lafayette, Indiana, and the one in his hometown of Decatur, Illinois, in September. All weekend, the kids would run

back and forth for meals and to buy more tickets for the kids'
play area. They loved stopping and seeing their Bebop. I held
down the fort while Dad bought himself a corn dog or a lemon
shake-up, and when Dad was busy talking to one customer, I'd
often start a conversation with the next person waiting in line.
Mom would come in for a few hours in the afternoon and then
leave again—or bring a book and hide out in my living room,
making the occasional appearance, just enough to say she was
there and go out to dinner at Little Mexico at the end of the day.
Because the festival was held in Indiana in June, inevitably one
afternoon there would be a bad storm and tornado threat, when
I'd run back across the street to quickly pack up Dad's booth.

Luckily, that was easy to do because Dad's system was so
simple. He certainly wasn't an engineer—but he had learned
carpentry from his father and he could build things. The six
panels fit together so that from above, the booth was shaped
like a letter *H*. Some of the panels had pegs and some had holes
drilled into them. By connecting the peg marked *A* with the hole
labeled *A*, and *B* with *B*, we got the whole thing to slot together
neatly, and then he topped it off with a wooden brace across the
top and some concrete-filled plastic tubes, attached with bungee
cords to hold the display steady on windy days.

His creative thinking and carpentry skills came in handy
when we decided to buy a new house.

UNRUFFLED CALM

20″ x 14″

Description: An egret
standing among lush, green,
tropical Florida foliage

"Dammit! The sink doesn't fit! Now what?!" I cried, exasperated.

With his usual calm, Dad said, "Well, let's think for a minute."

He stepped back and wiped his forehead with his T-shirt sleeve. I gulped from a bottle of water. We were in the kitchen of the new-to-us-but-hundred-year-old house Tim and I bought. The house had good bones but it was a mess—cobbled-together additions made by the previous owner, who didn't know a thing about construction. The house was filled with ugly fake-wood paneling on several walls, towel rods glued on top of wallpaper in the bathrooms, peeling wallpaper or mint green paint on most of the walls, gold sculpted shag carpet covering original hardwoods, doors boarded up to divide the house into several apartments.

The price was low, as you might imagine—but the amount of work needed to make it into a nice home was huge. Still, it shared a driveway with my sister's house and it was just around the corner from our current house. And it had five bedrooms instead of just three, so our kids could spread out a bit. We hadn't been planning to move, but when Kerry told us her neighbor's house was for sale and she wanted me to see it, all of our best-laid plans went out the window. Well, most of the windows were painted shut, so I guess they went out the doors instead. Much like the discolored cast-iron tub Tim had to break apart with a sledgehammer and carry out to the trash pile, heavy piece by heavy piece.

While electricians completely rewired the house, and the kids and I worked to scrape carpet adhesive off the old hardwood floors, Tim did much of the handyman work—installing new light fixtures, replacing a door, removing the metal cabinets and fixtures in the front room that had been rented by the previous owner as a separate apartment … that kind of thing.

Dad volunteered to help me with the kitchen. It was a mess. Stained ceiling tile sat in a bent metal grid, faux wood paneling lined the bottom of the walls while peeling wallpaper adorned the top. The appliances were arranged strangely, with the sink right next to the stove. No dishwasher, peeling linoleum floor. The cabinets were mostly solid, painted wood, but some of the doors were hung so they opened in the wrong direction. It was grungy and ugly and overwhelming.

I'd put together a design board and chosen colors and countertops and flooring. I had a plan, and Dad helped me make it happen. Let's be clear—I have zero carpentry skills or experience. That's what Dad was for. I was just there because he was doing it all for me, and he needed someone to hold things and hand him tools.

This thing with the sink wasn't our first problem. We'd had dozens. Throughout the summer, Dad would call me and say, "I'm on my way. Meet me over there?" I'd finish up an email to a client, throw on some old clothes, and walk the block to the new place, waiting until Dad drove up in Ol' Blue (his dented old red pickup truck).

Kerry was busy finishing nursing school, but whenever she was home she'd make us some cold drinks. Mom, with her usual sense of snark, named our congruent properties the Compound, as though we were Waco. Mom would stop by on her way to the library to see how the remodeling was going. Usually Dad and I were there alone since Kerry's husband, Doug, and Tim had to work, but our kids were always passing through. The boys (our son, Bobby, who was seven, and Kerry's son , Luke, who was eight) climbed up on the cab of the pickup truck where it was parked in the shade and played their Game Boys. Their main job was to stay out of the way.

Reilly, Kerry's daughter, was ten years old and always attached to her Bebop's side. He'd never been able to say no to her. When she asked him to pinch the loose skin under his eyes, which would then remain pinched in a weird line, he did it. When she popped his collar and asked him to make his signature funny face—which I can't figure out how to describe, but consists of him scrunching his mouth into a tight little half-moon smile—he complied. Later, when she was a little older, he let her drive his convertible through the yard, directing her to stop by the porch and grab two chair cushions so that she could see over the dash.

The cabinets were solid, and we had spent way more money on the other renovations than we actually had. Our credit cards were maxed out, so new cabinets were out of the question. Reilly wanted to use Dad's power tools, so he taught her how to unscrew the hardware on the kitchen cabinets and sand the doors so we could repaint them. I ordered new handles and hinges, and Dad filled the holes from the old ones, then rehung the doors so they opened in a more logical direction. He and I had torn out the lowered ceiling and he plastered the 10-foot one. He'd replaced the fake wood paneling with crisp white wooden wainscoting. I'd ordered new countertops, and they'd just been installed. But when Dad and I went to drop in the new stainless steel sink, we discovered that the cabinet below it wasn't deep enough to hold the bowls of the sink. The cabinets were handmade and not a standard depth.

"What in the world?" I kept saying, wanting to cry. I couldn't handle one more problem.

"Hey, honey, hand me the tape measure," Dad said.

And before I knew it, he'd designed a boxlike structure that extended beyond the original cabinet to enclose the sink. Once he finished, we painted it and mounted a cast-iron decorative piece on the front, and it looked like it was always meant to be there.

Mom wandered in one day, looking around. "Huh. I never thought it could look this good. Did you?"

My eyes rolled up into my head and I took a deep breath. She never saw what Dad and I could see.

But maybe she got under my skin so easily because I was already stressed: As a self-employed graphic designer, I had a somewhat erratic income. We put all the renovations on credit cards, anticipating that we would sell our other house for a nice profit and pay them off. And then the 2007 real estate market crash happened within weeks of listing our house. Old houses are notorious for requiring unexpected, expensive repairs, and we were scrambling to make the monthly payments on our cards. Our other house was a beautiful historic home on a stately corner—tall ceilings, original windows, great location. But no one wanted to even look at it.

Still, we pushed through the renovations, and the whole family pitched in. We moved, even though we still didn't have any offers. Finally, the realtor called with good (and bad) news. Someone made an offer, but it wasn't even enough to pay off our mortgage, let alone touch the credit card balances. Before I could celebrate—or be upset—a large, unexpected refund check arrived in the mail, I found out I was getting my first-ever tax refund (I'm self-employed so I always owe), our realtor offered to waive his fee, and we were now only $1,000 shy of being able to say yes.

I called Mom, not sure what to do, and she offered to hop in the car right then to bring me a check for that last $1,000. She may not have had a vision for how the house would look, but she always knew when I was in a financial bind. And this was one thing she could do to fix it.

You'd think I would have been relieved, but instead I was distraught. Nothing had worked out like I'd hoped. I mean—two years to sell a gorgeous old house, and then to not even be able to pay off our mortgage? Ugh.

But we celebrated anyway—what else is a person going to do? I posted pictures on Facebook of the *Sold* sign in the yard, and we settled into the new place. One big happy ~~family~~ Compound.

Living in the new house was good, even if the process of getting here hadn't been easy. Once I got through the financial mess, I didn't really think much more about it, except when people would comment on how much they wished they lived next to *their* sibling—or how glad they were that they did not. I enjoyed the convenience of borrowing needed ingredients from Kerry's cupboard and sitting on her couch sharing a bottle of wine, of having someone sign for packages if I wasn't home, and more. Our living situation was unusual, but it didn't seem all that remarkable until nearly ten years later, when my dad got really sick—and I understood the real reason why Kerry and I needed to live next door to each other.

UNTRODDEN

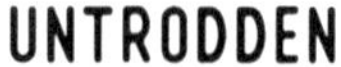

20" x 30"

Description: Mostly white
negative-space painting of a barn
on a hillside, the roof and ground
covered with undisturbed snow

"I'm not sure we've ever actually hugged," one of us said. I can't remember whether it was Kerry or me who made the admission, or even exactly when this happened—maybe a few years before Mom died? Our book club friends had been meeting nearly every month for at least ten years by that time. Kerry and I were two of the original members. Maybe our friend Peggy said something about her sister that led to the topic. Perhaps Kerry mentioned that she's just not a hugger. I'm not sure.

All I know is that suddenly our friends were determined to make us hug each other.

Kerry and I met in the middle of the room and lightly patted each other's backs. *Yay, okay, we're done.* Even though I was in my 40s at the time, and consider myself a hugger, I didn't particularly like it. Neither did she.

If the Hallmark Channel's portrayal of the sisterly relationship is any indication—sisters holding hands, gently sweeping the loose curls off the other's tear-stained face, wrapped up in a cocoon of pillows and watching a movie marathon late into the night—well, let's just say we're not very sisterly.

I mean, it was hard enough to admit that we were friends. Which we were, against all odds.

A few years before that, Kerry worked for me part-time as an assistant in my graphic design business. Her degree had been in therapeutic recreation, but she needed something to do while staying home with her first child, and I was always overloaded and wanted the help. I made her business cards with the title "Director of Special Projects." Sometimes that included changing one of my kids' diapers, but it also included billing, bookkeeping, getting printing estimates, making minor revisions requested by clients, stuff like that.

It worked well because as the younger sister, she was used to being bossed around.

Going back a handful of years before that, when Tim and I had only been married a year or so, Kerry was the "troll in our basement," as my husband so lovingly referred to her. We lived in Indianapolis then, and she was interning at a nearby children's hospital and working as a server at Applebee's in the evenings. She lived with us while I was pregnant. Once Katie was born, we appreciated having a built-in babysitter—but neither Kerry nor I can remember how long she stayed with us after that.

Maybe we don't remember because I had only started liking her around that time. Kerry spent one summer of college working at the American Embassy in Russia, taking care of the children of the American diplomats. I'm three years older, so I was working my first full-time job after college as an art director for an Indianapolis ad agency. I'd studied abroad in college (a term in England after a month of backpacking around Europe). Although England didn't seem as foreign as Russia, her travel made me realize that perhaps Kerry and I were more alike than I'd realized. I got permission to call her from work (because she was only reachable during certain hours, and those were within my office hours) and have the long-distance fees taken out of my paycheck, and I started sending her care packages.

I have so few memories of Kerry when we were young. Most of my early life I was just focused on trying to find ways to be alone and do my own thing. I don't remember actively disliking her, but she's simply not often present in my early memories. She says now that it was because she was constantly with Dad, doing whatever he did.

In high school, though, I do remember her. She was popular, tiny and skinny, athletic, part of a large circle of friends, even a cheerleader and class president—in short, everything I was not. She was a Future Homemaker of America; I was in Future Farmers. She was a thin blonde; I was a big-boned, awkward redhead. She ran track and cross-country, started in basketball, and made cheerleader. I played softball until eighth grade and had a not-impressive year in JV basketball in ninth grade.

All of those things mattered in middle and high school, and my strongest memories of those years include never fitting in. Being ostracized for being different. Dating the "wrong" boys. Screaming cuss words at my mom. Locking myself in my room and playing '60s and '70s folk and rock—Pink Floyd, Led Zeppelin, Neil Young, Peter Frampton, John Prine. Kerry liked Van Halen and Guns N' Roses. In younger years, I filled my walls with posters of Shaun Cassidy and Andy Gibb. Her walls were covered with Scott Baio, Leif Garrett, and Steve Alford (an IU basketball player).

We were nothing alike.

Granted, Kerry wasn't as mean to me as her best friend, Jennifer. Together, they harassed me at every opportunity. Our parents were best friends and we saw a lot of each other. Kerry and Jennifer loved to stand on the railing around the second-floor landing to peek through the stained glass transom window over my bedroom door and spy on me. If I left my room, they snuck into my closet to laugh at whatever I'd recently written in my diary, which they always found.

Once I turned 16 and could drive to school, I sometimes had to take Kerry and Jennifer with me. But I didn't have to like it.

I made them sit in the enormous back seat of my red 1974 Mercury Montego with a black landau top and gigantic V-8 engine. (Guys loved my car, which may have been why I picked it.) Every time those two laughed, I was convinced they were making fun of me, so I kept turning up the knob of my stereo trying to drown them out. I mostly played Pink Floyd, my favorite—maybe made even more so by the fact that they despised it. When Jennifer and Kerry would laugh at me—because they delighted in pushing me to my limits—I would put my right arm over the back of my seat and blindly swing, trying to swat them, all the way to school.

Other heartwarming childhood memories include the time I bent down to get a towel out of the bottom drawer in the kitchen and Kerry and Jennifer burst out laughing. I knew they were making fun of my butt, so I turned around and slapped the middle of Kerry's back. Hard. She was wearing a halter top, with skin exposed, and it left a red handprint. She was probably eight or ten at the time. Naturally, she got all the sympathy and I was seen as the bad guy.

That just proved what I already knew: Everyone liked her better than they liked me.

Except Dad.

Whenever one of us would call him, he'd answer the phone by saying, "Is this the pretty one or the smart one?"

When he asked, I'd usually answer, "Both," because that's how he made me feel.

Kerry had followed in the footsteps of my mom's family. My grandfather was a radiologist and my grandmother was a nurse. Kerry earned a degree in therapeutic recreation (using play to

work with children) and later, like Mom, returned to nursing
school to become a registered nurse. She worked at the local
dermatology office, fielded our medical questions, and has long
had the privilege of studying the whole family's odd-shaped
moles and strange rashes. When it comes to medicine, she is the
smart one.

Most of the time, though, Kerry was assumed to be the
pretty one, and in most practical matters, I was considered the
smart one. I handled all tasks related to business and finance
and art—helping Dad calculate his sales tax payments, typing
the consignment lists of paintings being delivered to a gallery,
designing his promotional brochures, updating the materials
list for his next workshop, submitting photos of paintings for
juried exhibitions, telling Dad the right way to spell a word he
invented for a new painting title. An unbiased observer might
say Kerry and I are equal when it comes to intellectual abilities,
and her grades in college may have, in fact, been better than
mine. But I am *not* unbiased, and I am a firstborn, so I hold tight
to the idea of being the best.

Even when I was actively doing marketing or design for Dad,
correcting his spelling, or trying to fix his phone or computer—
being the smart one—I always knew that, to him, I was pretty,
too. He kind of owed me, since I looked so much like him. No
woman wants to have her father's muscular, freckled calves. I
remember one morning when I ran across the street to help Dad
set up his booth at the festival near my house. I didn't have on
my usual eye makeup yet, and felt blah, but Dad commented
on how pretty I looked. (Perhaps without the makeup, I looked
more like him.)

Because Kerry and I grew up in such a small community,
every achievement was documented in the local newspaper—
honor roll, 4-H ribbons earned (mine in photography, hers in
baking), photos of me as an FFA officer attending state and

national conventions, photos of her dribbling the basketball when her team won a game, and so on. Kerry is good at nearly everything she does, but has never craved the spotlight, which is good because most of the time when her name made it into the paper, they spelled it with *l*'s instead of *r*'s, assuming someone had just written it down wrong.

If they'd stopped to think about it, they would have known I could never have set a cross-country record. Few things get under Kerry's skin, but my getting the credit for her achievements is one of them.

Mom and Dad always switched our names around—I was Kerrelly, and she was Kellery. The worst was when Kerry got married and opened a wedding present—a personalized Bible on which scripty gold-leaf letters spelled out "Doug and Kelly Dunham." Doug colored through the *l*'s with a black Sharpie, but still, that's not something you can really hide.

The thing that was so brilliant about my dad's question for my sister and me—*Is this the pretty one or the smart one?*—is that, by asking the question that way, he found a way to let us both know we were special.

When I remember spending time with Dad, I don't picture Kerry there at all; I thought she was always at sports practice or hanging out with one of her ten best friends. So imagine my surprise when Dad got sick and I discovered how close he and Kerry were. Dad's been gone now for years, and I'm still trying to rewrite what I know about their relationship. Because deep in my soul, I always felt I was the *real* favorite. Kerry felt the same way. She and Dad went together to the airstrip to fly model planes. She rode with him on the lawn mower. And so on. Maybe they spent more time together than Dad and I did. I honestly don't know. What I do know is that when I wasn't locked in my room hand-drawing my own magazine, or reading, or simmering with teenage anger directed toward my mom—on those occasions when I came out and spent time with family—I knew my dad adored and understood me, just as I was. It takes a special kind of talent to convince each daughter that she is the favorite. That was one of his greatest gifts to us.

Yet no matter how close Kerry and Dad were, I still believe I had something special and unique with him. It was more than the masculine calves or the matching red hair or the tendency to get sunburns. Dad was my safe place. Unlike the entire rest of the world, he was on my side no matter what. We were connected by our creativity, by that indefinable thing inside that pushes us to express through our creations the beauty we see, the wonder we experience by observing the world around us. My art looks different from his—I use a computer for design and paint visual images with words, and he was a master with a paintbrush or pencil. I have a short temper and perpetually choose to live in a state of high stress, whereas Dad was laid-back and slow-paced. We weren't exactly the same. And yet we fit together without effort.

In many ways, I'm more like my mom. We both loved to read and loved all-things-words. I have her uncanny ability to buy just the perfect weird gift for nearly anyone in my life. We were amused by so many of the same things. I'm skeptical and sarcastic, but she was downright cynical. My friend Peggy calls me the rule-following rebel because I will always follow the rules until I decide they don't make sense. I got the rebel gene from my mom. She was usually mostly quiet about it, but it was there. Most of my teen years I listened to Joan Jett's song "You're a Nag" at full volume, hoping Mom would get the message. When I fought with a friend, Mom left the book *How to Win Friends and Influence People* on my pillow. I promptly carried the book downstairs and threw it on her bed without opening it.

We constantly clashed. She asked too many questions (when I was trying to do my own rebelling). She was annoying precisely because she always knew exactly what I was doing that I shouldn't be. She knew when I had too much debt and spent too much, when I went to Target to buy clean clothes for my kids for preschool pictures because I was so far behind on my laundry and couldn't find a thing for them to wear, and when I should have been working but instead was meeting friends for lunch. She was critical about everything, and I refused to be that way.

When she died, I was more lost than I'd ever been.

Still, even then, I knew that Dad believed in me. He understood me in a different way. The parts of me that come from Dad seem to run deeper, to the very core of who I am. But in truth, I'm a pretty good blend. I'm one of them. And the other. Both. Neither.

I'm talking in circles. I am a walking, talking mass of contradictions that I can't define, but I so badly want to. I just want to be able to put a name to it, to all of it—what I'm feeling, what I've lost, who I was, who I am, who I'm becoming. I want to tame this pain and stop missing them. I want to give it a name so I can be in control of myself again.

I want to let go of this *missing*.

When Mom died, the moment was quiet and peaceful, but inside I don't think she ever stopped kicking and screaming against the injustice of it all. I should have been relieved that her pain-filled, diminished existence came to an end. But I remained unsettled. When God yanked her away from us against all of our wills, it felt like cruelty, not compassion.

What kind of God does that? The faith that had brought me comfort for years suddenly seemed like a sham. Did God "take" her or did she simply go? Was it divine cruelty or heavenly compassion?

I was still wrestling with these questions, still trying to figure out who I was and who I wanted to be. I struggled to reconcile my questions about God's character, nature, and sovereignty, to figure out how much or little he had to do with taking my mom away from me. It felt like I was still in the early, raw stages of grief—when suddenly it was six years later, and I was setting up my dad's deathbed in my sister's living room, right next door to my house.

Rob O'Dell, who is very sensitive to the moods of nature, sees the whole truth of nature in the subtle monotones of Winter, the gold of Autumn, in the quiet of Spring and the rich warmth of Summer. The mood always quiet and peaceful portraying the tenderness and affection revealed in even the most somber of nature's moods.

—Art show brochure, Welna Gallery, 936 Michigan Avenue, Chicago, Illinois, 1969

FAIR WARNING

14" x 21"

Description:
Sunny summer landscape
with storm clouds rolling in
from the distance

In 2014, several years after we moved into our new house and three years after Mom died, Dad was diagnosed with esophageal cancer. It shouldn't have been such a shock after his lifetime of heartburn and indigestion, after decades of smoking cigarettes and drinking Manhattans before dinner (while Kerry and I fought over who got the maraschino cherry soaked in whiskey and vermouth), after years of sleeping propped up to lessen his reflux.

But no one (other than my mom) really ever *expects* this kind of news.

Once Dad was diagnosed, he and Rita sought the best medical care in Florida, where they lived. The doctors advised an extensive surgery to remove a portion of his esophagus, with a year (or longer) recovery and many permanent limitations—and Dad said, "No thank you." He'd watched Mom be miserable throughout three years of treatments, and if he couldn't play golf or enjoy a glass of wine or eat popcorn at the movies, he wasn't interested in gaining a few more months.

I understood to a degree, I did. But also, I did not. Why

wouldn't he fight?

Although he put his foot down about surgery, Dad agreed to try chemo and radiation at a Mayo clinic a few hours from their home in Bonita Springs. Kerry and I flew down on alternate weeks to be with him.

At first, he was thinking the worst, but before long, as the treatments worked as planned, he felt optimistic about recovering. One morning, I walked with Dad to his radiation treatment. He slipped his feet into his sandals. His feet were startlingly white—at home, he always wore tennis shoes or golf shoes, so his size-13s never saw the light of day. But now he wore sandals. Sometimes even loafers with no socks. Rita took him to get pedicures to keep his toenails looking decent. All I knew is his bare feet looked weird to me.

I looked away, embarrassed.

As we walked slowly in the beautiful bright-summer Florida light, dappled palm tree shadows making a pattern on the sidewalk, he grabbed my hand. Maybe to help him remain steady, but he'd held my hand like that my whole life, so it was just as likely an expression of affection. I loved how his hands, large and freckled and much like my own, were always soft but never delicate.

Dad's hands were soft and uncalloused, but making his art was an active, physical process. He stood at his drafting table, and sprayed water, and mixed colors, and tilted the board to let the colors run in the right direction. He moved quickly, before the paint could dry, adding some sepia or burnt sienna, using an old butter knife to scratch weeds into the foreground. He liberally sprinkled on the crystally salt at just the right moment, and flicked the bristles of the toothbrush to create a splatter that mimicked seed heads on the grasses, getting paint under his thumbnail when he splattered it to create wildflowers or snow. But that day he was moving slowly, and his thumbnail was clean.

While we sat on the padded bench outside the treatment room, he and I found ourselves both looking up at the same big, modern abstract painting across from us. I can't remember details now—I just remember it contained a lot of yellow. There was one particular spot that had caught my eye all week, and while I can't remember the reason now, I do remember that, without my saying a word, Dad pointed to the very same spot and said, "Why do you think they did that?"

I loved it when I saw the same things he did.

I loved that he wanted to know what I thought.

That afternoon, Dad gave Rita a break from caregiving to make phone calls and pay bills, and he and I went to lunch together. After slurping down bowls of soup at Panera, we spied a Michael's in the nearby strip mall. Detour! Dad wanted to do some sketches, and I needed something to fill my time. We wandered the aisles, looking at brushes and soft lead drawing pencils, discussing brands of watercolor paints. He always preferred Grumbacher Academy brand, a student-grade pigment that was more granular than the higher-end brands, and he was able to pick up a few colors he needed. We felt the smoothness of the paper in the sketch pads, added a large kneaded eraser to our basket. I grabbed a colored pencil set and a book of intricate geometric patterns, much like the coloring books Mom bought me when I was a teen, to entertain me while I waited through Dad's appointments. We were like kids in a candy shop. I hadn't seen him so happy in days.

Then we went to the movies. I wish I could remember what we saw, but I know the matinee was sparsely attended, just a few retirees. We sat in the fancy reclining seats, ate popcorn, and lost ourselves in a world without cancer.

Afterward, as we ambled back into the public gathering spaces at Mayo, several fellow residents (all battling esophageal cancer) saw Dad and motioned him over to say hi. When they saw our bags, they asked what we'd been doing. After Dad told them, we started to walk away when someone mentioned that they were still serving dinner in the dining room. Dad said, "Nah, I had popcorn at the movies and I'm full." I glanced back at the looks of surprise on their faces. Popcorn is one of those foods that most people who have or have had esophageal cancer cannot eat because it's difficult to swallow. Dad just smiled and grabbed my hand again as we walked toward his room.

I smiled and thought, *My daddy is the coolest.*

Even after Dad's treatments were complete, he had to permanently give up his predinner/cocktail-hour Manhattans— the whiskey was too harsh—but he could still drink a glass of red wine before dinner and enjoy all his favorite meals. If he'd opted for surgery, those foods would have been literally off the table. After he and Rita went back to Bonita Springs, they continued to play in golf tourneys, dance at the country club, eat dinner with friends, take drives in his convertible, swim in their pool.

And of course Dad painted whenever he had a free morning.

Turns out, refusing surgery seemed to be the right choice. Dad's life—while different from the one he'd led in Ladoga—was full and good. He had regular scopes and checkups and was in remission for three years.

All was well until his heart started acting up.

Artists like O'Dell are to be treasured in today's changing world. He does in paintings what a poet like Robert Frost did in words. He preserves not just the images but the spirit of the land that makes Americans unique and strong. There is peace and beauty in all he paints.

—*The Commercial Appeal*, Memphis, Tennessee, October 1970

DETAILS, DETAILS, DETAILS

28″ x 14″

Description: Single painting with three painted rectangles of images, each a close-up view into the windows and doors of an old wooden barn, with different patterns of light and shadows

About that time, I learned a new term: AFib, or atrial fibrillation. This is when the heart beats erratically, with the upper and lower chambers out of sync. Untreated, it can lead to blood clots, stroke, and heart failure, among other things. Dad's heart had always been healthy and strong until cancer (or at least the cancer treatments) ruined that, too.

In late April 2017, Dad flew "home" (to the studio apartment) to mat and frame paintings for an upcoming art show in Decatur, Illinois. He had dinner at the Compound several evenings, saw his grandkids, and ordered the Speedy Gonzalez, his favorite lunch combo at Little Mexico. But we all noticed how quickly Dad got winded when walking. Or talking. Or doing pretty much anything. And he had a really bad pain in his upper back that wouldn't go away.

After his show, Dad returned to Bonita Springs. A few days later he left me a voicemail. "Call me. I need to talk to you."

That was weird. I called right back, and Dad put me on speaker. Normally, Dad and I would chat while Rita puttered around in the background, doing her own thing, occasionally laughing at something Dad said or adding a comment.

This time, though, Rita was right there beside him.

She took great care of Dad, researched his meds, monitored his numbers, scheduled his appointments, but worried about minor side effects and potential complications that hadn't happened yet. I half-listened to her telling me about Dad's latest appointments—*uh-huh, yep*—while I picked up the living room and wiped down the kitchen counter. Until she said, "Kelly, this is serious. I need to make sure you understand that."

Oh.

I stopped in the middle of the dining room and sank into a chair to actually listen. Dad wasn't feeling right, so Rita had taken him to the cardiologist's office and refused to leave until they could see the doctor. He was having trouble breathing, and his lungs were filling with fluid. His heart was in AFib again, which meant he couldn't go off his Eliquis, the blood thinner that kept him from having a stroke. But in order to have the procedure that would drain the fluid, he had to stop taking it for at least five days. On top of all that, Dad had a strong pain in his back, so bad that he couldn't sleep, which they thought might be a compression fracture. The doctor sent Dad straight to the ER. When those doctors couldn't get Dad's heart back into rhythm, they admitted him to the hospital. Kerry got on a plane the next morning; at that moment, she was the smart one.

Every time I said, "Promise me you'll let me know if you think I need to be there," she assured me, "I think he's fine."

Dad's health didn't improve. The procedure to shock his heart back into rhythm failed. They performed a thoracentesis to drain two liters of fluid from around his heart—which made them think perhaps he had congestive heart failure. But the fluid came right back, which didn't make sense. His heart was jumping all over the place. He felt terrible.

I was terrified Dad would die before I could get to Florida

to see him, so I volunteered to swap places with Kerry when she needed to go back to work—and then I was terrified to have to make medical decisions without knowing enough about it.

After Kerry picked me up from the airport, she detoured to make sure I knew where Target was in case I needed to escape for a bit. Along the way, as I looked out the passenger window at all the palm trees and upscale shopping centers, I found myself in completely new territory. Suddenly she was acting like the big sister. She gave me a rundown of Dad's meds and conditions and how they affected each other. She told me what to watch for, what the complications might be, and why certain things mattered. Every few minutes, she interspersed some form of "Kelly, you can totally handle this. You'll be fine."

My good-natured dad was short-tempered and struggling to be kind to the people taking care of him. He was rude to the nursing staff—saying, "*Ouch, that hurt me*," when they moved him, complaining about the food and his pain, ringing his buzzer the moment pain meds were due to ask for more. I'd enjoyed being there for the first day, but before long he was even stressing me out.

The doctors battled constantly—each specialist declared (but without much confidence) that it was ____ (fill in the blank with something within their specialty), but none of their treatment plans helped. It was a constant struggle to balance meds and side effects. Fluid continued to accumulate around his lungs, but the CAT scans (and X-rays and ultrasounds and cultures) were clean. Nothing pointed to malignancy, or anything at all. He had to be off the blood thinner while the drain was in, but as long as his heart was in AFib, they had to worry about blood clots. And now he was getting worse: oxygen levels decreasing, shortness of breath increasing, pain and more pain. Now they were saying he might have pneumonia from all the fluid. IV antibiotics, heart going in and out of rhythm, constipation. His right lung collapsed.

And then, suddenly, the room lit up and the angels sang a hallelujah chorus—because in walked a beautiful Italian-looking man in a white coat. I sat up straight in my chair. When Dad and Rita complained about the heart doctor that sent them to the ER and didn't seem to want to be bothered by them, *this* was not who I imagined. And on top of that, even though he'd just returned from vacation, Dr. G was impressively well-informed about what was happening. I've always liked it when people get straight to the point, and he talked, thought, and moved quickly. He proclaimed that Dad needed exploratory surgery to see what was really going on. He'd already requested a transfer to a Naples hospital with a thoracic surgeon; once Dad was accepted as a patient and the hospital arranged to transfer him, they would schedule surgery.

We'd been in the hospital long enough to know this would take some serious time. Since it was Thursday afternoon, we assumed he'd be moved on Friday, see the specialist on Monday, and, hopefully, have surgery on Tuesday. I encouraged Rita to keep her plans in Ohio with her grandkids, ushered her out the door, and sat down to wait.

Instead, the aides came in to transport him immediately. I scrambled to gather all the things we'd accumulated over the past week and hauled them in multiple trips to the car. The ambulance left before I did, so I drove like a bat out of hell toward Tampa, plugging in the address while I drove. Before I could find a parking place, the thoracic surgeon wrapped up his initial consultation, ordered more tests, and told Dad he'd be back in the morning.

After Dad fell asleep, I drove the 30 minutes back to his empty house, crying all the way, hitting the steering wheel and cussing. This was too much for me. *Kerry is the nurse, dammit.*

The next morning, I backed out of the driveway at 6 a.m.

to be there when Dad woke up—only to arrive as they were prepping him for video-assisted thoracic surgery (VATS) to check for cancer in the lining of the lung and to seal it to stop fluid from re-accumulating.

From that point on, it's a blur. *Is Dad gonna die? Why in the hell am I here by myself? How can I deal with everything happening at home (issues with Bobby and chronic migraines and fed-up administrators and last-chance-finals-week) when my dad might be dying? Please, God, don't let him die.*

A nurse comes out to tell me they'd had to make a short incision instead of just the tiny hole they'd described earlier. *Oh, shit. I can't remember why they said they might have to do that— something about the drainage catheter? Or an infection? Dammit. Why isn't Kerry here?* I can't Google it because one of Dad's golfing buddies has come to make awkward small talk—*What do you do? Do you have children? How do you know my dad?* I'm saved by a nurse leading me to a private room to hear the results of the surgery.

The minute Dr. Solomon walks in, I know. *Fuck.*

You'd think I'd remember the surgeon's exact words, but they went something like this: "We opened up his chest cavity and it is completely full of cancer, like a mass of cobwebs we couldn't get through."

He maintains sincere eye contact, which I notice instead of processing his words. "The cancer is in his lungs, wrapped around his heart. There is nothing I can do. I am so sorry. We closed him back up but we can't do anything for him."

I fight to keep my voice steady, but I can't see through my tears. My brain tries to retain the slippery medical terminology, but I don't even know what to ask.

How much time does he have left? (Could be days, could be two or three months.)

Can they do anything for him? (Just manage his pain.)

Dad will need PT to regain his strength, so he will likely go to rehab before he goes home and will need home health care to drain the fluid twice a week.

I somehow manage to choke out the most urgent question. "Will you tell him or do I have to?" A sob burst from my chest with the words.

The doctor assured me, "I'll tell him once he wakes up. You don't have to."

Thank you, Jesus. Because I just *can't.*

I pace the hallway outside the waiting room while I call Kerry, who tells me I asked all the right questions, and then Rita, who asks, "Do I need to get on a plane?" I tell her to take this time to do the things she'd planned with her family because it's going to be a long haul and we'll need her later.

She cries when I tell her, "It's not all on you, Rita. Kerry and I are here—for both of you."

Finally the nurse guides me into a cramped cubicle in recovery. Dad drifts in and out of sleep while I look at the machines and IV fluids and curtains and everything except him so I don't start crying. I fidget, waiting for the surgeon to come in and give Dad the bad news.

One of the nurses pulls me outside. "Honey, Dr. Solomon won't be back until morning rounds. The pain meds will make your dad sleep through the night. Go home and get some rest."

"Are you sure? I don't want him to be alone when they tell him." My voice rises as I choke on a sob.

She pauses until I regain control. "I'm sure. You need your rest, too."

I kiss Dad on the forehead and tell him I'll be back in the morning, but he doesn't stir.

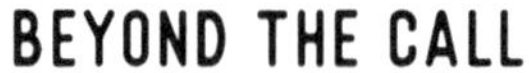

BEYOND THE CALL

20" x 29"

Description: Quiet country
cemetery with an American flag
flying on a pole

On the way home from the hospital, I stop at a little Italian market to get dinner. As I climb back into the car, my phone rings. Dr. G wants to know if I have questions about the surgery. He mentions something about how Dad had taken the news.

"What? No! I wasn't there. I was supposed to be there when they told him. Crap!"

Dr. G says, so gently, "You need to go be with him."

I drive like a madwoman all the way back to Naples, arriving right at 6 p.m., only to discover that no visitors are allowed between 6 and 8 p.m. The nurse lowers her voice. "I didn't expect Dr. Solomon to come in today. It was pretty harsh the way he gave him the news. I'll let you in as soon as we finish shift report."

Shit.

When I finally walk back into that little room, Dad and I both burst into tears.

"Honey, I thought you were avoiding me." His voice gets all high-pitched and squeaky when he cries.

"They told me to go home. They told me they weren't going

to tell you 'til tomorrow. I'm so sorry!"

"I'm glad you're here," he manages to say. I pull up a chair and hold his hand.

I don't want him to see me crying, but I can't stop. We talk about how much this stinks.

"I wonder if I'll ever get to go home," he wonders—and whether "home" would be Rita's house or one of ours. "She shouldn't have to take care of me, and it would be wrong to take over your lives. You girls are so busy."

The surgeon told Dad to see an oncologist, so we speculate about what treatments might be an option—and whether he wants to feel like crap the rest of his life. Mom felt like we made her suffer through treatments that she didn't want, so this time, I step back and let Dad lead. "We'll be glad to give you our opinions, but the final decision is yours."

He is almost giddy with triumph to have an explanation for the scapula pain. When I tell him they decided not to do a cardioversion for his AFib, he throws back his head, laughing. "Is it wrong to think a clot wouldn't be such a bad idea right about now?"

I sit and hold his hand—oh, how I love his big, freckled hands—and pretend to be strong. *Please, God. Help.*

As I drive back to Rita's later that night, Dr. G calls again. "I understand your pain," he says. He'd lost his dad a few months earlier. "I see how much you and your sister love your father, and I'll do whatever I can to help. But I think he needs to be at home with you."

He tells me that after he met Dad, he looked up his website. "I'm so impressed by your dad's talent," he says.

That doesn't surprise me, but still, all I can think is, This is so weird.

And then it gets weirder.

"You believe in God, don't you?" he asks me.

My eyes open wider and I'm glad he can't see my expression. I tell him that I write about prayer and faith, and he asks where he can buy a copy of my book. I promise to bring him one.

"You have my number. Call me anytime—even if it's 3 a.m.— if you need anything at all."

I cry as I drive the rest of the way home—and again as I fall asleep—but I'm just so grateful, too. *Thank you, God, for showing up in this hell.*

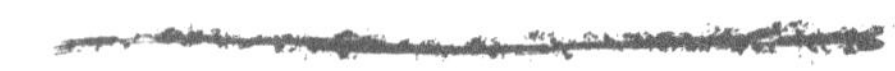

The next morning, Dr. G walks into Dad's room and smiles— at me, not Dad. "Oh, good! I wanted to catch you so I could get my book."

I'd gone back and forth about how to sign it for him—it felt awkward to use his first name, so I finally wrote, "For Dr. G with gratitude." He says he'll treasure it, then starts toward the door before turning around.

"Give me a hug," he says.

Dad's eyes get really wide as they meet mine over the doctor's shoulder. I may have mentioned that this man is just slightly older than I am, handsome and intense and successful and confident and lean and, well, beautiful?

The instant he leaves, Dad starts laughing. "Wow, that was weird. He kept looking at you and smiling. I think he likes you."

When the nurse comes by, I ask if Dad can have chocolate on his cardio diet. She goes to catch Dr. G, and returns with a raised eyebrow. "He says your dad can have a Big Mac, chocolate, Steak 'n Shake, whatever he wants."

Dad says, "I guess there are perks when the doctor has a crush on your daughter."

I text Kerry about it all, and she writes back, "Hmm. Sounds like there must be a little of that going on. Did he have anything to say regarding Dad and cardiac stuff or was this just a social call?"

It feels so good to laugh.

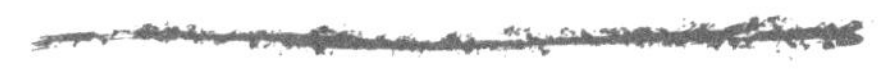

That night, the night before Dad's 79th birthday, I stayed up late to bake a chocolate cherry cake—because "my" doctor was allowing Dad to have chocolate and this was his favorite kind. Some friends stopped to visit, and though Dad wasn't hungry, he shared his cake. He was in a better mood—there was still more he didn't know, and he was worried, but he finally had some answers.

He sat in bed, talking on the phone to Rita, Kerry, his sister, and whichever friends called to check on him—but his room faced right into the bright, setting sun. So he talked on the phone, wearing his green hospital gown and his sunglasses. Breathing into a spirometer, wearing his shades.

Such a cool daddy. And fitting, since Dad included the sunglasses emoji in every text message he sent after he moved to Florida.

Doug arrived and offered to sit with Dad at night so I could sleep. One morning, Dad cried his eyes out telling me about Doug holding the water cup for Dad and offering to pray with him. "I just can't believe he was so sweet to me. We're lucky to have him in the family."

I agreed, then went into the bathroom and sobbed—how can any daughter not cry in response to her dad's tears?

GOING HOME

6″ x 9″

Description: A lone barn, straight on, with a purple-and-orange sunset shining through the open hayloft door

A few days later, Kerry went to Florida to relieve Doug. Dr. G called her to say the new combination of meds was successfully regulating Dad's heart rate and blood pressure, so he should "take this window of stability and get the heck out of here while he can."

Before hanging up, he mentioned that he had a signed copy of my book, and then said, "Rob reminds me of my dad, and I want to take care of him the same way I would for him."

Rita (and Kerry and I) thought that the responsibility for Dad's care shouldn't fall solely on Rita—plus, we wanted to be with him. He needed to get home, but it's a long way from Florida to Indiana—16 hours under the best of conditions. We looked into renting a full-size van, but he was in so much pain he couldn't sit up in the seat. Would an RV be better, if we could find one? At least he could sleep. But the jostling would kill him. An ambulance? Better care, but same issue with bumpy roads.

After a flurry of phone calls with doctors and social workers and hospice agencies, Kerry found out that we could fly him home in a private medical plane for $16,000. It's a ton of money,

but we didn't have a lot of time, and we needed to move him
now. Whatever it took. What was money for if not to make
things like this possible for someone you love? Dad agreed with
the plan, though he insisted on paying for it himself.

While Kerry coordinated things from Florida, I called
around to find a specific Tempur-Pedic mattress model that
could be raised and lowered like a hospital bed. Dad was
apprehensive about what it would mean for Kerry and me to
care for him, but he felt well enough to draw some different
furniture configurations for the room on a napkin while they
waited for the flight.

I bought a wheeled hospital table, scheduled oxygen delivery,
laundered new sheets, procured a walker and toilet seat, had
Tim install a handheld sprayer in the shower, contracted
with the same hospice agency that had cared for Mom, made
an appointment with the local oncologist, and transformed
Kerry's family room into a sick room for Dad, complete with
room-darkening curtains and a futon for us to sleep on. In the
last stages of preparation on this end, as I walked through the
grocery buying food and protein shakes, a bouquet of sunflowers
caught my attention. They made me think of Van Gogh's
sunflower paintings, and I put them in a red glass vase on the
mantle to brighten up the room.

I texted Kerry pics of her transformed house, and she replied
with the emoji of the muscled arm: "Sissies for the win!"

vignette

Rob O'Dell has found beauty all around him as he has walked an open field and touched the aging wood of a broken fence. He has seen a country road in winter partially covered with snow drifts and cold weather birds perched on power lines. He has studied the appearance of barns and farmhouses and all that is the essence of rural life—that which he knows is passing.

—Cheryl D. Peck, "O'Dell Paints Scenes of Disappearing World," *Herald & Review*, Decatur, Illinois, August 2, 1971

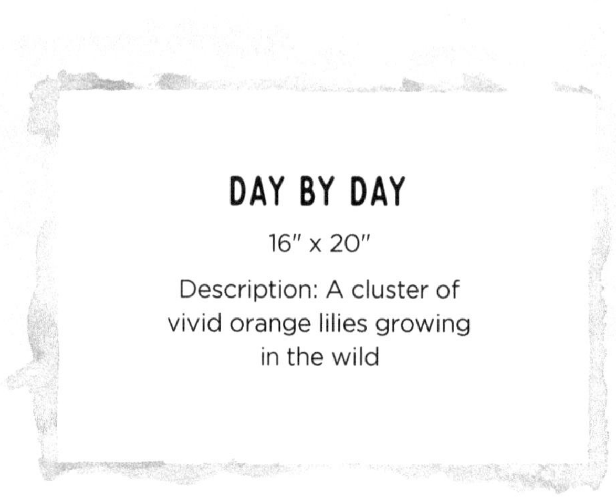

Within days, we'd settled into a routine with Dad's care.

I designed a daily calendar, which we three-hole-punched and placed in a thin binder. Every morning, someone (usually Kerry) wrote out that day's schedule—most often decorated by the non-artistic sister—so Dad could see at a glance who would be taking care of him and during which hours. When he would have a visit from hospice and get a bath. Which friend was scheduled to stop by that day. When the fluid would be drained from the tube still in his side. Who was sleeping overnight with him on the lumpy futon, the bright light from the bathroom shining in our eyes, dozing fitfully in between the mental recalculations/countdown to the next dose of oxycodone.

We tried to get Dad to walk five feet into the bathroom when he had to go, but he was content to stay in bed with a urinal.

Kerry's and my kids—his grandkids—wandered in and out. One day Katie, my oldest, stopped to visit her Bebop.

"Come and sit and tell me what's new with you," Dad said.

She perched on the edge of the bed. "Am I sitting on

your oxygen?"

My dad suddenly went still, his head nodding like he was
falling asleep. Then he flopped his hands over his head and acted
like he was dead.

He'd do anything for a laugh.

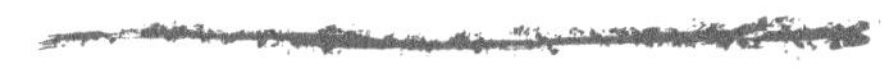

Periodically, I ran next door to my house to answer emails
and finish projects for my clients. Kerry and Doug and Tim went
to work and came home, and whoever was there gathered beside
Dad's bed whenever we could.

Every morning, we served him breakfast—an applesauce
and the Ensure shakes Rita bought for him and maybe a strip
of bacon, which he wouldn't eat—and then left the room as he
called Rita.

She had spent the first few days with her family in Illinois,
and then came to Indiana with us for a week or so. When she
saw that everything was under control, and it looked like it
could go on like this for a while, she went back to Florida to take
care of some things at home, planning to come back soon. But
as the days went on, she still hadn't made plans to return. Kerry
and I thought it was probably just too hard for her to be there.
Rita had lost her husband Jim to cancer several years earlier. She
wanted to be there for Dad, but she'd already lost the love of her
life and father of her children—and then her friend, my mom.
She couldn't bear to watch her other great love leave.

When Dad was talking to her on the phone, we had to
stay nearby in case he needed anything. He didn't always wear
his hearing aids, so he played all phone calls on speaker at full
volume—anyone in the house could hear their conversation. One
morning I typed a mini transcript into my phone from the next
room when Dad was talking about us.

"They're at my beck and call, and what if I didn't have this? I can't believe that I get to do this, that they're willing to do this as long as they can stand it."

He paused, voice straining to get the rest out without crying. "I didn't even realize this would happen. I can't even comprehend. They don't seem burdened at all about it. Everybody's on board."

Rita told him, "Rob, this is what the girls wanted. I hope my kids can do something close to this when my time comes, but even then it would only be one person and their spouse at any given time in one place." Her kids all lived in different states—no Compound for them.

Dad said, "What an amazing thing to happen, to have them like this—next door."

After several years of living in this new house, after the months of physical labor, the money worries of trying to renovate this place and sell the old one, our kids hanging out together, Kerry and I borrowing sugar and sharing wine and everyone gathering in the Compound—it all made sense.

The reason why it all happened had led to this moment, setting us up so that we could all be physically present for my dad during this awful—and wonderful—time.

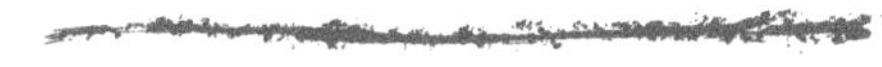

When the oncologist appointment finally came around, Kerry and I knew what the doctor would say. Between her nursing training and my hours on Google, we were too well-informed—and fresh out of hope.

Dad, however, was like a little kid, an eager, expectant look on his face, wondering if this would be the time he would get the giant lollipop.

We borrowed a wheelchair to push Dad into the tiny

examining room, everyone all too aware that this same place is where we came with Mom to get her cancer-related bad news. Kerry and I perched on the plastic chairs crammed into the corners.

Dad tried to be cheerful and charming. The doctor made small talk, not sure why we were there because we'd already been told how far the cancer had progressed.

Dad said something like, "If there's something I need to do, I'll do it. But if not, I won't. Just let me know."

The doctor looked Dad in the eye and spoke directly to him, not to us.

"I'm really sorry, but there's nothing more we can do for you. Do you need anything? How's your pain level?"

Dad swallowed and looked from Kerry to me, instinctively wanting to protect his girls. But he had to ask.

"How much time do I have?" he asked.

"It's impossible to say. Maybe three months?"

"Three months? Okay! Okay, that's good!"

He smiled at us, happy with the new info. I looked at Kerry, and she looked away. We both knew Dad had already been dealing with the symptoms for several months. That three-month counter started three to four months earlier, but Dad was oblivious to that fact.

I spoke up. "We've been making him get out of bed every day and sit in a chair and walk to the bathroom, but it hurts him."

The doctor, still looking at my dad, answered. "Rob, if you don't want to get out of bed, you don't have to."

Kerry asked, "What about eating? He's lost his appetite and we're giving him Ensure shakes ..."

Again, looking directly at Dad, the oncologist answered, "Eat when you're hungry."

Then, to us, "Any other questions?"

Since we had none, we all shifted as though to leave. The

oncologist approached Dad and held out his hand, saying, "I'm sorry there's not more I can do."

Dad looked the doctor in the eye and replied, "Thank you, sir. Your bedside manner is really calming. You're really good at what you do. Thank you."

Kerry and I turned away so Dad wouldn't see our tears. His death sentence was just confirmed—and Dad is thanking the doctor for being so good at sharing that news?

This—life, cancer, all of it—this just is not fair. Dad is too good for this.

"I like to paint weathered objects particularly," he said. "I'm fascinated by how things deteriorate, the patina that forms. It tells a story. I think a barn has all of the elements and shapes of a good painting in it, with the added bonus of the seasons. The same barn looks completely different in the winter than in the spring."

—Donnette Beckett, "Having an eye for detail," *Herald & Review*, Decatur, Illinois, July 6, 2017

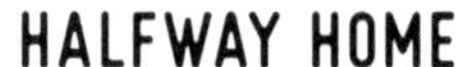

HALFWAY HOME

10″ x 28″

Description: Old barn
in evening light, with a tiny V of
ducks flying through

The days blurred together, turning into one week, then two, then three. Once the doctor told Dad he wasn't going to get better and he didn't have to get up if he didn't want to, he simply gave in and stayed in bed. No anger, maybe a little disappointment and surprise, but mostly peace.

"Honey, the last time I played golf, I never would have imagined it would have been my last time."

And glimpses of his corny humor. "I sold another painting. I guess people've heard."

When a Decatur, Illinois, newspaper announced that Dad was the recipient of the prestigious Herb Slodounik Artistic Merit Award (a lifetime achievement award named after an Illinois photojournalist), he threw back his head and laughed. "Unexpected death benefit!"

As I emptied the red vase of sunflowers on the mantle, he commented, "Those flowers make me want to paint. It's hard to believe I'll never paint again."

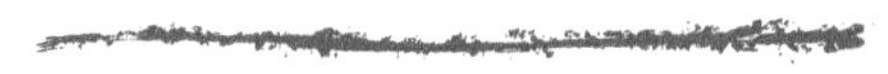

The overnight shifts were the hardest, but those were the sweetest moments, too. Dad would wake me up—"Babe, come over here for a minute"—and he'd hold my hand and start talking. "I need to talk about this incident in my class this morning."

He started describing a woman in one of his workshops, and what a troublemaker she was. She was upsetting others and trying to take over. Dad couldn't be sure if he kicked her out of the class or not, and he was quite upset to think he had done such a thing. I explained, not for the first time, that this was something he dreamed. I was trying not to say the word *hallucination.*

He was incredulous. "That's not real? Honey, I am just ... shocked."

"How about this, Dad? Whenever you're not sure if something is real or not, tell me and I'll let you know."

A minute later, his thumb rubbing my hand over and over: "My ladies were really protective of me."

"Yes, Dad, they always take care of you."

Then, "I haven't thought about art for three weeks and it's kind of nice to be back in that world."

Throughout that night, he asked me questions: *Did this person say that? Did I really go there?* And I would answer, "No, Dad, it was a dream."

Finally, in the early hours of the morning, after another such exchange, Dad softly said, "Honey, that's kind of annoying." So the rest of the night, I kept my mouth shut as he fretted and worried, making noncommittal sounds so he knew I was there.

One night, as Dad was getting ready to go to sleep, he said, "I'm just really sad." Kerry and I were both in the room so we walked over to his bed. She kissed him on the forehead and we each held one hand.

Kerry said, "Dad, it's okay to be sad."

His eyes full of tears, he said, "I love you both so very much."

Another night, Kerry was alone on overnight duty and he asked her, "See those people standing over there with all the shirts? Right behind you?"

It reminded me of how Mom, in her final days, kept looking at the corner and saying, "Ooh, I don't like those scary men in the white shirts." Later, I realized that throughout the Bible people were afraid of angels in all their terrible beauty, falling on their faces in fear when they appeared. So this wasn't scary, this was really beautiful.

Except that it was also terrifying.

As Kerry and Dad discussed the people in white clothes, she asked him, "Is there anything I can do for you?"

He replied—the man who had only recently started going to church, the one who never spoke about faith or anything else, someone who had probably never uttered these words before: "Just lead me to the promised land. I'm trying to get home."

NEVER ENOUGH TIME

30″ x 40″

Description: A farmstead with several barns, sheds, and silos with a tractor parked in the barnyard

Dad came back to Indiana on June 16, and by Kerry's birthday, on July 9, he had declined significantly. That morning, I had breakfast next to Dad's bed and then left for church. Kerry stayed with him, but almost as soon as I got to church I felt this urgency to get back home, so I took the car and left Tim to get a ride from someone else.

Kerry was sitting in the recliner next to Dad's bed and her goldendoodle, Tucker, was sitting upright, alert, in her lap. She said, "This is so weird. Tucker has been right here all morning." In the previous three weeks, we'd often commented on the way Tucker would sleep beneath the hospital bed as though he was protecting Dad.

Shortly after I got there, Kerry and I confronted the hospice nurse when she was away from Dad in another room, telling her we could see a substantial decline. Could she please tell us the truth about how long this could go on like this? Dad wasn't awake. We weren't able to give him meds most of the time. He was in pain and moaned in his sleep.

She assured us Dad probably had another week or more.

Another week of this agony? Damn. We were too embarrassed to let her see our disappointment. We weren't looking for hope, we were looking for relief. For him, but also for us.

I'd been asking Nathan and Peggy, my pastors and friends, to come pray for Dad, but Dad was always sleeping when they had time to visit, so it hadn't happened yet. But once church let out that day, they came to see us. Amy, a close family friend, was there fixing lunch. My son, Bobby, came and sat with us.

Nathan positioned himself at the foot of Dad's bed, his hand wrapped around Dad's ankle through the blanket.

Another couple arrived to visit. Kerry was in the other room greeting them, when Nathan suddenly sat up straighter and said, "Where's Kerry? Go get Kerry." Amy and I looked at each other, eyes wide, and she went to the kitchen, bringing Kerry back.

Kerry said, "What's the matter? What's going on?"

Nathan said, "Where's Doug?" Doug had run to Kroger to grab a few groceries we needed. Kerry tried to call Doug, but he didn't answer.

We stood around the bed, alternately looking at each other and watching Dad breathe. The hospice nurse was in the front hallway talking on the phone, trying to get a doctor to update the dosage of one of Dad's meds.

Nathan said something to the effect of, "It's time."

Kerry—the nurse—argued. "No, he's been like this. Has something happened? Nothing has changed."

I would find out later that Nathan, a fireman and medic, was monitoring Dad's pulse.

I sat beside Dad on the edge of his bed and held his hand. Amy and Kerry were on the other side of the bed, also touching Dad. Peggy started praying softly out loud, holding on to Dad's other foot. I looked over at Bobby, who was standing a few feet away trying not to cry, so I held out my arm to draw him close to me. It didn't occur to me until weeks later that I should have called Tim and Katie, who were at home next door.

I didn't know what to do with the terror and confusion and uncertainty I felt, so instead I got ticked off at the nurse for continuing to talk on the phone. *Isn't this where she's supposed to be? Shouldn't she help somehow?* "Somebody needs to tell her to get in here."

Within three or four minutes, Dad's breathing slowed way down. Every time he exhaled, we all held our breath, too, waiting for him to inhale again—praying that he would. The space between breaths grew longer and longer. We were all crying, telling Dad how much we loved him.

A couple more breaths, and then there were no more.

We knew who to call when Dad passed, because Dad had been friends with John, the man who owned the local funeral home, for years. He has a second office in the tiny town of Roachdale, about ten minutes from Ladoga, and we arranged a time to meet there to discuss options.

My GPS fails me because there's no cell signal, so I drive up and down the handful of streets until John steps outside an unmarked storefront and waves at me. Kerry is already there. He leads us into a nicely appointed room and seats us at a table with a glossy catalog in front of us. Along the left-hand wall, decorative urns are on display.

Tall and thin, John walks with the manner of a funeral director—softly, unobtrusively, a little bit bent over so as to take up less space. He speaks gently. It must be hard to do this work when the body in question was your golfing buddy and breakfast partner. He takes his seat across from us. John directs us to a premium section in the catalog, since he's sure we'll want something really nice for our dad.

We'd already decided on cremation. Mainly because that's

what everyone else in our family had chosen. Kerry and I fully agree with Mom's sentiment—this body is failing me, so why in the world would I want to preserve it?

Kerry and I turn the pages. *Nope, no, no … definitely not.* Our eyes skim over the oriental cloisonné vases, the big clunky enamel ones with Asian-looking scenes inscribed on them, the shiny brass, the heavy florals. She and I look and look, then go back to the beginning and flip through one more time.

"Dad just would like something plainer, simple. These are too froufrou." Kerry laughs. John adjusts his tie and shifts in his seat. Apparently, we're not being properly reverent. I try to rearrange my face into a nonsmile.

"This is one of our most popular ones," he says as he points to something in the catalog.

"Nope," Kerry and I declare simultaneously.

"Well, umm, what about this?" He gives up on the fancy ones and points to a clunky pewter urn. There's nothing any better, but it feels wrong to put Dad's ashes in something so ugly—and cheap. Shouldn't we get him a high-class container for eternity? Except he isn't going to be in it anyway, and the expensive ones are the ugliest.

They all feel too hard. Too artificial for Dad.

Kerry flips through the catalog again as I look at the ones on display. I glance up at John. "Don't you have, like, I don't know—a pretty wooden box or something?"

I can tell he doesn't know how to respond, but he reluctantly turns to another catalog showing a simple rectangular walnut box. Smooth, straight lines. Simple, clean wood, richly polished. Quality craftsmanship.

"Yep, that's the one," we say. "Anything else?" Kerry and I reach for our purses.

"Well, yes, there are several more things." We sit back in our chairs.

"Would you like to have his name inscribed on the urn?"

Kerry and I glance at each other. "Uhhh … no?"

"Are you sure? It's a very nice touch, and most people do this."

One of us—I don't remember who—says, "Well, it's not like anyone's going to see it!" We both laugh, but John's obvious discomfort makes us feel like we've disappointed him.

"We're not trying to be cheap. I promise. We just know Dad, and we don't think he would want or need all this."

John nods, begrudgingly agreeing. "Okay, as you know, the urn goes into a larger container to protect it from the elements. How would you like his name to read on this?"

I look at Kerry, and she says, "Do we have to do that? Again, who's going to be looking at it?"

John clears his throat and finally meets our eyes. "I'm going to go ahead and throw in the engraving on that." We shrug. Fine. I suppose if the cemetery ever gets dug up, they need to know who they're dealing with.

He tallies up our expenses on the preprinted form—lots of blanks in the price column since we skipped all the extras—and I write out a check. Kerry and I thank John for everything, and leave, promptly bursting into laughter as soon as the door closes behind us.

"That was awful," Kerry says. "John has to think we're the *worst*."

But we both keep laughing. Such a different experience than when Mom died. I don't remember picking out the urn. Maybe Dad did that part all by himself. I bet he didn't laugh.

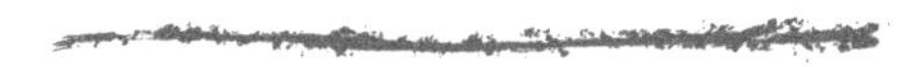

What I do remember is the small cardboard box Dad brought home one day, with a thick, clear plastic bag full of her ashes. Mom had asked that some of her ashes be spread around the homestead, the place that she loved—land that had been in her family for generations with the house built by her great-grandfather, George S. Otterman, that she and Dad renovated and repaired. She spent countless hours on the front porch, the chains of the wooden swing creaking as they shifted in the big metal hooks that held it. She folded and refolded flimsy newsprint pages. Turned the pages of library books, plastic covers crackling. In the distance, tractors chugged by. Farm trucks drove too quickly down the lumpy "country-paved" road—patched with asphalt, no painted lines, barely wide enough for two cars to pass, so most people drive straight down the center until they meet another vehicle. Crickets chirped, bees droned in and around the hollyhocks growing at the end of the porch. Mom resided there, in the noise of the silence.

Dad, Kerry, and I walk down the steps from the porch into the front yard. He opens the box, balancing it as he struggles to get the heavy plastic bag inside open.

I'd never seen human remains before. I thought it would be like the name implies—a pile of sooty ashes. I am startled by the white, irregular chunks nestled in the ash. I can't let myself think about what they are. Instead, I bite my lip. Hold my eyes wide open, hoping the summer breeze will evaporate the tears gathering in my eyes.

We walk slowly down the slight slope away from the house toward the road, Dad and Kerry chatting, me unable to make a single sound or else I will let loose a guttural wail. Words would be a gateway to a place I dared not go.

As we near the pine tree in the corner of the yard, where the front yard meets the side pasture, Dad says, "This is the last walk I'll ever take with her."

I pull back, slowing my pace so I'm a step or two behind. Kerry, being the strong one, keeps sifting ashes and ... bits ... onto the grass in the yard that takes Dad about four hours to mow. With a tractor that will drive right over ... her ... until there is no trace of her to be found.

vignette

The result is a body of work which radiates the peaceful beauty of natural surroundings and places. For many, the appeal of O'Dell's work is his remarkable ability to create a real sense of belonging which is readily experienced by the viewer.

—J.M Mallon Galleries, *ARTlook Indianapolis*, Winter 1993

STANDING ROOM ONLY

13" x 9"

Description: Vertical stalks of
pale pink and red hollyhocks
crowding the page with a splashy
green background full of leaves
and shadows

In November, four months after Dad died, we were all set to host our big sale. One hundred and eighty-seven paintings were on display. There were the landscapes that are instantly recognizable as paintings by Rob O'Dell, but also some more unusual ones: Arizona cliff dwellings; studies of antique toys, ears of corn, and rusted milk jugs created early in Dad's career; nude figure drawings. Not to mention countless trees, Maine boats, rocks, creeks, wildflowers, Florida birds, and foliage. A few were created when Dad was in art school; some were painted weeks before he passed. Of all the subjects Dad painted, hollyhocks were the only thing missing, because they were so popular he sold them as quickly as he could paint them.

The studio was ready. The spotlights glinted off the shiny hardwood floor. Easels perched strategically in corners, proudly displaying an abundance of riches. Paintings were stacked on the antique wooden church pews that lined both walls, snacks set out on the large beige flat files. My daughter Anna sat at an antique desk near the front doors with a calculator and money box. Outside, rain was pouring down, and people huddled on the sidewalk under the awning, waiting for us to raise the blinds and unlock the doors.

My cousin Kathy and I looked at each other and high-fived. "We did it, #2," she says.

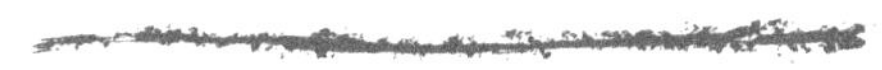

Kathy's dad, Terry, was my dad's younger brother. In the exact middle of the six siblings, Terry and Dad were always the closest, but maybe that's just because the house was so full they had to share a bed. Kathy's family lived in Decatur, Illinois, where Mom and Dad had grown up.

Kathy and I had always been the artistic ones. Kathy Ann O'Dell was born first, so by the laws of nature and cousinhood, she got to be KAO #1, and I, Kelly Ann O'Dell, became KAO #2. As teenagers, we sent each other drawings and paintings and designed business cards for the KAO Club. While she was stationed around the world during her Air Force career, we'd always found time to visit each other in interesting places (England, Arizona, Italy), and we still handwrote old-fashioned letters on paper that we sent through the mail.

When Kathy's dad died, she was 19 and living in Germany, about to give birth to her son, so she couldn't come home for the funeral. Her adoration of my father was fueled by how much she missed her own—and the fact that our dads were so much alike. When we brought Dad home to Kerry's house for his final weeks, Kathy lived in Austin, Texas, but happened to be visiting her sister in Decatur, Illinois. They came to see him one afternoon, a week or so before he passed, and giggled at how silly he was.

Right after Dad died, I got an email from #1—for once she'd foregone snail mail:

> Your dad ... shaped who I am. He inspired me to dream I could be an artist even though life went in another direction for me.

You have the good fortune to have inherited his red hair and amazing talent. I guess we are among the few that retain some of the goofy O'Dell humor. I love that he showed a little of that last week. I'm here for whatever you need. I know you will let me know as the details unfold about the funeral. I plan to be there.

I love you, cuz.

When Dad died, there were more of his paintings than Kerry and I had wall space to hang. We knew Dad wouldn't want his artwork to sit and molder in racks in the back of his damp brick building, so we began planning a big sale. But it was a lot to undertake. During that time, Kathy decided to leave her paralegal job, move into the studio apartment to help us, and then find a place of her own in the Midwest when we were done. She could live nearer to her sisters and we would have her help.

Thank God that even though we had grown up, we still laughed like silly kids whenever we were together. Oh, how I needed that. I loved her even more than I always had because she got it. She, too, had lost her parents. She, too, admired my dad and his talent. She knew how much this mattered to me, to all of us, because of how much it mattered to her.

The KAO Club got to work. #1 and I ordered mat board and stacks of frames. We drank wine and reveled in the comfort and companionship unique to family members who are also friends. Kathy is a careful, disciplined perfectionist, so we intuitively delegated the tasks requiring fine craftsmanship to her. She learned how to cut mats and assemble frames. I tend to be impatient and impulsive, so I did things that I could do in short bursts of energy: wrapped watercolors and prints in plastic shrink-wrap, made a catalog of images with sizes and titles, and priced it all on a spreadsheet, then printed price

tags, picked up pieces of glass for the frames, placed orders
for supplies, designed promotional postcards and social media
announcements, and so on.

Along the way we discovered Dad wasn't as good a craftsman
as we'd once believed. As we took apart existing frames to repair
water-damaged mats, we learned that Dad used random scraps
of different colors of mat board to hold the painting in position,
rather than simply cutting one clean piece. That sometimes he'd
cropped out several inches of sky or foreground because it hadn't
turned out well. And so on.

Still, we didn't want to disappoint him, so we felt pressure to
get it just right.

The hard part was figuring out which paintings were hidden
away in Dad's drawers because he didn't like them, and which
he had kept because there was something he wanted to work on.
Should they go in the sale, or would he be horrified to let the
public see them? Were they bad, in his opinion, or did he simply
run out of mats or frames and throw them in a drawer, planning
to pull them back out again when he had more time (or ordered
more frames)?

As the designated "smart one," I worked with the attorney to
settle his estate. We went back and forth, consulting with CPAs,
other attorneys, and an appraiser about whether we needed to
have formal appraisals to be able to accurately value the estate.

Brady, the appraiser, wondered how much Dad's personality
factored into his art sales. For instance, did he travel to locations
to be present to help sell his art in gallery shows, or did the
galleries just randomly find a buyer who was interested and sell
them that way? Did people buy them because they liked Dad or
because the art was independently good?

Yes, I said. Both. Of course, Brady didn't trust that I had an objective opinion.

"If they bought because of his personality, we might have trouble selling the remaining works," he informed me. He speculated that we had a limited window in which people would want to buy, while the loss was still fresh, and that people would soon lose interest.

I took it all in. *Oh, Brady, how you underestimate my dad.*

By November, we'd worked through all those questions, made our best guesses, and let family claim whatever they wanted, within reason. The night before the large public sale, we'd opened the studio to a small group of friends and family. We mailed a few dozen invitations to Mom's and Dad's longtime friends, Dad's golfing buddies and breakfast companions, our cousins, and our best friends. There were too many hugs to count, lots of sweet stories, and loads of sales. We offered a discount across the board because Dad always gave one to his close friends and family.

When the big day came around, we filled the empty spots on the walls from the paintings we'd sold the night before and shuffled around the art that remained. For this sale, we'd sent close to a hundred invitations. We knew we'd likely missed lots of people we should have included, but we were at the mercy of our memories and Dad's random file folders of customer names and addresses to determine the invitation list. We tried to include everyone, though, by posting about it on social media, and word of mouth had spread. It felt like this gluttonous excess, the all-you-can-eat-buffet to beat all buffets. Almost four months of effort on our part. Kerry had handled the medical stuff earlier, but this part belonged to Kathy and me.

You might think Kerry and I would be feeling sad, but we were giddy—and had been that way most of the time since Dad died, if I'm being honest. He was no longer suffering. God, in his compassion, had taken him, and we got to show our love for him right up until the very end. We were proud of him, proud to belong to him, and we had the opportunity to let other people get hold of these amazing paintings made by our talented father.

We felt generous. Exhilarated. Inspired. Happy.

That night, Kathy and Kerry and I, and our families, stood in the center of the gallery. The pleated window shades were pulled down over the large plate glass windows at the front, keeping us and the studio's contents hidden until we were ready to open. Five minutes ahead of schedule, we took pity on the people crammed under the wooden awning during a deluge of rain and opened the doors.

The front "gallery" room of the studio measures about 30 feet by 20 feet and feels huge with its high ceiling and large windows. Though the room was completely full, more people were pushing to get inside. My husband, Tim, had worked as a bouncer in college, so we gave him the job of monitoring the number of people allowed inside and offered him an umbrella to help people back out to their cars at the end.

I stood on the church pew along one side of the room so everyone could see me.

"Wow! This is absolutely amazing! Thank you for coming. We're gonna do this on a first-come, first-served basis. If you want to buy a painting, ask one of us to remove it from the wall and you can take it with you tonight. Dad always gave a 20% discount to repeat buyers, so we're offering the same to you. If you own other paintings, tell them at the desk. You're on the honor system … and go!"

It was like a Thanksgiving Day sale at Walmart—well, let's say Macy's because it's a little classier. As Kerry looked around, she kept saying, "I wish he could have seen this. All these people. Why didn't we do this while he was alive?"

But would they all have come then? We didn't know. What we did know is that these people had loved his art, but they had loved him, too—every single person crowded into that room. Everyone felt connected to my father (or mother), and therefore we felt connected to them. We told stories, sipped wine, hugged people we hadn't seen in years, and moved paintings around to fill empty spots on the wall.

Kerry and I took turns pulling each other aside, negotiating unplanned discounts and gifts. She told me she'd promised a friend's parents a special deal, so I whispered that to my daughter Anna, who was taking payments at the desk as people left. One of my close friends picked out a small painting of a wooden decoy for her parents. Her husband couldn't stop looking at one of Dad's more recent Florida bird paintings, but while he was trying to talk himself out of spending the money, someone else grabbed it and took it home. Other friends of mine bought paintings for their adult kids and for themselves. Longtime customers, old family friends, people who'd lived in Ladoga all their lives—everyone seemed to be there.

Kerry and I approached one of the men who farmed the land previously owned by my grandparents, and now by us, around Mom and Dad's house. Just a couple of years younger than my parents, Bob had always been a good friend to our family. He lived just around the corner from them and was the one they called when a raccoon got into our upstairs bathroom. He arrived promptly with a shotgun and a shit-eating grin— and loved to repeat the story to anyone who would listen. He was color-blind and he and his wife had a light blue car, which looked pink to him, but he drove it anyway. Wearing his dress Wrangler jeans and polished boots, Bob had bright, pale blue eyes, sun-weathered skin, and crinkles around his eyes from always smiling.

We told him, "Pick any painting you like—as a gift. Mom and Dad would want you to have one." Not surprised in the slightest, he nodded, looked around for a moment, and then pointed to one of the largest paintings hanging on the wall, a big, beautiful summer barn surrounded by lots of green grass. He didn't play the game of choosing a lower-priced option. He knew what he liked, and we loved the grin on his face as he carried it out to the car, head held high.

Some people chose more paintings than they could carry in one trip. Others held tight to their selections, hugging them to their chest as they waited in line to pay. Still others deliberated as long as they dared, worried someone else would grab the painting off the wall in front of them before they decided. A few whispered to their spouses, debating whether to get the one they really liked or the one closer to their budget, because some of Dad's paintings were big-ticket items and they were practical people.

One young man, a local farmer, bought the largest painting, a 40" x 30" winter barn showcased in the prime position in the center of the show—along with five or six others. This was unusual and intriguing, even more so because this was a young man and we weren't sure how someone his age could afford them, and why he wanted so many. As he loaded them into the cab of his big pickup truck, we glimpsed the name of his family farm painted on the door of the truck.

"Oh my gosh! That's the last name of the girl that Mom used to take care of, isn't it?"

As a high school nurse, Mom had her favorites, people who ducked into her office to take refuge from the noisy cafeteria and became her friends. One girl who was particularly close to Mom was undergoing treatment for cancer. Mom administered her daily meds and visited her at home near the end. She was heartbroken when the girl died. Kerry and I looked at each

other, our eyes filled with tears. "That must be her brother!"
Now we understood why he wanted those O'Dell paintings so
much. Tonight's sale was presumably about Dad, but not only
about him. In that moment, Mom was just as present.

In addition to bouncer duties, Tim used my 35 mm camera
to take photos of each person with their purchases after they
paid. Later that night, I dropped the film at the one-hour
Walgreens. We didn't know everyone's names, but nearly all
the faces were familiar. Going through the photos, we wrote
people's names on the backs, and when we were stuck, we cross-
referenced the titles of the paintings people held in the photos
to the invoices and checks they had written.

As I flipped through those photos, I was struck by the big
smiles on everyone's faces. Some were likely first-time buyers
who'd never spent money on art, or who thought there was
no rush because Dad was always around. Some were longtime
collectors, with dozens of paintings filling their walls at home,
greedy to get as many as they could—and anxious to tell us
exactly how many they already owned.

We'd already had a memorial service for Dad, but this event
was so much better. Besides the high-end take-home treats
and the inevitable tears, there was even more laughter. Stories,
friends reconnecting with each other. Everyone wanted to tell
us exactly what painting they had at home, when Dad sold it
to them, and what he said when they bought it. Everyone had a
story. Everyone felt like it was a treat to have known Dad, and a
bigger treat to own his work. They were claiming a piece of him,
remembering his talent, the way he saw the world, how he made
them feel.

At the end of the night, the studio was much emptier than
it had been before. In the two nights, we'd sold or given away all
but about 20 paintings.

The walls were emptier, but my heart was full.

<h1 style="text-align:center">vignette</h1>

You're standing on a dirt road. The path continues ahead of you, two muddy ruts worn in the snow. To your right is a dense tree line, and the left side is lined with broken rows of corn stubble remaining in the field after the harvest. Off in the distance, a snowy hill is striped with the purplish shadows of the trees. And if you look closely, deep into the dark, dense woods on the hill, you can see a tiny barn among the trees. In the 21" x 14" painting, the barn is only about one inch wide. It is subtle, yet it looks as though it took root right there, part of the very fabric of the landscape.

After watercolor dries, if you carefully apply clean water with your brush to an area of dried pigment, wait just long enough, and blot with a paper towel, you can "lift" the excess pigment, leaving a shadow of the original color—which in this case looks like weathered barn siding.

The barn wasn't painted onto the painting; it was subtracted. An area of darkness was transformed by light. What wasn't there at first is now there, forever tinted by the shadow of what remains.

FRIDAY FLURRIES

6" x 9"

Description: Minimalist, nearly abstract
piece from the early 1970s, consisting
of two clouds of gray-blue, several
delicate trees with bare branches
indicated by a few simple delicate lines,
and big white drops of falling snow

After the big sale, Kathy moved into an apartment near
Indianapolis. I repainted the studio walls , scheduled movers to
lug boxes of design books and art supplies to the building, and
settled in.

Now I go into the studio daily, waking up early. Which is
something of a miracle, to be honest. I'd go just about anywhere
in my quest to stay busy, but I really do want to be *there* and it's
been years since I woke up early on purpose. Hop in the shower,
throw on clothes, gulp down some coffee and a bagel, and after a
15-minute drive through cornfields and trees and creeks and big
open skies I arrive in Dad's space.

My space, my husband keeps correcting me. It is, but it isn't.
And I kind of like it that way.

In 1990, after Kerry and I were no longer living at home and
Dad no longer had constant interruptions at home, he bought
and renovated a historic storefront building in town. He wanted
to have a place to work where he would be more visible, where
people could stop by and talk to him about art (or life or golf),
and where he could host workshops. He loved to teach people

to paint. He didn't see a need to keep secrets; people either had
talent or they didn't, and it had nothing to do with how many of
his tricks he shared. He wasn't threatened by competition.

A narrow, deep two-story brick building in the middle of
the two blocks that are "downtown," the studio was built in 1900
for a butcher, but it had been empty for years before Dad bought
it. I have a photo pinned to my bulletin board of a hand-lettered
banner he hung on the building during renovations, accepting
the slur his buddies always used to refer to his work: "Rob
O'Dell's Paint-By-Numbers Gallery."

Since I'd already lost Mom years before Dad sold the house
I grew up in, I panicked at the thought of letting go of Dad's
studio. Kerry didn't have a need for it but wanted it to stay
in the family, so when we divided Dad's assets, I claimed the
building.

Thick plate glass windows line the entire face of the
building. A four-foot-wide sidewalk and some angled parking
spaces separate the building from the two-lane highway running
through town. (Incidentally, a town that has no stoplights.)
Under the metal-roofed awning, a plastic owl swings from a
piece of wire that once securely tethered it, meant to deter birds
from roosting in the eaves. Now it is used mainly as a landing
pad for the pigeons that return yearly to nest there.

When you step inside through the ten-foot-tall oak door,
you will find yourself in the midst of a brightly lit gallery space
with a 14-foot-high, white-painted decorative tin ceiling. Below
the ceiling hangs a rectangular frame, fashioned from PVC pipes,
which supports the industrial spotlights positioned to shine on
the paintings hanging on every wall, their light reflected in the
golden-oak, shiny hardwood floors. Dad added country-blue

beadboard and a chair rail along the bottom three feet of the
walls, the top painted a neutral tan—colors that complemented
his art and most country homes around here. Those colors
are not my style, so I hired a guy to repaint the walls (a bold
eggplant purple and warm gray), but couldn't help feeling like I
was painting over Dad. Erasing him.

Even temporarily moving his painting table out of the space
while the walls were being painted felt like a betrayal. I came
home and fell into bed, trying to hide my tears from Tim.

After all, it had been months since Dad died. You'd think I'd
be over it by now.

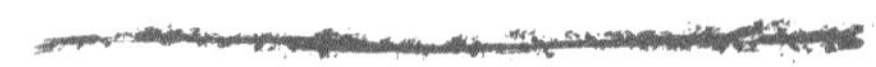

While we prepared for the sale, my cousin Kathy and I tried
to do things exactly as Dad would have done, steadfastly refusing
to move a thing on his credenza. It was like if we didn't disturb
his brushes and paints, we could hold on to him a little longer.
I think it was hard for some of my family to see me make any
changes to the space, and we're all absolutely certain that Dad
never imagined his paintings on a purple wall. He'd probably be
horrified.

Believe me, if I could go back to having him here, I would
happily accept the country-blue walls. On the other hand,
preserving his studio as a shrine isn't really sustainable.

I think Dad would love it that I want to be here, that I feel
comfortable in this place, that I want to hold on to whatever I
can that was his.

I've done a decent job of finding a balance. One wall is
dedicated to the remaining original paintings we still have.
They hang above and are stacked along the 12-foot-long church
pew that Dad had placed along the left-hand wall. At the end
of the bench, at a 90-degree angle, is the drafting table where

Dad painted. The credenza beside it still holds his white enamel antique trays of brushes, pencils, paints, masking fluid, and water containers. Inside the top drawer are the same rows of crumpled foil tubes of watercolors, organized by color.

Beneath that, a drawer contains stacks—hundreds, no thousands—of photographs that Dad used as reference for his art. Barns and trees and silhouettes at sunset and gates and roads and foliage and hollyhocks and Florida marshes with egrets. I need to be able to function in this place, but although I've gingerly flipped through the photos, I'm not ready to blatantly disturb them. There's something holy about that little bubble of universe where Dad once created, and I'm just not ready to mess with that.

Farther back, a short wall—about seven feet tall—divides the space into two rooms. Dad built the wall when he converted part of the building into a living space. Along the ledge at the top, I've propped my antique signs: my initials, the letters taken from large plastic signs, a hand-painted "Advertising Dept this way" sign Mom and I found in an antique store, and several more. A four-foot-tall kite—an old-fashioned sailing ship with three masts—hangs in the air above the wall. Dad made it from a kit Kerry, Mom, and I gave him one year on his birthday. Made up of light balsa wood ribs and clear epoxy, the thin, semitranslucent paper covering it makes it airworthy—well, maybe it isn't all that airworthy since you can also see all the patches and repairs Dad made to it, presumably after trying, and failing, to fly it.

Originally, before he added the wall, Dad's drafting table and credenza sat in this area. Bold with a paintbrush but not with his interior decorating, Dad covered the floor with beige flecked linoleum. Old fluorescent lights hung from the ceiling, which was crisscrossed with a maze of exposed pipes with peeling paint. A large, boxy, industrial heater dominated the space, clicking on and off to blow heated air throughout the winter. The back wall held Dad's antique signs and advertisements—signs from the Monon and Wabash Railroads, a huge Copenhagen metal thermometer, a framed 1950s ad for cigarettes, and, always, an IU basketball calendar.

After Dad sold the house and became a Florida resident, he took down the signs, moved his drafting table into the front of the gallery, carpeted the middle section, and added a kitchenette. The space was just barely large enough to hold his king-size bed, a dresser, two La-Z-Boy recliners, and a small TV stand. In one corner near the kitchenette sat the antique wooden table from Mom and Dad's kitchen. The pie safe that had once been my grandma's served as the pantry.

Before I moved my office in here, I hired someone to enclose the peeling, dilapidated ceiling. He replaced the unsightly fluorescent lights with recessed spotlights. We kept the industrial heater because it would cost a fortune to add ductwork for more conventional heating or air-conditioning, but added a sleek ceiling fan to move air about. We sold and gave away Dad's furniture and turned the space into a workroom containing Dad's framing table, flat files full of prints, and a couple of old desks. I kept our old kitchen table with the ugly brass-accented armchairs—the table we sat around to help Dad name paintings, play Tripoli, and eat our ordinary suppers.

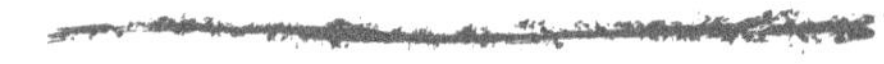

Most mornings, I sit at my desk in the big, open front room in the soft light—no bulbs on, just ambient daylight coming through the enormous windows in the front of the building. Large farm trucks with noisy engines rumble through town. People park in an angled row and run in to the market across the street for cigarettes or a Mountain Dew. Farmers slam their truck doors after they finish breakfast at the Laughing Cow Diner, four doors down. (They only take cash and they close at 2 p.m. every day.) Occasionally someone will park their pickup so that it's blocking the alley next to this building and they'll run into the hardware store next door, holding a broken bolt in their hand that they need to match. And then they're gone again.

It's busy, but it's not hectic.

Unlike my life. I've always hurried from place to place, defined by how many things I cram into the little squares on my calendar. Right after the sale, I scheduled myself for five speaking events plus a weekend-long writing retreat—all in the span of five weeks. I scheduled doctor's appointments, manicures, hair appointments, lunch with friends, meetings to finalize the estate—something, anything—every day. I started a bullet journal just so I could neatly check off every task on my detailed to-do lists—because when I'm stressed, I like to get organized.

And oh, was I ever organized.

I don't know how to be any other way. I feel compelled to keep moving, to add one more idea, another task or accomplishment. It feels irresponsible not to bring to fruition the ideas and concepts and creations flowing through my mind.

So I keep rushing to the studio, attempting to avoid the *missing*. It's an ache in my chest, a physical pain that emanates from the center of myself. Will I ever feel whole again?

But anymore, all that activity has become too much. Many days, I stop moving and just sit here in the quiet, muted by the weight of an indescribable longing, hoping the peace of this place—of my dad—will seep into my soul. That it will give me the rest I so desperately need. I look at all the people, going to and fro, oblivious to the jagged hole that was torn in my universe.

I sigh as I continue to sit here, all alone in this holy place.

WAITING FOR THE WIND

21" x 14"

Description: Simple landscape
with a gray, cloudy sky, an
unremarkable field, and a
delicate, detailed windmill within a
small fenced-in enclosure

Since Ladoga is in a no-man's-land of cell service, I kept
Dad's landline. Since no one knows where I am at any given
moment, most people still call my cell. But when my girls or Tim
knows I'm in Ladoga, or when a customer from years ago calls
to inquire about the value of their paintings as they're planning
their estate, the cordless handset rings. From time to time, I get
the standard calls from Disabled American Vets and annoying
spam calls from people trying to sell me health insurance. The
phone is still in Dad's name (even though, when I called, they
assured me they'd changed it), so when someone calls me from
the studio, my caller ID still reads "Rob O'Dell."

One evening, as I'm concentrating on a project on my
computer, the phone rings.

"Hello, may I speak to Rob O'Dell, please?"

I don't feel like getting into it right now, so I try to be
vague. "No, I'm sorry, he's not available." I keep clicking, typing,
tweaking the newsletter layout I'm trying to finish so that I can
go home and cook dinner.

"Is this the best number to reach him?"

"Umm, no. This is his daughter, actually. May I help you with something?"

"Are you authorized to make decisions on behalf of the business?"

I finally look away from the computer screen and lean my head back against the chair. Take a deep breath—how to answer?

"His business is closed."

"Oh, that's all right. We don't have to talk to him. Are you the owner of the new business?"

Now I'm getting annoyed. "Yes, but I'm not interested."

"We can enhance your Google listing and give you a free website. All we need ..."

"No!" I shout. *No, no, no.* Tears spring into my eyes. "You can*not*! Because. HE. IS. DEEEAAAAAADDDDDD!!!"

vignette

When I'm asked to comment on my art, the words come hard. Perhaps this is why I paint. What I paint is commonplace—places and things that I'm comfortable with. Watercolor is my medium.

Watercolor is very fluid. Things happen along the way that are unpredictable and exciting. My hope is to gain control along the way. Just to let things go is not my style. I strive for something called "realism," because with realism I can begin to communicate. To this end I utilize composition, color, and most importantly, drawing. These basics are achieved in different ways, and not always with traditional methods. The end result is all important. It is very rewarding for me to know that others share my interest and deep feelings for the often-neglected places of my art.

—Rob O'Dell brochure

CHANGE OVER

20″ x 18″

Description: Thicket of tall vertical
trees on a hill behind an unobtrusive
gate, an abundance of yellow
and green leaves changing into
a vivid orange

In so many ways, I feel like I stepped into my father's life. I work in his studio. At the diner over lunch, I speak briefly to the farmers and retired men who were Dad's friends. I couldn't tell you most of their names, but they all know me. This is a typical small town. Everyone knows exactly who I am—and they probably recall which boys I dated and that time my car was seen on the wrong side of town while their wife called my mom to report on me. They remember that I got good grades and that my sister was a runner and that I played softball with their daughter—and even if none of that was true, the physical resemblance is clear. I'm tall (5′8″ compared to his 6′1″) and have Dad's hair color, though his was curlier than mine, becoming kind of Afro-like in the '70s and '80s or when he simply let it get too long, and then turned gray. We have the same dark brown eyes, complete with puffy bags beneath them, and freckled skin. We're both sturdy, solid, with big bones, large hands and feet. Nice and Irish.

But I'll be darned if I know who *they* are. I've gotten pretty good at pretending recognition, but I've learned to hate it when the front door opens and a strange face smiles in at me.

"Do you know who I am?"

Even if I did know them once, isn't it likely that they've changed since I last saw them 30 years ago? When they tell me their name, though, I usually know it, even if I don't recognize their faces. The visits go something like this.

The big oak door swings inward and the traffic sounds grow louder. I look up to see a man standing there looking uncertain. Shy. He's usually wearing a button-down plaid shirt and faded jeans. In his 60s, maybe 70s or 80s. (Sometimes 30s. Okay, they're all over the place age-wise.)

"Are you Rob's daughter? I knew your dad."

After looking at the paintings (sometimes remarking, "I think I have that one," which of course they don't because each one is one of a kind, no matter how similar they might be), these gruff old men ease themselves down on the couch with a big sigh, awkwardly looking anywhere except directly at me.

"Your dad was something else."

"I miss him, you know. He used to let me watch him paint sometimes."

Or "We played a lot of games of golf."

Several have told me, "He was a good guy. A good friend."

"He was pretty good at them paint-by-numbers. That's what I always told him."

"I used to sit with him while he painted."

"I took one of his workshops, and I'm not much of an artist, but he always humored me and said I wasn't bad. I always loved looking around in here. Ooh, I love that tree!" (pointing to a painting on the wall).

"I'll never forget the last time I saw him." (This was a month before they found Dad's cancer.) "He came over because I was working on my building. He was winded, and he had to kneel down and catch his breath. I knew something was wrong."

I've had dozens of visitors. But the stories are all nearly the same.

"I just loved talking to him. He was such a good guy."

"He was always so nice. Never said a mean word about anyone."

"He always made me feel so welcome."

"He treated me like an equal, and I ain't nobody special."

"He was so down-to-earth."

"He always made me feel like he was happy to see me."

Some express surprise: "I didn't know he was sick."

"I just heard he passed. I don't know where I was when it happened, because it's been a while, hasn't it?"

"I missed your big sale, and I'm so disappointed. I always wanted one of his pictures and couldn't afford it."

One man walked in, confidently navigating the step just inside the entrance that most people trip on. "Rob around?" Forgetting to be sensitive, I blurt out, "Umm, no. He died almost six years ago."

"No! Really?"

"Yes, unfortunately."

"I can't believe I didn't know that. We was good friends," this man says, using the sleeve of his T-shirt to wipe his eyes.

Good friends? I thought to myself. *How good of friends were you if you hadn't noticed he was gone for so long?* He stretches out his hand, introducing himself.

"I worked at the children's home over there." He points toward the edge of town. "I used to stop in from time to time. I brought kids here to watch your dad paint. He was one of the finest artists and such a good man."

Naturally, I have to agree.

"Well, that just tears me up. I'm so sorry. Thanks, hon," he says as he heads back to the door. "I'm so glad this place is still here."

This man wasn't from Ladoga, but I hear the same thing from lots of locals. "It's nice to see life in this old downtown." Or "We were all afraid this building would sit empty."

Another common question: "So do you paint, too?" *No, I'm a graphic designer and writer.*

Nearly everyone comes back to: "It's such a shame about your dad." Then they continue, "Did he ever tell you about the time …?" Finally, no matter how they knew him, they all end with this same line: "I sure miss him."

When their voices crack or tears threaten, they hurry off, suddenly having someplace they have to be—these old, rough, gruff men with big, soft hearts.

Most of the men and women know they weren't best friends, so they tell me about their relationship shyly, a little bit embarrassed to admit how much it meant to them. Still, they hold tightly to their claim on him, even a couple—or six—years after his death.

Looks like Kerry and I aren't the only ones who thought we were his favorite.

END OF A DAY

14″ x 10″

Description: Country road extending
straight ahead, barely visible in the
shadows, lined with trees on either
side. Stark black leafless branches are
silhouetted against the radiant purple,
orange, and yellow sunset.

About two years after Dad died, Rita flew up from Florida to spend a couple of days with Kerry's and my families. She wanted to see what I'd done with the studio and apartment. She stood in one place, slowly looking around, then hugged her arms against her chest, tears in her eyes.

Finally, she said, "I just like to imagine Rob and Annie being happy somewhere together. I had the privilege of loving both of them, and I'm just so grateful."

A minute later, she added, "I'm so happy that you guys invited me back here and loved me."

Sometimes I forget that this loss belongs to other people, too.

My neighbor, the man who owns the building next to the studio, tells me he keeps running into a friend of Dad's at the Laughing Cow. This man would like to come see me, but I'm never here when he is in town. A few days later, when I see a big, tall man stop and reach for the door, I know right away who he is, even though I haven't seen him since I was a kid.

Dick is wearing brown Carhartt overalls, a red-and-black buffalo plaid flannel shirt, and a single gold pen clipped in the center front pocket. On top of that, a red Lands' End jacket, lined with gray fleece, and a ball cap. He opens with, "I can't stay too long. I've got my dog in the truck."

I offer him a seat on the couch because I suspect he'll be here a while.

He says, "I'll sit over here in the tall one," the high office chair with wheels at Dad's drafting table. He slowly eases himself down and I jump up to help, knowing the chair will roll back as he drops his weight onto the seat. It does, but he is more in the seat than not. I sit back down; close call, but all is well.

"Me and your father were good friends," he says after he gets

settled. "I remember you like this," and he holds out his hand
to indicate a small child, maybe three or four. "Of course I held
your mother in high regard, too."

He starts right in with the stories, and I know I want a
record of whatever he will have to say. "Okay if I take some
notes?"

He nods and gets right to it, telling me a story I didn't know.
I'd heard bits and pieces—probably all of it, over the years—but
I didn't remember the details.

Dick's father-in-law, Bill, was chairman of Indiana National
Bank in the early 1970s. As the 33-floor tower was being built in
Indianapolis, he decided he wanted that many of Dad's paintings
for the building, one per floor, positioned so you would see them
when you got off the elevator. He recognized quality and he
recognized talent—and he saw both in Dad.

"What were the paintings of?" I ask.

"Whatever your dad wanted to paint," Dick replies. He holds
his arms open wide to show me the size—I'm guessing 30" x 40"?
The size Dad would call a full sheet. Dick says he believes they
were mostly barns in winter, which makes me laugh.

"Bill gave him half the money up front and said to bring
them in as he painted them. He'd give your dad the other half
upon completion. For a young artist, that was a big thing. A lot
of money."

After all the paintings had been delivered, Dick said his
father-in-law sat Dad down. "Now I'd like to have you do one
more thing: Double your prices. You're too damn cheap."

Dick laughs. "And just like that, Bill's investment doubled
in value!"

Dick has one of those original 33 paintings in his office now,
he says, but his "favorite is an old barn with a rickety basketball
goal mounted on an old tree trunk, with branches growing up
behind it. The backboard was all beat up, like from kids playing

on it. And he called it *Double Overtime.*" He smiles.

"I just hold him in real high regard." His chin trembles slightly and he looks off to the side to compose himself. "I imagine we have a total of twenty-five of his paintings. I see them all the time and can't tell you exactly what they are right now. Whenever I didn't know what to get Kitty for Valentine's Day or Christmas, I'd buy her one. Finally, she said, 'I don't need any more of those,' so I stopped."

He tells me about his family's cottage in Northpoint, Michigan. "It was big, like twelve, thirteen bedrooms." Dick never knew what to get his father-in-law, so one year he commissioned Dad to paint the cottage. Dad told him, "Give me all the pictures you have," then asked Dick to stop by every evening to check his progress.

"You've gotta be my eyes," Dad said.

"So I gave him everything I had. All the photos. One side faced Lake Michigan, one side faced the golf course." Dad sketched it from all different angles, and Dick corrected him when he drew too many windows on one side, but otherwise he captured it perfectly. The painting he ended up doing showed the west side in summer, and the east side in winter—two different vignettes on the same paper.

Dick shakes his head in wonder. "Yeah, that one of the cabin in two seasons ... I tear up just thinking about it. It's really good." He tells me about some of the others he has. "The sugar shack's a good one. It's got the buckets hanging on the trees. I like that one."

As we continue talking, he asks me about Dad's sketchbooks. "You still have any of those around here? He used to have a whole bunch of them."

I walk to the bookshelf and place a stack of discolored, oversized, spiral-bound books on the table in front of him. "Now that's talent," he says, leafing through them. "I'm so glad you have those."

We talk about all sorts of things. His family, and mine. My upcoming trip to see the grandkids. What I do for a living, all the many businesses he's run, and how he first came to this community. He tells me about going snowmobiling with Dad and Bob, the farmer who lived around the corner from Mom and Dad, and about how Dad took a sketch pad in his pocket when they went out on their three-wheelers.

"He changed my opinion of an artist. I'm a farmer and I always thought of artists as being …" He makes a vague, flighty gesture with his hand. "But your dad looked at life through a different prism than most of us. He could see beauty in a pile of junk."

As he prepares to leave, he grabs Dad's drafting table to steady himself and pushes off the chair, which rolls back behind him. He takes a few slow steps toward me, his body stiff and sore from all his years of hard work. Earlier, I told him about my writing and gave him a copy of my first book, which includes pictures of a couple of paintings along with some stories about Dad and his art. He picks up the book, walks over to my desk, and extends his hand—not for a traditional handshake, but palm down. I reach up and he grasps my hand. Sincerely, he looks me in the eye. "You're a credit to your father, and I mean that."

"You're making me cry," I manage, as I try to smile back at him.

Then we both have to look away. I sit in my chair trying to hold back tears as he slowly walks toward the door.

vignette

When I have a terrible need of—shall I say the word—religion, then I go out and paint the stars.

—Vincent van Gogh

LIGHT OF DAY

21″ x 14″

Description: Enlarged
detail of hinges on a barn door
with strong shadows
cast by the sun

Until 1990, when he moved into the Ladoga building, Dad worked in a two-room shed about 50 steps from the back door of the farmhouse where our family lived, across a gently rolling yard. Growing up, I was never, ever told I couldn't be in the studio or that I needed to leave Dad alone (that I can remember, anyway). And yet there was something exhilarating—a tiny bit naughty and a little bit scary—about going into Dad's studio when he wasn't there.

The first thing you'd notice was the olive-green-and-black checkerboard carpet. Very 1970s. Vertical racks corralling mat boards and frames and assorted dusty pieces of glass lined the left wall underneath a long countertop that Dad used for framing and matting. Above that, the walls were cluttered with rows of colorful ribbons—purples and blues and reds, yellow s, pinks, and whites: First prize at the Indiana State Fair, Best of Show for the Hoosier Salon, Honorable Mentions and Purchase Prizes and Firsts and Seconds and Thirds from art fairs, exhibitions, and more. On the countertop were strewn tools, metal rulers, screwdrivers, and pieces of corner frame samples.

Underneath the second counter, horizontal shelves held pieces of watercolor paper and scraps of pebbled mat board and paintings that had been abandoned but not discarded because Dad knew there was something there that he might want to go back to.

In the left-hand corner by a large single-paned picture window, Dad's drawing table took advantage of the natural light pouring in. A paint-dabbled piece of plywood sat on top, to which Dad taped sheets of watercolor paper as he painted. Just outside the window grew a great big maple tree surrounded by tall, scruffy weeds—and just beyond that was the edge of the neighboring cornfield.

Next to the table was a credenza covered with the same white enameled paint trays he would later use in the downtown studio, several shallow trays full of brushes and art pencils and tubes of Grumbacher Academy watercolors and small rectangles of cardboard. There were sponges covered with random brushstrokes of paint and rusty Folger's cans filled with water. Inevitably, stacks of photos would be scattered across the top of the credenza, the scenes sometimes cropped by strips of beige masking tape or L-shaped pieces of cardboard. My favorite implement was the gray, amorphous blob of kneaded eraser, usually sitting next to the rubber cement pickup and small bottles of Miskit masking fluid.

Two shelves along the back wall ran the full width of the room. Picture books about the Midwest in general (and barns in particular) leaned against the curly metal spines of the dog-eared sketchbooks Dad had filled over the years, antique metal toy trucks and trains interspersed among them, beside a small gold plaque that read, "It's hard to be humble when you're as great as I am." We must have bought it for him because he used to love to sing the Mac Davis song.

The gallery room was one step lower than the rest, separated by a half wall made from a hand-hewn barn beam. Sunlight from the skylight beat down in squares onto the hideous carpet. Dad's antique train collection ran in endless loops around the narrow ledge around the top of the room. Paintings hung on the walls and sat in stacks around the edges of the floor. One wall had an old wicker couch with very uncomfortable cushions—people didn't sit there to be comfortable, but to decide which painting they couldn't live without.

In one corner, a rough wooden ladderlike staircase led to a small loft over the first room. The upstairs was particularly unnerving because you never knew if you'd encounter an old mouse carcass—or worse yet, a live creature. I shudder just thinking about it. There were boxes of books and papers, some old frames, and Dad's old art school portfolio. Once after venturing up the stairs with Dad, I carried a stack of his dusty typography books into the house. I loved turning the pages, examining the shapes and designs of the letters. I held pages up to the light of the picture window in the living room, tracing them for the newsletters I hand-decorated for various pen pals.

As risky as it felt to be in the loft, the rest of this tiny building was a place of wonder. The dust motes swimming in the light coming through the skylight made me think of light pouring through stained glass in a vast, carved, beautiful church somewhere. Once or twice, I took high school boyfriends in there when Dad wasn't home to hide from Mom's chaperoning eyes. I loved being there with Dad, naturally. Looking back, though, the times I remember most were when I was all by myself.

What was I looking for? What was I longing to find?

There was just something about being in a place where beautiful things were created, set apart specifically for that purpose, giving the act a kind of gravitas.

A sanctuary, if you will.

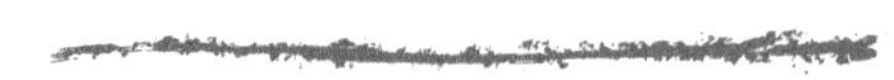

When Dad was in treatment for cancer the first time around, he told me about a meditation class he attended at the cancer center where he was living during his treatment. The instructor asked them to close their eyes and picture the most beautiful mansion they could imagine. She then guided them through the rest of the scene: *Notice the peak of the mountain in the distance behind it. Look at the sky.* And so on.

Afterward, she said, "Rob, you're creative. This should be right up your alley. Tell us what you thought about."

He said, "Well, I started with Downton Abbey. It's the most beautiful house I can imagine. But then you said mountain and there are no mountains there, so you lost me."

She said, "You could have just gone with that. It's okay."

And he said, "Well, I did. I pictured one of my barns, you know, like I like to paint. With the patina of the wood and all that. Because it's like a sanctuary to me. When I paint it feels like that. I'm just there. My mind isn't anywhere else. So I pictured that instead."

I immediately recalled one of my favorite Bible verses, from the Psalms[4]: "The one thing I ask of the Lord—the thing I seek most—is to live in the house of the Lord all the days of my life, delighting in the Lord's perfections and meditating in his Temple. For he will conceal me there when troubles come; he will hide me in his sanctuary. He will place me out of reach on a high rock."

Dad's description captures what I believe is the most profound reason to create art. Finding that place inside yourself, a place where you can quiet your mind and open your heart and breathe. A protected space where you can dwell, taking your time and delighting in what you've found. A place of safety and of peace.

A local journalist who was one of Dad's greatest fans wrote, "I have no idea how his paintings affect other people, but for me there is always a 'safe place' in each one. The snow scenes almost always include a weathered barn where animals have been sheltered from the storm or where a human could take refuge from the weather."[5]

I think that sense of safety is what I sensed as a child in my dad's old studio. Perhaps it's what I have also found in his "new" studio building in Ladoga—different location, same spirit. I feel it beckoning to me as I sit here, day after day, longing for the father I've lost.

And yet, I find that—somehow—he's still here.

FALLEN TREASURES

26" x 20"

Description: A jumble of life-size
maple leaves in mottled reds,
purples, oranges, and yellows
scattered on the ground

A year or so after losing Dad, I stood in my usual spot in the second row of my church, letting the words of the song wash over me.

> I'm not going back, I'm moving ahead
> Here to declare to you my past is over in you[6]

As we sang the chorus, I felt something unexpected rising up within me—hope. That maybe I could become new and whole again. That maybe I would someday stop hurting.

When people talk about wanting to put their past behind them, I think they're usually talking about mistakes they've made, people they've hurt, behavior that was destructive. Their regrets.

But the truth is that the past, by definition, is behind us even if we don't want it to be. No matter how good it was or how much I want my dad to still be here.

And although it's tempting to try to hold on to the memories—to create a monument to Dad, to tiptoe around the studio, blowing the dust off his things so I don't risk accidentally disturbing the way he left it—that won't bring him back.

It doesn't make me miss him any less. It doesn't help me heal, nor does it erase the sorrow.

And yet there is healing in inhabiting this place. In adding my own sketchbooks to the stacks of his, and the computer on which I create my art, and hanging my travel photographs alongside the art my dad made. I'm there, and so is he.

I get lost, sometimes, staring at details in his artwork, wondering how he created that texture or got such rich, dense colors using such a watery medium. Studying his composition, his colors. Driving to and from the studio and observing the way the light hits the trees at a certain time of day, and the way the storm clouds rise up to reveal brightness. Noticing the colors of the shadows, the nuances of the landscape lined with rows of crops and tufts of grass in the ditches. The wobbly telephone poles that line the edges of the roads.

As I excavate articles and brochures and booklets, stuffed in every nook and cranny of the storage areas in the studio, I'm reminded of accolades and accomplishments I'd forgotten. I came upon the printer proofs for the 1980 Indiana Bell Telephone Directory. Dad was named Artist of the Year, and the company commissioned a painting called *Reaching Out*, an image of a leafless sycamore tree against a cloudy blue sky, with my mom's name and a heart carved on the trunk of the tree. The Indianapolis Decorator's Show House brochure from 1987 features two commissioned paintings of the featured homes. I have photos of Kerry and me holding a painting alongside Joe Allen, a NASA astronaut originally from Crawfordsville. The school corporation wanted to send a piece of home back with him, so Kerry and I were asked to present the painting on their behalf at a school-wide assembly.

There are also things I'm not sure I ever knew about. When I paged through a 1975 *Better Homes and Gardens* magazine, wondering why it was stuffed in the box of clippings, I discovered a multiple-page spread for the feature story, a beautifully designed home with a large Rob O'Dell painting on the wall. I've uncovered Indiana Artists Club brochures, catalogs from the Kentucky Watercolor Society and Hoosier Salon featuring Dad's paintings reproduced in fuzzy black-and-white printing with callouts for Best of Show or Honorable Mention awards; letters regarding purchase prizes from numerous corporations; Indiana State Fair brochures with his name in the list of prizewinners; postcards from one-man shows at galleries in Michigan, Illinois, Kentucky, Pennsylvania, Tennessee, Arizona, Ohio, Colorado, Connecticut, and California. I found a photo of one painting being presented to a businessman in a boardroom in Japan.

Through the years, as I designed promotional brochures and a website for Dad, selecting the best of his recent images and writing new copy about his art, I typed in his credentials, over and over, until I can nearly recite them verbatim: Member of the Watercolor Society of Indiana, Indiana Artists Club, Indianapolis Art Center, Crawfordsville Art League, Madison Art Club, Brown County Art Guild, Indiana Federation of Art Clubs, Indiana Realists, Montgomery County Council of the Arts, and the Crawfordsville and Indianapolis Art Leagues.

In 1995, he was awarded the Sagamore of the Wabash award, the highest award given by the governor of Indiana. The term *sagamore* was used by the American Indian tribes of the northeastern United States to describe a lesser chief or a great man among the tribe whom the true chief would look to for wisdom and advice, and it was quite an honor. The enormous, framed certificate still hangs on his (my?) studio wall.

But there's more: Rob O'Dell's art is in public and private collections worldwide—Australia, England, Japan, Holland, and Canada, among others—as well as in some organizations a bit closer to home, such as Indiana University, Purdue University, University of Illinois, Rose-Hulman Institute of Technology, Wabash College, Indiana State Museum, Art Museum of Greater Lafayette, Saint Meinrad Archabbey, WISH-TV, A.E. Staley, Archer Daniels Midland, Mayflower Moving, Nipon Corn Starch (Japan), Eli Lilly, Stokely-Van Camp, Boehringer Mannheim, *Indianapolis News*, Simon Properties, Citizens National Bank, and so many more. Most of them have been around long enough that they have been purchased and merged and changed names. I thought I knew most of them, but just last month I stumbled upon three paintings in a local bank that I'd never noticed.

I've found articles and brochures I don't remember seeing before—and while nothing is really a surprise, because I already knew who Dad was and how far his art reached, occasionally there is one new detail or story I didn't know and it makes me feel one step closer to him.

While Dad's talent continues to astound me, I'm most proud of the type of person he was. I am the very fortunate daughter of a truly remarkable man. I wouldn't change that for the world. I take great comfort in knowing that parts of him are written in my very DNA. But I wonder, sometimes, if simply belonging to him is enough. Dad never expected me to be just like him, to do the things he did.

So why am I wrestling so hard to determine who I am without him? Why does it matter so much to me what parts of him I carry forward? How can I honor him and still be uniquely my own person?

I wish I knew how Dad would answer those questions.

vignette

Frequently, his paintings evoke a kind of contemplative nostalgia. Time seems to stop momentarily but its effects are evident. And one suddenly becomes more fully aware that the familiar objects in the natural environment which make up the subject matter of O'Dell's paintings—the tree stump, the coon's den, the field of wild flowers, the snow-covered pasture—are steadily becoming less familiar. Indeed, the mood is often one of loneliness, and while nature and the objects of man's creation appear repeatedly, man himself is completely absent from the scene.⁻

—Howard E. Wooden, Director, Sheldon Swope Gallery, Terre Haute, Indiana,
"Recent Watercolors," October 1970

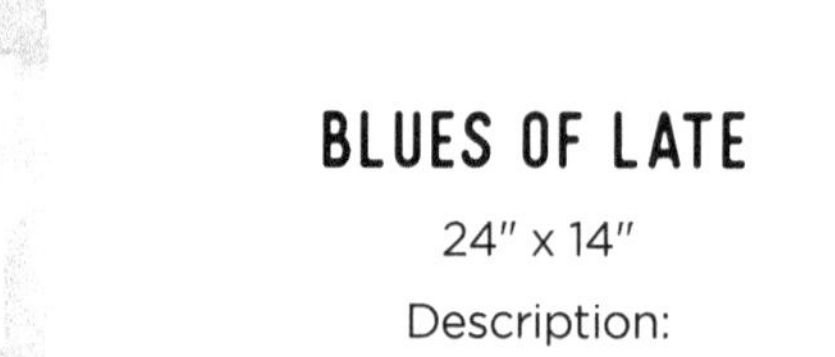

My freckled skin and I sit in the shelter of the umbrella, but I'd lathered myself in sunscreen anyway. With my skin, you can never be too careful. Just a couple of feet away, the Mediterranean Sea wraps around us, lapping against the rough stone wall encircling our Maltese hotel. The sunlight is bright, garish, the kind of perfect pure light you'd expect on a tropical summer morning. I close my eyes, savoring the breeze and the snatches of tourists murmuring, laughing, and shrieking in a jumble of languages as they reapply oil to their bronze skin, reprimand the splashing children, contemplate another cocktail.

I am in Malta with my friend Peggy. Our teen kids are off somewhere else, old enough that we don't have to remain vigilant. It is paradise.

Which I can only afford because my parents are both dead.

Today is the seven-year anniversary of the day my mom ceased to be. In four days, I'll be "celebrating" the one-year anniversary of my dad's death. Thanks to their life insurance, I can commemorate these dates in style, far away from home.

Deep breath. Focus on the beauty.

I can't keep my eyes open against the sudden flood of tears.

There's something incredibly garish about scenery like this juxtaposed against such depths of sorrow. The light is too bright, the colors too pure. It's a shock to my senses, a completely different sight than the ones I see driving to and from the studio through rural Indiana.

And yet the hope in the air cooling the sweat on my skin as I soak in the sun just cannot be ignored.

What is it? A sense of justice, a cosmic balancing of the scales? We're not talking about gray skies and winter barns. The impossibly blue water and the wide-open, sunny skies and the colorful doorways and the lush foliage and the breezes across the water finally break through—or at least begin to crack—the dense and dark, cynical and ugly grief that goes with me everywhere.

It is beautiful. The trip is wonderful.

But I can't shake the sense that it's all just an extravagant consolation prize. If I hadn't lost Mom and Dad, I wouldn't be here.

And that's the problem with a consolation prize: No matter how grand, you always know it's a stand-in for the thing you really want. Your heart's desire—that remains just out of reach.

MELANCHOLY DAYS

14" x 28"

Description: Rusted
Coca-Cola sign in the
window of a run-down
grocery store

In late fall, early winter—a year after the big sale, nearly a year and a half after Dad died—I see Dad all around me.

I drive the 15 minutes from home to the studio, watching the landscape gently undulate around me. But I see it as though it's a painting. The slashes of sepia and raw umber defining the fence line, from which the bare branches of the trees reach up into the cerulean sky. The Naples yellow and sap green, intertwined like some kind of scratchy camo, the detritus of the harvested fields and dying grasses.

The sight of it all evokes such a visceral longing I can hardly catch my breath.

And it reminds me how lonely I am. How much I miss him.

Most of the rest of the year I miss my mom, but right now, all I can see is him. It's a privilege to be able to see the world through eyes like his—the same dull, dark brown, the same eye for composition and light and shadow. But at the same time, it reminds me just how lonely this life is that I've stepped into. I'm like a kid playing grown-up. Wanting to feel connected to my daddy. I have his walls, his building, literally surrounding me every day. His art decorating those walls. Friends who knew him nodding at me from the street as they walk past.

But he isn't here. He will never be here. The landscape changes with the seasons, but the missing doesn't.

Fall is my favorite, but in winter, I see a lot of Dad around me, too. Winter strips everything down to its bare bones. If an artist doesn't understand the structure beneath, they can't portray it in a realistic way, and in the winter, what lies beneath comes to the forefront.

I see the truth and beauty of the Midwest in the skeletal tree branches, the gentle hills. (My husband says they're not actually hills because he's from Pittsburgh, where they have Hills-with-a-capital-H). There's a simple, stark beauty in the frost reflecting off the rows of splintered corn stubble. In the strength and design of the barn frames, even those slowly falling down. In the geometry of the patchwork fields lined with trees and crisscrossing fences. In the early-morning sunlight reflecting off the puddles of spring rain in the corners of a field.

Indiana winters are not lush and indulgent like a tropical paradise would be. They're simple and honest and true. Pure.

But if winter is the bare bones of the landscape, summer overwhelms with its impossible decadence. The green is so extravagant it's almost embarrassing.

The scenes around us change constantly, growing, fading, transforming, renewing. The only thing that remains consistent is the underlying structure.

Dad wasn't about dressing things up to make them look better, but about portraying the truth of things at their most vulnerable. At their most real.

Just as he captured that which lies beneath, I think his work appeals to those people who do the same thing. Who meet the needs that people take for granted. The ones who raise the crops, feed the cattle, make things run when they're broken, and feed you when you're hungry. The ones who are rarely in the limelight, but are the core of our quality of life.

The ones who are pure and steady and honest and true.

Much like he was.

vignette

Those viewing the works in the current museum exhibit will notice a change, however. ... He calls it breakout. All of a sudden there are skys [sic], horizon lines, foregrounds, and they're breaking randomly out of the rectangular painter's plane.

"If I didn't change I'd go crazy," O'Dell says. He feels the breakout technique has put a new sense of freedom and excitement in his work.

—Kathy Matter, "Artist Returns with Breakout Works," *Journal & Courier,*
Lafayette, Indiana, October 6, 1986

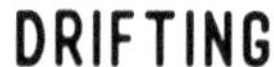

DRIFTING

16″ x 20″

Description: Winter landscape with tufts of weeds pushing through snowdrifts. Featured in the ad for an exhibition at Wabash College.

The back of the studio building is a world apart from the bright, gleaming hardwood floor gallery space in front. Behind the gallery and a functional workroom, the next room was once Dad's closet, where he hung all of his IU sweatshirts, "ugly" golf shirts, and the assortment of quirky T-shirts we gave him over the years. "My favorite people call me Bebop," read one. "Daddy-O," said another. I bought Dad and myself matching shirts once that said, "Go to your studio and make stuff." One of my favorites was the gray T-shirt that read "Hoosier Daddy" (based on the legend of how Indiana got its nickname: when people came upon someone new, they would ask, "who's yer daddy?").

After Dad died, my friend Peggy accompanied me on a drive to Florida to retrieve his things from Rita's house. Kerry and I mainly wanted his T-shirts. But when we arrived, Rita showed me the closet full of button-down shirts with designer labels. I asked about his T-shirts, and she pointed to a small drawer containing a neat stack of boxer briefs and plain black dressy T-shirts—he had a different wardrobe down here. I couldn't bear to ask if he had thrown them away or she had.

But at least the Hoosier Daddy and Bebop shirts were still in this closet up north, safe.

After boxing up Dad's things, I packed the closet with large filing cabinets, boxes of note cards featuring Dad's paintings, extra copies of my books, an array of tiny drawers of beads and wire, and totes filled with random craft and art supplies.

Beside the closet sits a large bathroom with a stand-up shower and stackable washer and dryer. The plain wooden door at the back of the closet leads to the dark side.

Once you step down into the space, you reach up blindly in the dark to feel for the spark plug hanging from a piece of ratty string, which Dad called into service as a pull cord for the fluorescent lights. Keep your eyes peeled for bats—and potentially other rodents, which I don't like to think about. The exposed brick walls are crumbling in spots, dribbling peaks of terra-cotta dust in little mountains along the side walls. A partial loft overhead is stacked full of wood scraps, unnecessary doors, a few antique bicycle fenders, and who knows what else. There's not enough light up there to really see, and most everything is specked with bat guano, so I'm not inclined to explore in depth.

The long, narrow room contains stacks of boxes and extra furniture. The unsealed concrete floor is grungy, and when it rains, water pours down the brick wall on the left side (the wall this building shares with the hardware store) because of how the owners "fixed" their roof leak years ago. As a result, we've had to put everything important on top of durable plastic drop cloths. The room smells of damp and of mice.

Dad had two six-foot tables set up back there, topped with stacks of his barn and hollyhock prints wrapped loosely with torn brown paper. The prints on top were stained with the kind of black dust that filters down in a building like this. A second framing table with storage beneath it is tucked into the corner, no longer fitting into the workspace up front, holding L-shaped frame molding samples and old T squares.

At the back of this room, another door leads to the final section, a one-car garage. The ancient wooden workbench is strong and solid, supplemented by a floor saw and drill press, plus another boxy, industrial heater. The left-hand wall is lined with shallow, low shelves holding tackle boxes, spare hardware, coffee cans full of screws and nails, dried-up cans of paint, a couple of dirty plastic funnels. Dad's art-show-booth panels lean against one wall along with the table he used for workshop demonstrations, which has a clunky wooden extension to hold his painting utensils and a frame to support a heavy mirror above it so that people throughout the room could watch Dad paint.

A large platform by the doorway between the rooms holds toolboxes with the servos and controllers Dad used to fly his now-decaying radio-controlled model airplanes.

When Dad was dying, he got a letter from Scott Bradley, the younger brother of Jennifer (the friend of Kerry's who rode in my back seat while I swatted at her on my way to school). Kerry and Jennifer are still best friends, and in a weird twist of fate, she's one of my closest friends now, too, and a fellow graphic designer. When Jennifer told Scott about Dad's health, he immediately sat down to write him a letter—which revealed to Kerry and me things we didn't know.

Such as this: While I was at college, Scott, who was seven years younger than I am, used to hang out in Mom and Dad's nasty basement to build RC (remote-controlled) airplanes. Dad had pushed an old Ping-Pong table into one corner, a runway of sorts on which he parked his model planes in all stages of completion and repair. Old-house basements are damp and full of mildew—much like the back room of the studio building in

Ladoga, come to think of it. The ceiling was unfinished, so you could see nails poking down from the kitchen floor above, and spiders built webs in the windows along the ground level of the house. Dad had workbenches in the corner and a shelf full of controllers. Rolls of pinstriping tape hung from dowel rod racks, and hooks in the ceiling suspended the random biplane wing.

When I still lived at home, sometimes I would timidly make my way down there, trying not to look in the dark corners or at the sump pump in the floor, slapping at the random displaced cobwebs, while Dad showed me what he was building. He carefully cut emblems and signs and letters, enjoying the decorating of the planes as much as the building.

What I didn't know until Scott wrote that letter is that he and Dad spent countless hours building planes together. On summer evenings, they hung out at Scott's family's airstrip, a grassy area in the middle of a cornfield with a red wind sock, flying their RC planes. Afterward, Scott and Dad would go back to the house to fix or rebuild the planes.

As an adult, Scott became a small-plane pilot and an airport manager, so the time he spent with Dad made more of a difference than I had imagined. In his letter, Scott thanked Dad for the time they spent working together and said he was grateful for the way Dad believed in him.

When Kerry and I were cleaning out the back of the studio after Dad passed, it seemed only natural to offer the airplane stuff to Scott. He backed his big pickup truck up to the garage door at the back of the studio, and we carried out numerous planes and toolboxes. As he reached for one of the last planes, he glanced up at the wall.

"Oh, hey, that's the prop from Rob's Ultralight!"

I'd noticed the six-foot-long wooden propellor on the wall, but I hadn't registered it any more than one might notice the random implements screwed to the wall in the local Cracker

Barrel. I had no idea Dad had saved anything from those days.

He bought (and built from a kit) a full-sized Eagle Ultralight aircraft. Rainbow-colored wings sheltered the engine and the precarious-looking seat hanging below. This kind of craft isn't like a plane; it's a hang glider with what might as well be a chainsaw engine. The pilot sits in this net, his hands on controls that adjust the rudders. Now, as I look back, I wonder what he was thinking. A powered hang glider? As a husband and father of two young girls?

It was a one-seater, thank God, because there is no way any of us would have wanted to go for a spin. Other than a flimsy triangular frame on which were attached three tiny wheels for taking off and landing, nothing substantial existed between the pilot hanging in the air and the ground far below.

I know Mom didn't like it, but I was 14 and engrossed in my own world, so I'm not aware if they fought about it, or if Dad had her full approval. The Ultralight just seemed like a natural extension of his forays into building flying machines as a kid, racing dirt bikes in his 30s, and then flying his RC planes. Kerry went with him to watch most of his flying adventures—both hang glider and model planes—but I do remember going to the little airport where his Ultralight was stored to watch him fly it, the little engine buzzing as he swooped past us and then brought it down onto the bumpy, grassy runway.

I don't remember many details, but when I think about those times, I picture him smiling and laughing with his friends, who were also standing around watching to see what he would do and to be part of the adventure.

ON THE EDGE

28″ x 36″

Description: Dramatic vignette
of a hillside with a
majestic tree perched on
the edge of the slope

My parents went to Ireland several years after Kerry and I had both left home. They spent two weeks in a little cottage, eating meals at the local pub, wandering around and exploring. Dad even did some *plein air* painting there, which simply means painting outdoors, on location, instead of working from photographs. Typically, he avoided that—watercolor, after all, is fluid and runny, so you can't use an upright easel, and as he said in a newspaper interview once, "It's no fun when you're out in the field painting and dust or a bug lands on your work and leaves tracks."[7]

When Mom and Dad came home, I flipped through the stack of 35 mm photos they'd picked up from the photo developing place. I put them down on the kitchen table while I ran upstairs to my old bedroom. I came back with the ivory leather photo albums from the three months when I studied abroad and traveled during college.

"There! Look!"

I turned the photo album toward Dad and placed the top image from the stack of photos I had been looking at right beside it. We had both visited the same town—I think it was in County Cork, a harbor—and had taken virtually identical photos. The same rocks in the foreground, a similar pile of rope, the same angles in the background. Yes, it's true that if two people visit the same landmark location—like the Eiffel Tower, for instance—it's likely that their photos will look similar. But this was some random, obscure corner of a harbor, several years apart, in a tiny town off the beaten path. Yet the similarities were uncanny.

I suppose, having been surrounded by Dad's work for so long, it's not surprising that our sense of composition and what we noticed were similar. Everyone always said I was Dad's mini-me, but still, it amused me. Yet the way we saw the world felt safe and ordinary.

As a longtime graphic designer, I see Dad's art much differently now. And it turns out, the reason for his initial success had a lot to do with the chances he took.

Although Dad's personality was laid-back and peaceful, taking risks was part of his personality. We heard stories about his numerous attempts to build contraptions that he launched off the garage roof as a boy—hoping, but failing, to fly. When he and Mom met, he was (as she put it) from the wrong side of the tracks—a bit of a bad boy. He wore Levi's and white T-shirts with cigarettes rolled into the sleeves, with his curly auburn hair slicked back. While working in his dad's cabinet shop, he put all the money he made into buying newer, faster automobiles every year.

When he joined the Army a couple years after high school, he initially wanted to be a paratrooper.[8] "After five weeks of airborne school I quit," he said. "It was too much. You were on call all the time." Instead, he went into the President's Honor Guard in Washington, DC. The group served at the inauguration and as the guard at the Tomb of the Unknown Soldier—but with the honor guard, he had more time to draw and enter shows than he would have had if he had served as a paratrooper.

When I was in elementary school, Dad raced dirt bikes. I have photos of him standing on the seat of his motorcycle, leaning over to grip the handlebars, popping wheelies across the yard. The RC plane phase started before the hang glider and lasted years beyond it. (He flew his Eagle Ultralight for only two years or so.) He had other, safer hobbies, too—fishing, playing (and coaching) softball, and building elaborate villages for his model trains.

For his 73rd birthday, Dad had two requests: a new all-terrain vehicle (ATV) and a CD of Katy Perry because, as he told people with a wicked grin, "She kissed a girl and she liked it." Since Mom was in the middle of her cancer diagnosis, she bought him exactly what he asked for—and some small helmets so the kids could ride with him.

With his adventurous personality, maybe it's not a surprise that he took the initial giant leap to become a professional artist. It's not a career for the faint of heart.

His early paintings were bold. Dramatic vignettes—triangles of green representing a hillside. Trees, bare branches snapped by nature's storms into extreme shapes. Snow fences slashing entire canvases of mostly unbroken white. Broken things—rusted pails, a patchwork of boards and light and shadow in a dim interior or a barn. Deserted homes, an elaborate composition of shadows and branches striping the wood. His paintings were done in a realistic style, and the objects themselves were easily recognizable, but he put them on the page in a way that was unusual.

Nancy Noël, a woman who went on to have massive success with her oils and pastels of Amish children, angels, and animals, owned a gallery in Indianapolis in the early 1970s. She said in the *Indianapolis Star and News* in December 1971, "Anyone can learn to draw, but design is harder to achieve. We look for something that's creative, well-executed, and, of course, everything we carry is original." Her gallery included several contemporary artists, but also a realistic one—my dad. "His art has a contemporary flair," she went on to say. "Like Andrew Wyeth," whom she considered the best practicing fine-artist in the United States today, "O'Dell may paint just a barn, but the way he takes it and makes a design of it says, 'I want you to look at this as if you were looking at it for the first time.'"

Dad's personality was playful, but never pretentious. Dozens of articles and interviews described him as low-key, humble, down-to-earth. And he was.

Chuck Gleason, a local newspaper columnist, stopped by the studio in Ladoga one day in 2002 and wrote about it: "After meeting and sharing conversation with him, I was able to understand where the calmness to his art comes from."

As Dad's talent evolved, he moved from more dramatic compositions into some less risky ones. Not because they were boring, but because they were beautiful. Because it was what he saw every day. Because they worked and people liked them. That mattered more than anything else to him.

In his early career, he used a stark, dark color palette—mostly black and brown—and then added some cadmium yellow and crimson and sap green light. As he explored different subjects, venturing into abstracts and multiple images, he challenged himself with the textures and patterns of rocks, leaves, and plants. His work evolved from minimalistic and graphic to well-rendered, more traditional representations. In his later life, he explored graphic, tapestry-like geometric shapes to depict cascades of leaves, flowers, and ferns.

It took me a lifetime of watching, followed by three years

of closely studying details of his work and career and life after he died, before I truly understood how he had forged his own path. He wasn't just seeking a paycheck; he knew what subjects fascinated him. He understood how to use his talent. He did exactly what he wanted to do, and he loved doing it.

I was much the same. I started working as a graphic designer, and before long started freelancing—like my dad, I worked from home, setting my own hours to make my career more compatible with family life. Along the way, I discovered my love for the written word and authored four books. I thought I was happy and fulfilled. I had already built the life I wanted.

But suddenly, after losing Mom and Dad, I found myself wondering how I might reimagine my life. Was it what I wanted? Was it enough? I didn't really have time—or the inclination, if I'm honest—to start all over with something new.

Yet the thought kept sneaking in and I couldn't help but wonder: Could I paint? Would I ever want to?

vignette

"Watercolors are unpredictable. Happy accidents occur when I use them. I'll be painting something and I will find that I have created something else that wasn't planned. Watercolors are very fluid."

—Rob O'Dell quoted by Cheryl D. Peck, "O'Dell Paints Scenes of Disappearing World," *Herald & Review*, Decatur, Illinois, August 2, 1971

JUST ADD COLOR

14" x 20"

Description: Irises painted in graphic
black and white, overlaid with
translucent squares of green and
purple highlighting the flowers

I stand in front of my dad's drawing board. Ever since I moved into the studio in 2018, I've resisted this compulsion to paint. But two years is long enough. Today is the day—even if I still can't bring myself to mess up Dad's work area, to wipe away the final mixture of sepia and cadmium yellow still on his enamel mixing tray, to disturb the order of the watercolor tubes in the top drawer of the credenza (interspersed with a few random items like a bright yellow Matchbox car, placed next to a tube of yellow ochre, rather than the cadmium yellow deep that was a closer match). I lean over and for the thousandth time blow the dust off the brushes aligned in their white enameled trays—without touching or changing a thing. Another puff of air removes the accumulated dust on the cracked, dried wells of pigment in the little rectangular and circular indentations of his palette.

I go to the storage closet in back and get the brushes and plastic paint tray Dad used in Florida. Rita's house had two guest rooms, but the light wasn't good in there, so he wedged his painting table into the dining room and kept his supplies to a minimum. I wasn't afraid to use these; they've already been displaced, and since I wasn't there in person for most of it, his Florida life didn't feel like his *real* "real life."

In other words, the thought of using these and potentially messing them up doesn't make my soul cringe.

And that's the thing. I know I'm going to mess up. I know I won't paint like Dad did—anything I do will be a cheap facsimile of him.

When I told a friend that I was thinking about painting, she replied, "Oh good! I bet you'll feel closer to your dad when you paint."

Not really. The defiant teenager rises in me, just as it did when I went to Italy after Mom died. Mom would have been thrilled about my going to a writing workshop with one of our favorite authors, happy that I was exploring my talent, but she would think I was spending too much money on myself, and she'd criticize me for leaving my family home for a week to fend for themselves.

I wanted to give painting a shot, but I was convinced that, if he were here, Dad would offer plenty of criticism about what I did, helpful or otherwise. I might show some promise, but I would only ever be an amateur—never as good as he was. But I can't shake this determination to try. It doesn't have to be a competition.

I use one of Dad's sponges to evenly wet the surface of the watercolor paper. I dab some cerulean blue paint onto the mixing surface, dulling it down a bit by adding a touch of sepia, then swipe a summer sky onto the glistening paper with a wide, flat brush. I watch the color bloom. I swish the brush around in the water, then dab some sap green onto the paper, the beginnings of a rudimentary landscape. I reach for the saltshaker and sprinkle the little white crystals onto the grass I just painted, knowing the salt will soak up the pigment and make shapes that give the impression of weeds and flowers if you apply the salt at just the right time.

Which I didn't, apparently. Nothing happens. Must have been too soon.

I wait a minute for the paint to dry a bit, then try again. *There.* I see the little starbursts forming in the paint. I know I have to wait for the paint to fully dry before I can move on to the next steps, but when it does, I see how faint and pale the colors are. My touch was too light, but I can't fix it now that the paint has already dried.

I squint my eyes, trying to be objective—only to realize this looks like a preschooler did it. The blue and green, while pale, are unnatural, unrealistic colors. I might as well be using a Crayola set of eight basic colors and a plastic brush.

I turn off the light above the table and go back to my computer to do something I know how to do.

There is no surprise in the fact that the exhibition's top prize—a $500 merit award for the outstanding work in any medium—went to watercolorist Rob O'Dell for "Offspring," a super-realistic depiction of three dying tree stumps with newborn treelets growing out of them. O'Dell, who has entered two previous Hoosier Salons and won something in each of them, is one of the state's most competent and original artists, if the number of people who lately have taken to painting like him is any indication. Imitation, they say, is the sincerest form of flattery.

— Marion Simon Garmel, "48th Hoosier Salon Opens," *Indianapolis Star*, 1972

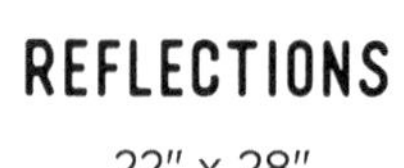

In the 1980s, Dad started teaching other artists. He'd been asked to teach a workshop or two, and initially said no. "But he acquiesced after looking around and seeing no one using his techniques, and also as a result of his father-in-law talking him into it, saying it was his turn to give something back to watercolor for the next generation," according to a 1992 *Montgomery Magazine* interview.

Once he started, he found teaching to be rewarding. He taught at various galleries, art leagues, and schools, and a big reason he moved into the studio in downtown Ladoga was to have space to host his own workshops.

People tell me that what made him such a good teacher was he didn't hold back any secrets. He believed that if you had talent, that would come through, and if you didn't, the techniques alone wouldn't carry you. He wasn't in competition with his students; he just wanted to help. In an interview in a Decatur, Illinois, newspaper in 2006, he reflected, "There are a lot of artists there that have taken my workshop. It's nice to know that I've possibly had an influence on their work."

A friend of Dad's, Sue Powell, took his workshops and served as gallery director for the Decatur Area Arts Council. She said, "He is just the ultimate gentleman in my mind, a humble artist who is so appreciative of the fact that he could earn a living with his art. He's a very low-key individual who loves to meet people who are interested in watercolors, and I believe you can see that low-key nature in the gentleness of his work." She went on to say that his paintings are veritable master classes on watercolor technique. "He is a master of understatement, in ways that only other painters would be likely to recognize," she said. "When he demonstrates, he makes it look so effortless. He has certainly made a following of friends who come to see him and look at his work every year."[9]

Dad continued his conversation with the *Montgomery Magazine* writer. "I can tell if someone is good or not," he said. When asked whether he would recommend that someone leave a stable career to pursue painting full-time, as he did, he said, "If they've got the ability, then I have to find out if they've got the drive. If they want it bad enough then there's no problem. But if they think they can just paint whenever they want to, it just won't work."

And then he wrapped it up by saying, "I still slap myself in the face every once in a while and say, 'Boy, you're lucky.'"

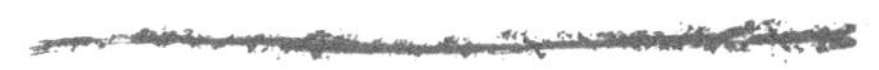

About nine months after Dad died, I stopped by County Market, the local grocery, to get a donut. Okay, two, but who's counting? This cute little woman wearing a County Market uniform and a huge smile ran over to me. She looked familiar, but I couldn't place her. She told me to stop by the local Athens Gallery because she'd dedicated something to my dad in her art show.

Intrigued, Kerry and I went, not entirely sure what we were

going to see.

We took a quick look around the gallery and zeroed in on a watercolor of a weathered gray barn surrounded by snow. "There!" The composition was similar to Dad's, although the colors were more gray and less brown than his usual palette. The rusted metal roof covered with snow, the crooked lightning rods, the stark sycamore tree standing up behind it. Yep, definitely a Rob O'Dell knockoff, as we'd come to call them.

Next to this painting—which was nicely done, by the way (you just never know until you see someone's work in person)—was a laser-printed page of text. Kym Bushong (now we knew her name!) had dedicated the art show to the people who had inspired her to pursue her art. Under the "Rob O'Dell" heading, we read this:

> Several years past my daughter gave me the gift of two Rob O'Dell workshops. ... The night before the first workshop I was so excited I didn't sleep. After all, I was set to learn from a master of the art I was pursuing. Soon after the class began, I knew I was in over my head, but I took detailed notes and way too many pictures. By the end of the weekend, I was hooked. I went home, looked up the dates for the next workshop, and mailed the check on Monday morning and my journey began.

She went on to explain that several years later, she overheard a discussion in which some women wondered why another woman was absent. Dad said she hadn't been invited, and Kym was horrified to discover that she'd been overstepping all these years by inviting herself back. She continued her story.

> I saw Rob at the Taste [a local food festival]. He approached me and asked if I had received my invitation. In the ensuing conversation, I asked why he had never said anything about me inviting myself. He told me, "Because I saw promise in you. I saw someone serious about learning. I'm not going to

live forever, and we have to pass the secrets down if we want
to preserve our art." I attended his last workshops at Old
Normal and he reminded me, "Don't take it all with you, leave
something behind." Rob helped me become the artist I am
today and though he has departed, ... life (and art) goes on.

I looked at Kerry through my suddenly watery eyes. "People
didn't have to be invited," we said, confused, but on reflection
we realized that in a sense people *were* hand selected. Dad had
long lists of people who had attended previous workshops, but
he only mailed info for the next workshop (what he apparently
called "invitations") to 45 people so that he would end up with
25 to 30 attendees. He didn't have space for more, so he was
selective about who he included. I don't think Dad ever flat-out
told anyone they could not attend, yet I know over the years
there were some people who were removed from his lists because
they were overbearing or rude.

Dad had earned a place in Kym's show because of his
kindness and encouragement. She had innate artistic abilities,
but I think what Dad responded to was her eagerness to grow, to
learn. When she shared her fear about overstepping, Dad showed
her how welcome she was, that he believed she had what it takes.
And now Kym never passes up the opportunity to tell that story
about Dad.

But it's not just her. Dozens of people have stopped by the
studio in the years since I've worked in that building for the sole
purpose of telling me how much Dad's encouragement meant
to them. He didn't treat them like he was better than they were,
even though they knew their talent didn't match his.

When it came to family, though, that wasn't always true.

I feel that there is nothing more truly artistic than to love people.

—Vincent van Gogh

FORERUNNER

24" x 20"

Description: A mostly white scene
of a snowy creek running across the
center of the page (one of four scenes
from the Prairie Heritage Print
Collection offered in 1974 by Citizens
National Bank in Decatur, Illinois, as an
incentive for account holders)

In college, I took an introductory painting class that was required for my graphic design major. With a combination of youthful arrogance and loyalty to my dad, I carried a strong bias against oils and acrylics—it didn't take as much skill if you could keep layering on more paint and covering up your mistakes. I'd seen the work of the instructor and was not impressed. She had nothing on my dad.

Our assignments were things like painting an 18" x 24" study of random, dull little pottery shards in shades of gray acrylic. Painting a stack of wooden two-by-four pieces of different lengths in the style of Van Gogh's *Starry Night*. And so on. We didn't do or learn anything I would consider "art."

I had better things to do with my time. Like sleep. The class, unfortunately, started at 9 a.m. during winter quarter. The art building was a 20-minute walk across campus from my dorm, and I have always believed waking up early is a peculiar form of hell. The only thing compelling me to go to class was the attendance policy, which only allowed me three absences, after which the instructor would dock one letter grade per missed class. I only missed three classes, but I may have come in late a few other times.

And yet, when I picked up my stack of canvases at the end of the semester, I discovered the instructor had given me a C in the class. One of the critique sheets said my lowered grade was due to excessive absences. I'd only had maybe one or two other Cs on report cards in my entire life.

But the semester was over, and I was just glad to be done with the class, so I didn't argue. I wedged the paintings into the back seat of my 1982 Chevy Cavalier, right next to the overflowing baskets of dirty laundry, and drove home for break. Dad carried my paintings out to his studio to store them in his racks. Out of sight, out of mind.

Until Dad mentioned that I apparently needed to go to class more often. He'd read my critique sheets (which I forgot were attached to the backs of the canvases).

"But I went to class! She must have counted me absent when I just came in late sometime!"

"Whatever you say," he teased. "Looks to me like you were lucky you got a C."

It stings a bit to remember this, but if I'd ever thought I could paint, I didn't believe so after that. I'd grown up knowing without a shadow of a doubt that my dad was extraordinarily talented, so I accepted his biases and opinions about art and talent as truth. Since I certainly couldn't do what he did, he was probably right about me, too.

Then again, I didn't really want to do what he did, so it all worked out.

I only tried to paint with watercolor once as an adult. It was 1996, and I was six months pregnant with Anna, my second child. Dad held workshops twice a year at his studio, and I'd stopped by to say hi a few times but never attended. I am not sure what prompted me to sign up, but I decided to give it a try.

Before every workshop, Dad asked me to scan his sketches of the paintings he planned to teach, format his materials list, update the registration forms with the new dates, and print 35 copies to send to the attendees. He made sure everyone knew the subject matter ahead of time. For this particular workshop, he'd chosen some "good" subjects—a painting of irises for day one and a barn silhouetted against the sunset for the second day.

Each morning of Dad's two-day workshops, he completed a demo at his painting table with the gigantic mirror above it. After lunch, his students tried to copy what he had done. Since this was before the days of everyone recording things on their phones, all I have now is a single page of notes scribbled with a Sharpie onto a page torn from a sketch pad. Just a few phrases, not even enough to help me re-create those scenes.

During that workshop, I did okay with the irises on day one, but when it came to the barn, all I remember is struggling with my initial sketch of the barn. The angles were wrong; the barn sat awkwardly on the page; my perspective was terrible.

Perspective is a way of conveying distances and space, which relies on lines that converge toward the horizon. As objects get farther away from you, they appear smaller, and the ones closer to you appear larger. When you draw a landscape with a building in it, the angles of the roof and side walls will usually be angled, not the parallel horizontal lines you might imagine. Dad had always told me that women were inherently bad at understanding perspective, that our brains just worked differently, so I didn't question Dad's need to correct the angles of my lines. (Years later, I took a drawing class from my friend Elizabeth to try to remember all that I'd forgotten about drawing, and she was horrified by Dad's opinion. I'd never thought to challenge it until then.) While Dad's opinion was sexist and misguided, I can't deny that getting perspective right was a challenge for *me*. Drawing isn't instinctive for me.

I have to pay close attention and stretch myself, but I'm often too impatient to really study the details and get it right. When something does not come easily, I rarely keep doing it long enough to get it right.

The day of the workshop, Dad sat down beside me, grabbed a kneaded eraser, and fixed my awkward lines. Just a few confident strokes, and suddenly the barn looked right again. He went on to help the next person, and I started adding color. The finished painting turned out pretty well. At first glance, someone might even assume it was one of his—which is fair, since all of us in the room did a variation of that same scene using his techniques and colors. I presented it to my in-laws for Christmas that year, and it hung over their mantle for years. The iris went to a friend. Shortly thereafter, I had baby number two while working full-time in my graphic design business, so there was no spare time to paint. I stashed my tackle box of brushes and paints in the attic and never looked back.

I did do some *other* arts over the years, though. My husband and I took a stained glass class—one night a week for a couple of months, in a building near Dad's studio in downtown Ladoga. Mom and Dad kept the girls, who were pretty small, so we could both get away. Tim has never been artistic, but he's mechanical and had the soldering down pat. Although I never really mastered the soldering with much finesse, I loved working with glass. I could design an image (no templates for me) and pick just the right colors and textures of glass to enhance the shapes. That year for Christmas I made an interpretation of one of Dad's hollyhock paintings out of milky white and pink glass, with triangular leaf shapes in numerous variegated greens. Dad loved it and built a wooden frame so he could hang it in the front window of the studio for everyone to see.

The only place at home where Tim and I could do stained glass was our damp, unfinished, old-house basement, which always kind of grossed me out. Besides, the kids always seemed to need me just when I would get started. So, after making stained glass panels for several people in my life, and a tulip vase for Mom, I packed away the grinder and pieces of glass in boxes. When we moved a few years later, the box was transferred to the new attic, and it has never been opened again.

Not long after I gave up on stained glass, Mom bought me a basic jewelry-making set with tools and a simple beginners' instruction booklet for Christmas—and I went crazy from there. I'd always bought artsy jewelry at the art fairs I attended with Dad, so I had a drawer full of cuffs and wire wrapped bangles and dangly earrings to inspire me. Why couldn't I make them too?

Bending wire was like bringing to life lines and curves that perfectly complemented the shapes and textures of the beads or stones. Jewelry making doesn't require artistic skill, necessarily— nearly anyone can string beads onto wire—but I like to think my jewelry was created with the eye of an artist. I crafted unusual combinations of design elements that made my jewelry look handcrafted and interesting. I loved sorting the little plastic drawers of beads by color and size. Loved experimenting with bending and twisting and hammering the wire. Creating tight spirals and wide-open ones. Triangles, squares, circles, ovals. Charms and dangles and handmade quirky clasps.

I designed business cards, started a Facebook page, held trunk shows, and attended a few art festivals over the years. Sold necklaces and earrings and whimsical charm bracelets to clothing shops and beauty salons. But the thing about doing jewelry is that when it breaks—which it inevitably will, unless you're soldering or firing your own metal pieces—you have to fix it. It seemed I never had the right replacement beads, or (let's be honest) the patience to mess with it after it was made. Over time, sterling silver tarnishes, and it took so much patience to hand-polish each little loop and connection. Eventually I stopped trying to sell it, though I've kept the tools and (literally) hundreds of little drawers of beads—way too much for someone who isn't actively making jewelry. But when I see a cool pair of earrings in a catalog or boutique and can't bear to pay that much for them—or just can't find a pair of earrings I like to go with a new blouse—I pull out my stuff. I'm not a super-meticulous or methodical craftsman, but I can get the job done.

Yet the easiest art for me, hands down, is graphic design. Yes, it's my career, but I also still enjoy it, even 30-plus years after getting my degree. Not many people can say the same. In college, I studied architecture—it was peripheral to art, but included math, and you had to be smart to do it. (That mattered to me then.) But my brain doesn't really think in three dimensions. One afternoon in college, as I melted down in the stairwell of the architecture building because I was unhappy and didn't know what to do about it, my favorite professor sat down on the steps with me. He suggested I consider graphic design because it was an application of the artistic principles we'd studied and I had a knack for it. I looked up to him, so if he thought it would be a good fit, I was willing to try.

At the time, it didn't register that I was going into the same field of study Dad had—probably because when Dad was in school it was called "commercial art." In his day, everything was done by hand, so craftsmanship was everything—perfectly rendering images in ink, carefully aligning the typesetting, using a T square and a fine-tipped ink pen. By the time I entered the field, graphic design work was done on a computer (which I loved), diminishing the craftsmanship aspects so that the focus was more on understanding composition and design, color balance, hierarchy, mixing fonts effectively, and leaving plenty of white space.

From the start, I was good at it. Before my senior year, I interned at one of the top design firms in Indianapolis, and after graduation I worked in some of the best ad agencies. In those first years, I spent hours and hours designing a new business card, envelope, and letterhead for Dad for Christmas. Printing was expensive, and hardly anyone could afford full-color printing in those days. But I was a master at using the tools available to me. If I couldn't have lots of colorful ink, I could select a gorgeous paper stock. I discovered a new family of papers that came in a variety of beautiful, natural colors covered with tiny black, irregular speckles. They reminded me of the little blobs and dots Dad made by flicking paint off the end of a paintbrush or toothbrush. The warm tan color nearly matched the walls of his studio, which were a perfect backdrop for his art. The final design had simple, black serif type—an old-fashioned font with an interesting low x-height—printed on that paper. To give it more character, I picked different shades of paper for the business card (off-white), letterhead (tan), and envelopes (rust brown). *Voilà*—the stationery was easy to produce and looked like Dad without expensive printing.

He loved it. The set was even selected for a book called *The Best of Business Card Design 4* in 1998 by Rockport Publishers.

After that, whenever Dad needed an updated brochure, an invitation for an art show opening, or whatever, he volunteered me to do it (whether I wanted to or not—though I nearly always wanted to). He didn't give me much guidance, just picked a few photos of his recent work, and then I gave him a few layouts to choose from. Once, I enlisted a friend who worked as a copywriter to write new brochure copy because I was tired of the same old artist statements and quotes from newspaper reviews. (I hadn't yet started calling myself a writer.) Dad gave her a beautiful painting as payment—and he gave me the

gorgeous snowy creek we'd used on the cover as payment for
my part. When Dad was running low on brochures again,
he would let me design a new one with different paintings,
updating the look and refreshing the colors. He probably would
have been just as happy to reprint the old ones (*same ol'* and all
that), but *I* was always ready for something new. As full-color
printing became more and more affordable, I used as much
color as I could get away with. Eventually, as I began to do more
writing professionally, I took it upon myself to write new words
about Dad and his art rather than simply reproducing the same
artist statements.

Besides, every time I designed something new, he'd pay me
with a new painting. And they were all "good ones."

PRIDE OF CRAWFORDSVILLE

14″ x 10″

Description: The Montgomery
County (Indiana) Courthouse and
monument, painted for the cover of a
hardbound book of county history

About two decades after my mediocre painting class, my middle child, Anna, signed up for photography in 4-H and attended a workshop to help her take better pictures. A few months before her project was due, she went to Italy and Greece with a group from her high school. Like everyone does, she fell in love with the Amalfi Coast and took numerous photos on the island of Capri. Her favorite featured a thick white column on the right side of the image, with tendrils of vines growing up its length and puffy clouds dotting the sky. Down below, you could see buildings stacked on the edges of the cliffs, surrounded by turquoise blue water. It was a little overcast that day, but the scene is so pretty that it doesn't matter.

She couldn't wait to show this one to her Bebop. When he came to pick up the 8" x 10" print so that he could mat and shrink-wrap it for the fair, he commented, "Anna, your composition is all wrong. You don't want this column to be cut off on the side. It should be in a little more—but not centered either. Do you know about the rule of thirds?"

This guideline for balanced compositions says this: Imagine

that the image is divided into three sections across and three
sections up and down. Important elements should be placed
on the intersection of those guidelines for the strongest
compositions rather than in the center or along the edges.

"Well, I like it," I said. Anna, like all the grandkids,
absolutely adored Dad and I was afraid she'd be devastated by
this criticism. I knew what it felt like when he didn't approve
of your work. Saying that feels unfair, maybe even disloyal. Dad
would have sworn he was supportive of our efforts. He was so
encouraging to everyone else, but he didn't have it in him to give
us false praise. I now think it was a sign of respect and trust, that
he was unerringly honest with the people he dearly loved. But
tell that to a teenager who felt like her beloved grandfather was
disappointed in her.

Not long after my brother-in-law, Doug, joined the family,
he spent a lot of time with my dad. One day he asked if Dad
would ever consider teaching him how to paint.

Dad said, "Nope. I can't teach you to paint if you can't draw."

"Well, can you teach me how to draw?" Doug asked.

"I'll tell you what. It would just be easier for me to paint the
painting and let you sign it."

Doug laughed, telling me the story, but it had to hurt a bit,
too. Dad's comments were always delivered in an affectionate,
joking manner, with a smile. I don't think he knew how much we
took his comments to heart.

My cousin Jodi Barnes had a very different experience. The
oldest daughter of Dad's older sister Jean, Jodi wrote about Dad
in 2010 in a piece about being dyslexic:

> And you are starting to hear the familiar self-scolding until
> you remember that one story from your favorite uncle who
> paints in watercolor. He told you when you were ten and you
> are just now, 40 years later, wanting to believe him. He showed
> you how he douses the board and what little control he has

over where the greens go, how the brown bleeds with the blues. He said: sometimes my best work comes from my mistakes. And you look at your haiku, a 7-5-7, not a 5-7-5, and you smile because it might be good.

A couple of weeks after Dad's comments to Anna, she got the results of the photography competition at the fair. She couldn't wait to tell him the news.

"Hey, Beeb, guess what? I got grand champion! My photo's going to the state fair!"

Her smile of triumph faded as he said, "Who do they get to judge these things? He obviously doesn't understand composition either."

Even though her photograph went on to win a blue ribbon at the Indiana State Fair, it's remained a sore spot. After Dad died, Anna went back to Capri with her husband, found her favorite column, and took a new photo—this time, though, the skies were bright and sunny. The column was fully visible, not cut off at the edge of the frame, and it was placed approximately one-third in from the right. The horizon line of the water is one-third of the way up from the bottom. The composition is perfect.

But Dad's not here to see it.

About four years after Dad died, many months after my first failed attempt to paint, I have a free Saturday with nothing scheduled, so I decide to try to paint a scene I'd photographed in Italy. I print the photo on my laser printer and draw a pencil grid on the canvas and photo to help me accurately draw the shapes and gauge the perspective. I feel like I'm cheating—the grid method is a basic technique used to enlarge an image and help maintain proper proportions (like if you were creating a wall mural from a sketch). If I were a true artist, I wouldn't have to rely on this method. I could eyeball it.

Anyway, since I had done so poorly in my last attempt with watercolors, I start blending some smooth, creamy acrylics, dabbing them onto the canvas in the right spots. The crisp edge of the building comes out wobbly and awkward, so I mix up more of the sky color to paint over my mistake. This isn't like watercolor; I feel such relief knowing I can fix whatever I don't get right the first time. I try not to obscure the pencil outlines I'd sketched, because I still need them as guides, but the acrylics are too thick to see through, so I have to keep letting the paint dry and redrawing the pencil lines on top. I go back and forth, working on different areas—the texture of the limestone blocks, the mottling and discoloration of the stone. My brushstrokes get looser when I add in the flowers growing out of the corner area, making the rest of it look too tight, so I add what might be the 15th layer of paint, trying to loosen up the stone blocks to match the rest.

When I'm done, I feel good about it. It's pretty. Vibrant, graphic, colorful. It took most of a day to create, but it's not bad.

I plop it on the old wooden church pew that lines one wall of the studio, between a painting of a giant sycamore tree and creek in the winter, and a meticulously detailed, falling-apart barn standing majestically in the snow.

Well, *that* was a mistake. Next to Dad's finesse, my detail work is clumsy. Thick, awkward lines, garish colors. None of the elegance or sophistication Dad had.

That's the thing about Dad's work. It's possible not to like his style or content matter, but it's nearly impossible to fault his technique. His drawings were meticulous and spot-on. Perspective, of course, was perfect. Details were tight, careful, and accurate. Even when he used techniques like salt sprinkled on the wet paint to create an effect, it was always just right.

I turn my painting to the wall so no one else can see it. It isn't terrible, but it isn't like Dad's, either. If someone isn't an expert, they might like it, but I can't fool myself (or my dad), who surely would roll his eyes at my amateur attempt.

But considering that the last acrylic I did was more than 30 years ago, as a 19- or 20-year-old college student—and remembering that Dad said I was lucky to get a C in the class— I still feel a tiny glimmer of pride. At least I tried.

vignette

O'Dell needs no one to speak for him or his work. His talent speaks for itself but so do the scores of people who have purchased his work.

They live in New York, California, Colorado and Iowa, these people who buy O'Dells. They hail from Indiana, Michigan, Montana and Maine. They're farmers, businessmen, rich and not-so-rich, but they all buy for the same reason ... Rob O'Dell has something to say, something they associate with whether they're important people in high places or average people living the way most Americans live ..., something they want to hold close. Through his paintings he tells them about a simpler time and place. His work speaks in plain, honest language that can be understood by anyone who views his work.

—Gaildene Hamilton, "Year's Trial Becomes Successful Venture," *Montgomery Magazine*, Crawfordsville, Indiana, February 1977

A ROAD LESS TRAVELED

14" x 28"

Description: A quiet winter day with
a snowy country-paved road, striped
with shadows, curving past strong,
bare trees, fenced fields, and barns

A woman who stopped at the studio said, "I've always wanted one of your dad's paintings, but I could never afford it."

A man leaned forward to read the price tag, then whistled under his breath. "Woo-ey, that's pricey."

Still another: "They're way out of my price range, but I always liked them."

In the years since Dad died, I've heard dozens of variations of this. A compliment (the speaker recognizes that the painting has value and that Dad had talent) nearly lost in a confession (they know nothing about art and don't feel qualified to judge it, or they're intimidated by the high price tags).

Which is funny, especially when you know the decisions Dad made about pricing his work.

He calculated his prices according to the size of the paper he used (regardless of how much of it was covered by paint). It didn't matter if it was a simple white field with a tiny tree perched at the top of a hill, or a complicated composition with five barns and a tractor parked in a shed. If two paintings were the same size, it didn't seem fair to him that one would cost more than the other. Besides, it was easy that way. That's not to say he didn't want to make money. If someone commissioned him to do a particular painting, he might suggest doing a larger size. Or he might give a customer two or three options, letting him explore multiple approaches to that subject matter and result in a couple of additional paintings to sell. But no matter how complex, the price for each size remained consistent. This always seemed particularly unfair to me when it was a negative-space scene and two-thirds of the surface was left unpainted, leaving the viewer's imagination to fill in the space.

In the mid-1960's, as Dad was painting on weekends while still working at his catalog layout job, he sold his first pieces for $10 and $20 to friends of my mom's parents. After he started going to art fairs, he set his prices by seeing what established artists charged, and selling his for half that. To maximize each piece of expensive watercolor board, he liked to do quarter-sheet-size paintings (15" x 20"), which he sold for $50 at the early art fairs.

In 1965, he attracted the attention of a Chicago gallery, DeMilo Art Galleries. The gallery owners convinced him to raise his prices by one-third or even one-half to compensate for the commissions that art galleries receive on each sale, so the price went up to $150. When that gallery closed a few years later, the Welna Gallery on Michigan Avenue offered to represent him, so he made the move.

When Welna offered Dad his first one-man show, they wanted to raise his prices quite a bit. The man said, "You're giving them away! Why not make them $3,000? Customers don't know they're $300 on Rob's personal price list."

That didn't sit right with Dad. He didn't think it was fair to charge different prices to different people, and he couldn't conceive of telling his ordinary customers these big prices, so he refused. He sold 15 pieces at that show.

Dad was young, passionate, and talented. His compositions were dynamic and stark and bold. His work was powerful. People began to notice, and after a while, the gallery owner told Dad they needed to let him go because his prices were too low. They had to make more on each painting to justify the wall space.

"Rob, you could probably get away with asking $2,000, $3,000, maybe even $5,000 or $10,000 per painting!" this man said. In 2023, those prices still seem pretty significant, so I can only imagine how enormous those sums seemed in the 1960s.

As Dad told me this story, he said he paused to digest that information, then asked the gallery owner, "Well, how many do you think I would sell in a year?"

"Maybe ten or even twenty paintings a year!" the man said, beaming.

Dad paused again, this rebellious boy from the wrong side of the tracks, intimidated a bit by the arts culture and yet knowing himself well enough not to ignore his gut-level reaction. He was starting to believe he had what it took, but he didn't deserve the higher prices—yet. He had talent, but not experience. And there was only one way to get that.

So he looked at the gallery owner and said, "Why in the world would I do that? I love to paint. I don't want to just paint ten or twenty paintings a year."

He wanted people to have his art. He didn't have to charge a fortune for a painting because he could paint another one, and it might be even better the next time. Besides, he was already making a decent living, at least by his standards. On one newspaper clipping about the 1968 Barn Colony Art Fair in Decatur, Illinois, Mom wrote along the edge in a bold red marker: "Bob sold $1,329 today!"

Art, as far as he was concerned, wasn't meant to be exclusive or unattainable. He didn't want to debate hidden meanings and symbolism. He wasn't all that interested in the intellectual side of it, or even aspiring to be cutting-edge.

He just wanted to paint.

And so he did. In 1977,[10] Dad estimated that he'd done 1,500 to 2,000 paintings since moving to Ladoga. And that was just in the first eight years of his career. If you do the math, that's anywhere between 185 and 250 paintings a year. Some years he probably painted more, others less. But over his 50-year full-time art career, that calculates to approximately 11,000 paintings. If someone doesn't absolutely love to paint, it would be difficult to produce that many—so his decision with the early gallery owners makes a lot of sense.

Dad told a reporter in 1974, "I sell to all kinds of people in all walks of life. I had no idea I could appeal to that many people and make a living from my work."[11] He never took his success for granted, though. In 2011, Jim Vorel wrote, "He sometimes feels he should have lived in an earlier epoch, but he is probably better off today when it comes to making a living as an artist." Dad said, "I would have liked to live back then, but I think I probably did come along at the right time to make a living and provide for my family. Besides, the barns would have been unweathered and unpainted. Those barns would have looked pretty sad."[12]

Dad kept a stack of cheap spiral-bound school notebooks in a filing cabinet at the studio. He didn't record the information I would have wanted—titles or a description of each painting—but he listed the date, the name of the purchaser, and the amount paid. The lists are written in a soft, probably 2B pencil ("2B or not 2B, that is the question," my dad often joked—the closest he ever came to Shakespeare), in his squat, all-caps letters, messy and hard to read. At the end of each quarter, Dad tallied up his total sales to fill out the state sales tax forms. While his records don't show us what he painted, they span his career and include many of the people who were touched by his

work. In another place, Dad kept small index-card-sized drawers
with people's names and addresses in my mom's handwriting,
an attempt early in his career to capture their information so
that when he had an art show in a gallery nearby, my parents
could hand-address the promotional postcards to invite them to
buy again.

Other boxes and drawers are stuffed with snapshots of his
paintings. In early years, those images were often on 35 mm
slides because juried art shows requested samples of the artist's
paintings submitted this way. It's also what printers used to
reproduce a painting for an art show invitation or a newspaper
article. I know he didn't take photos of all his paintings, but the
sheer number of photos is remarkable. That's nothing, though,
compared to the stockpile of images from which he painted. He
kept his 35 mm camera, an old Canon, under the driver's seat of
his vehicle, so whenever the light (or the angle of the corn rows
in a field, or the shape of a barn) caught his attention, he could
pull over and snap it. He cut scraps of mat board, labeled by
hand using a wide Sharpie, to use as dividers for each section—
boats, creeks, trees, flowers, fences, signs, tractors, wagons.
When he was ready to paint, he just had to flip through the
images and pick one.

Dad used white card stock frames to crop the photo in
the proportions he planned to paint. Next, in a sketch pad, he
made a detailed sketch, bold graphite strokes interspersed with
squiggles of notes about colors and technique: "Vermillion, sap
green, sepia." Or "scumble, cardboard, salt." After that, he taped
a piece of watercolor paper to an old wooden board covered
with blobs of various paint colors he tested on the board before
placing them on the paper. Next, he did a light sketch on the
page before any paint was applied. Watercolor is somewhat
spontaneous—you have to adapt on the fly—but Dad always
started with a plan. And then he watched and responded; waited

and adjusted. And it was nearly always beautiful.

That afternoon, he'd walk into the house and announce, "I just made $500 today." It drove Mom crazy; she knew he had to sell it first, but he was confident that he would. His work complete, he was then free to fish, or golf, or go fly his Ultralight, or help me remodel my kitchen.

What a life.

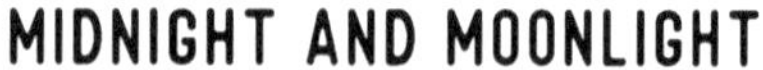

MIDNIGHT AND MOONLIGHT

10" x 14"

Description: Wintry
scene of tree and fence
at night with bluish-purple sky
and full moon

One night, maybe ten days before Dad passed, before I climbed into the futon next to his hospital bed, I kissed Dad's forehead. He looked up at me.

"Did I do the right thing?"

The question came completely out of the blue, but I knew what he was asking.

Instead of making $50,000 a year from selling a handful of paintings, he had chosen the harder route: earning perhaps $50,000 a year from 200 paintings, which sold for $100 or $400 or $700 apiece. There was an integrity to his art. Rather than selling hundreds of prints of each image, he chose to make the originals affordable, believing one of a kind was always better than mass produced. When he did finally offer some prints, I think it was mainly to allow everyone access if they couldn't afford an original.

Should he have gone for it? Tried to really be something phenomenal? Would it have worked? Made him more money? Made him happier? I guess we'll never know for sure, but I wouldn't have changed a thing.

"Yes, you did, Dad. You absolutely did the right thing," I whispered, as I patted his hand and tucked him into bed.

Within moments, he was snoring. I lay there, wide awake, for hours.

vignette

O'Dell confesses to never having been a starving artist, but has experienced a lean year here and there. The state of the overall economy has a lot to do with the state of the art economy, 'but the big buyers are always out there,' he said.

—Glen Cumbrella, "Rob O'Dell's New Studio Fulfills Lifelong Dream,"
Montgomery Magazine, Crawfordsville, Indiana, July 1992

NO HUNTING

11" x 14"

Description: Broken wooden gate
held together with barbed wire and
surrounded by drifts of snow.
A hand-lettered sign reads
"No Hunting Without Permission."

In the late '70s, Dad was asked in an interview by Gaildene Hamilton for *Montgomery Magazine* whether it was difficult sometimes to let go of a piece of work.

He said, "You see something in the finished piece, something you like. Then someone else sees that same thing and wants to own it himself. ... Sometimes it's hard to give up a painting because you realize it has so much of you in it."

By the time of that interview, he estimated that there were in the vicinity of 10,000 originals out there. The article continued:

> That's a lot of paintings, a multitude of barns, fences, daisies and other ramshackle buildings. And each and every one is a bit of Rob O'Dell. Every barn is a composite of barns he's seen and liked. Each fence has at some time kept the cows in and intruders out. Each sagging loft door saw tons of sweet-smelling hay pass through to provide feed for a winter. Every sagging roof has sheltered animals and humans from the storm.
>
> They're not hard to read, these Rob O'Dell watercolors. They're a place in someone's childhood; a faded barn in

someone's back pasture; or a golden woods in someone's dreams.

They're real, they're honest, they're a part of rural America, and they're so distinctive that anyone familiar with his style and talent could pick out one of his paintings in a gallery filled with hundreds of works of art.

No wonder I'm having such a hard time letting go.

While I am working one day, an eBay alert pops into my inbox: "Rob O'Dell: 2 new matches today."

I click over to see if they're good ones or not. Just saying that makes me smile, because it's what I would have said to my dad.

Whenever Dad completed a painting he was particularly proud of, one that was unusual, or even one he wasn't sure was up to his standards, he brought it along the next time he stopped by the Compound. He'd walk into my office, saying, "Hey, Kelly O!" Then he'd prop the painting on my desk or against the wall and ask what I thought. Usually, I think he was seeking affirmation, which I normally gave him, usually with plenty of teasing wrapped around it. Dad's paintings weren't always perfect, though I could rarely fault his technique, but it took more than that for us to designate it a "good one." A good one stands out, offers a surprising perspective or composition, has an unusual color palette, or depicts an uncommon subject.

I have more paintings than I can hang on my walls. It is downright greedy to want more, but I always watch for eBay and auction alerts, just in case. I see immediately that this is a standout. One painting is fairly ordinary, but the other awakens an indescribable longing. A feeling of homesickness. Loneliness. Melancholy.

I want it, but they're asking too much for it. People
always do.

I've emailed sellers telling them that a piece they've labeled
as original is, in fact, a note card that was framed, and it's
certainly not worth $400 (more like $40). Once I found an
original watercolor labeled *War Ravaged* that depicted what the
seller described as a "German World War 2 symbol on building
ruins." I guess I'm not the only person who makes up titles. Being
the annoying person (but loyal advocate of all-things-Rob-
O'Dell) that I am, I emailed the seller to say those were actually
Native American cliff dwellings in the southwest. Surprisingly,
he responded with genuine gratitude and some questions about
Dad, and he quickly updated the description. That painting is
still sitting unsold on eBay at least three years later, though. It's
not one of Dad's best.

But the one I discovered today is lovely. A dilapidated
wooden farm gate—a few weathered and broken boards held
together with rusted wire—sits among snowdrifts broken up by
long brown clumps of windswept grass. Tiny tufts of seeds adorn
the ends of the delicate stalks. A soft cerulean sky warms up the
piece—a winter day that's cold but clear. A small skeletal tree
grows beside the fence post anchoring the gate. The wire fencing
on the right is twisted and falling off the frame, but the other
side of the gate is wide open, no wire in sight. A small rusted
sign nailed to the post reads "No hunting without permission."

I don't have a painting like this. I love the ones in which
Dad included old signs. And the details are perfect—the tiny
seedpods on the ends of the individual blades of grass, the rusted
wires twisted around boards to hold them together, the shadows
cast onto the wood.

It occurs to me, as I stare at the enlarged photo on my
computer screen, that every new painting I find is like getting
one more glimpse of Dad. I'll never see him again, this side

of heaven.

But *this*. He didn't just touch this. He *created* it. I can see his process, hear his thoughts, almost as if he were right here. I want this one. I really want it.

My computer chimes as an automated email informs me that I was outbid. The auction has ended.

So close. But not close enough.

He remains just as far away as ever.

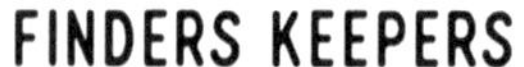

FINDERS KEEPERS

14" x 22"

Description: Junkyard filled
with a jumble of boats, doors, and
metal burn barrels in the "Lost
and Found" style

Three years after our big sale of Dad's work, a man I've known since childhood came into the studio to get permission to cut down some trees on the lane leading to one of my family's farms. He was wearing a worn, heavy flannel shirt, some dusty old jeans, and a faded hat. He walked straight to the back wall, on which hung a painting he and I have talked about numerous times before. He leaned forward, squinting to see it better.

"Well, now, you used to have one … this looks kind of like it but it's not the same one."

"The one of the house you grew up in?"

"Yeah, but this ain't it. The one you had before had different colors in it."

"This is the only one we have. I'm pretty sure it's the same," I said, knowing darn well that we hadn't suddenly discovered a second painting of some random house that he lived in as a child.

Then again, "seen one, seen 'em all," as my grandpa said.

He pointed out—just as he had before—the window of his parents' room, and his room on the back side of the house, and how Dad changed the lay of the land and put this tree where there wasn't one and moved the outbuildings around.

I marveled at the fact that this was his childhood home, and he knew Dad. He even brought a family member in once to see the painting and they agreed that it was their house. At that point, we were down to only ten original paintings left. But he never considered buying it. Maybe it's more money than he wanted to spend. Or maybe it's because though it's based on his house, the artistic license Dad took changed it, so it doesn't hold meaning to him.

He stepped back from the painting and looked around, as though to make sure no one else was listening. No one was there with us, yet he lowered his voice and smiled conspiratorially.

"Rob always said they'd be worth a lot more when he died. Is that true? Are they?"

I hated to disappoint him, so I broke the news gently. "Not really. I mean, it all depends on what people want to pay, but unfortunately, it doesn't really work the way he thought it would."

It's true that Dad can't make any more paintings, so in *that* sense they're valuable, but they're not inherently, automatically worth double. Dad would have been so disappointed because he had always joked with his buddies about his art: "At least they'll be worth something when I'm gone."

SCHMIDT GOOSE DECOY

22" x 29"

Description:
Large gray-and-black antique
wooden decoy against
a plain white background

"The damn decoy finally sold!!!" I texted Kerry and KAO#1.
Yes, I used three exclamation points.

When Dad lived in the studio after selling the farmhouse, he
filled the walls of his private living space with paintings—mostly
the art (both his and other people's work) that had adorned the
walls of the house. The largest one was a wooden goose decoy.
Beautiful detail, of course, gray, weathered wood, stark white
background. The whole thing measured about 40" x 30"—the
wooden frame was massive and there were multiple mats,
including a yellowed mat board covered in dusty burlap. It was
so large that Dad had added extra hangers on the back of the
painting and strung heavy-duty wire across it to distribute its
weight better when it was hung.

I'd never cared for it.

Don't get me wrong. It was well done. After all, Dad
knew what he was doing. Dating from the 1980s, this painting
dominated the others because of its sheer size. Did he keep it
because he liked it or just because it was expensive and had
never sold? The jury is still out.

In the '80s and '90s, Dad was asked to paint some rare duck decoys for prints produced by the Sportman's Classics of Traders Point in Indianapolis. He wasn't a hunter, but he enjoyed the textures, the details, the colors (browns, more browns, and an occasional gray). Many of the pieces were more like studies—a carved and painted wooden decoy on a plain white background, or with a simple wash of color behind it, or perhaps a wooden shelf and paneled wall. The details were meticulous: the grain of the wood, the subtle and perfectly rendered colors, shadows and light.

They were fine, perhaps even beautiful—just not really my thing. At one point, Dad painted a pair of small prints of two different decoys—one is perched upon a wooden box, the other with a plain white background. When Dad died, there were two tall stacks of prints in one of the flat files—literally hundreds of decoys. As Kathy and I prepared for the sale, we also found several matted original ducks in Dad's drawers. Decoys everywhere. Maybe if we were outdoorsmen, they would speak to us. Then again, it had been decades since he painted them, and they hadn't sold, so maybe we weren't the only ones who weren't in love with them.

One night after Kathy and I had finished our work, we opened a bottle of cabernet Dad left in his wine rack. The brand: Decoy. Seemed fitting. We enjoyed it much more than the paintings themselves.

It feels weirdly liberating to be so outspoken against something Dad did. They were beautifully done, but the subject matter left us wanting. We hoped they would appeal to someone ... yet after the big sale, we still had four of the seven decoy originals. I strategically placed them in the galleries, rotating them around, displaying them in the studio, reducing the price (more than once). One sold on eBay for a really low price. I donated one to a fundraising auction held by an art guild Dad had long been a member of, thinking it was a brilliant way to get rid of it, help an organization, and give someone a chance to own one of the few remaining originals. It received zero bids and was sent back to me.

Which seemed to make it official: *No one* wanted these damn decoys.

One of the galleries admitted they hadn't been displaying one of them, an unframed goose decoy (as opposed to a duck), because they only display framed pieces. They volunteered to reframe it at a discounted cost—even so, it cost us over $250. The painting had originally been priced at $2,000. By then, I'd lowered it to $1,000. It wasn't my favorite, but it was an original and Dad would be insulted that I kept marking it down. I still wanted to make some kind of profit on it. Then again, it's only a profit if it actually sells.

The new frame changed the look completely. With a softly polished, wide black frame and no mat, it wasn't quite as large and imposing, but the frame made the painting look bold and graphic. It no longer belonged in a rustic cabin but would now fit in a contemporary home because of the sleek frame and minimalist color palette. Still, no one showed any interest. Right before Black Friday, five years after Dad died, I posted a picture of it in the Ladoga Chatter Facebook group with a sale price of $800. The next day, a woman came into the studio and walked straight to where it hung on the back wall.

"How much for this?"

I sensed an opening, and I wasn't going to mess around. "I'd let you have it for $650."

"Really? I saw it was $800 and was gonna look at it and then think about it, but I'll take it for 650. Sold!" As she opened her purse, she proceeded to tell me her connection to my family. She was married to the son of a friend of my parents, and he'd passed away, but he always loved these ducks so she was buying it in his memory.

My enthusiasm was genuine. "I'm so glad this is going to someone who will appreciate it!"

I practically ran to my phone to send the text to Kerry and Kathy. I was still smiling when I deleted the eBay listing. I delivered Kerry her share of the sale in cash.

Dad loved cash sales. He kept a stack of $100 bills in a certain cookbook at the house, and after a good art show, he treated us to dinner at Red Lobster (if we were out of town) or at the nearby New Ross Steak House, which only accepted cash.

When we were kids, we ate there fairly often. A tiny place with Formica-covered tables, griege wood paneling, and amateur oil paintings with faded price tags on the walls. The ceiling was rimmed with colored fluorescent lights. Mom and Dad always knew people at the nearby tables, and the waitresses had been there for decades and knew them by name. The restaurant had good steaks, obviously, and hand-cut fries. Dad loved it because the owner kept a bottle of Martini & Rossi sweet vermouth on hand to be able to make Dad's Manhattan on the rocks just the way he liked it. The plastic-wrapped garlic breadsticks in the cracker basket were crunchy and delicious dipped into the individual tubs of margarine. Kerry and I drew on the back of the scalloped-edge paper place mats while we waited.

Inevitably, as we were starting to wonder why it was taking so long to cook our food, Mom and Dad would light cigarettes. Kerry and I would dramatically cough and wave away the smoke, complaining about how gross it was. But it never failed to work—once they lit up, the food would arrive. After we finished, a server would bring doggie bags of waxed paper to hold our scraps. Kerry and I would have to sit and wait through yet another cigarette, but at least the waitress brought us some mini Tootsie Rolls with the check.

I don't drink Manhattans often, but I order them sometimes,

in his memory, when we go someplace with fancy cocktails. Or someplace that only takes cash, particularly when I have a $100 bill from selling a painting.

And *especially* when the painting that sold was one of the damn decoys.

Not long after the goose decoy sold, my friend Lisa asked me to walk to her van after we finished lunch. She had something for me. Assuming it was another tin of her legendary chocolate-covered peanuts, I eagerly followed her out.

Her parents had recently moved into a senior-living facility and cleaned out the house. Her mom owned one of Dad's paintings. "It's so beautiful," Lisa tells me. "Remember, I bought it for her at the sale?"

I nodded vaguely, not remembering what she had purchased.

"Mom said it belongs with your family. You and your kids should have it."

"That's so thoughtful," I say, genuinely touched. Lisa's family has always been so kind and generous. "Give me her address so I can write and thank her."

She hands me the painting, tightly sheathed in Bubble Wrap . It's a small one, in a wooden frame. I don't have to unwrap it to see what is nestled inside.

Another damn decoy.

vignette

The influence of those commercial days followed in the form of the white backdrops—the negative space as O'Dell calls it—that dominated his early work.

"It was always the space I'd save for copy," he says. "When I started painting it seemed like a natural thing to save that space." He did and turned it into a trademark of his style.

—Kathy Matter, "Artist Returns with Breakout Works," *Journal & Courier*,
Lafayette, Indiana, October 6, 1986

In John Canaday's book, *What Is Art?*, he wrote: "The eternal function of realistic art is to reveal the familiar world in a vision that affects our experience of it."

A review in the Champaign-Urbana Courier (likely from 1969 or 1970) speculated on what made Dad's work stand out from that of so many other realistic watercolorists.

> Painted with a dry brush, there is very little of the loose, free look we ordinarily associate with watercolor. Except for some areas of sky, where the paper has the 'washed' look of watercolor, the artist has combined draughtsmanship and the application of the pigment, while retaining the translucence of watercolor. Although these seem the epitome of realism, and in the painting technique they are realistic and detailed, the scenes themselves are abstractions of reality. For the artist has actually eliminated all details which he considers nonessential, to give us the distillation of his view of reality. We forget that the original scene had, probably, a multitude of distracting elements, such as additional buildings, or landscape features, or haphazard accretions of daily life.

You could see Dad's simplicity and vision in the way he painted. Howard Wooden, who was the director of Swope Galleries in Terre Haute, Indiana, wrote, "O'Dell is a 'realist' in the traditional sense of the term, but one with a powerful facility for simplifying, for distilling the essence of his forms in order to better communicate his meaning."[13]

My father had a way of making life appear simpler, even when he included the broken and abandoned places. "The effects of age have always fascinated O'Dell, who seems to shun the furious pace of a modern world in favor of the life of a bygone time," wrote Jim Vorel in 2011.[14]

Dad's painting wasn't the only place we saw this. He was happy and only occasionally felt stressed. One time when I was home for a break from college, I stood behind him at the kitchen table while Mom was cooking, and squeezed his shoulders as though to give him a back rub. He jumped like I'd hurt him. He didn't carry tension there the way I did.

Once I was out of college and settled into family life, Dad and I talked regularly by phone most days—just a couple of minutes, usually, to see what the other one had planned for the day. Kerry and I often laughed about it when Dad would tell us how busy he was. For him, that meant he had one thing to do every day. Going to Crawfordsville (20 minutes from home) for a haircut one day, an oil change another. Golf with a foursome on Friday at Turkey Run, a trip to Indy to drop off paintings for an upcoming Hoosier Salon show, attend a soccer game for one of his grandkids. Still, with all that, he managed to fit in lunch with Kerry or me at least once a week, have breakfast at the diner on weekday mornings, and produce a handful of paintings most weeks.

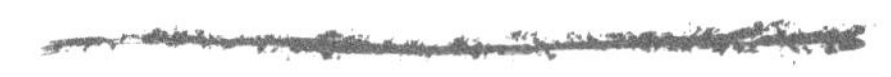

People often comment that Dad's paintings look like photographs, and he referred to his approach as realism, but he wasn't a photorealist who painstakingly and unerringly reproduces a photograph in such an accurate way that you can't tell it's not a photo. It wasn't until recently that I happened upon the term that I think most accurately describes what he did.

Marion Simon Garmel, an art critic in the *Indianapolis News*, wrote in July of 1978, "O'Dell works in a style known as 'magic realism,' whereby tricks of the brush create the impression of realistic painting when the realism itself is not there."

His "tricks" included rendering the weathered wood of a barn by dragging cardboard strips dipped in paint along the edges, sprinkling salt to replicate the lacy weeds growing in the landscape, and dipping a sponge in paint to create the leaves of an autumn tree. In a newspaper clipping which was cut out without including the publication name, author, or date, Dad told the interviewer that he disregarded all rules to create. "He uses a dry brush technique which means there is much less water involved. He can build a tree using his fingerprints and a bit of color. He can use the blade of a kitchen knife and make tall grass and weeds. A toothbrush comes in handy to splatter dots of color here and there and a sponge is another of his working tools."

I don't have memories of sitting down with Dad as a child and learning to paint, but I do know that when I was eight, Dad helped me make a painting for my grandparents for Christmas. It has a cloudy blue sky, which, if I'm being honest, nearly anyone can create if someone wets the paper properly and tells you when to add paint. Simply dab a few brushfuls of cerulean blue onto a wet board. Once it dried, I dipped the edge of a cut piece of cardboard into brown paint, which he likely mixed for me, and stamped an uneven row of vertical stripes—a rudimentary snow fence on its way to falling down, a common scene in rural Indiana—nestled into a landscape of scrubby weeds created with a dry brush. I signed my name, Kelly O, in fat, awkward cursive in white paint in the corner.

I thought it was just as good as any of Dad's paintings could ever be. It looked just like his, I thought. Dad framed it and then my grandparents displayed it in their formal living room, right above an early piece of his, as long as they lived there. Now it's propped on a bookshelf in my house, and every time I see it, my only criticism is the chunky signature. I love that painting.

But now it doesn't seem as easy to me as it did back then.

THE COLOR OF WINTER

10″ x 28″

Description: Extremely horizontal
negative-space painting of a snowy
landscape with a limb-filled burn barrel
and a lone tree near a fence

Just as the Midwestern landscape moves from the spare, desolate whites and browns of winter into the lush yellow-green of budding spring life, Dad's color palettes changed through the years. His earlier works were practically a study in white. Watercolor is not an additive medium, in which you layer color on top of color. It's more a subtractive one. As explained by Glen Cumbrella in *Montgomery Magazine* in July 1992, if Dad wanted an area to be light, he had to use less pigment so that the white of the paper would shine through. Dad explained, "The white is all-important to watercoloring and that's the trick of the medium."

The negative (or unpainted) space makes Dad's paintings distinctive. He would physically render the sides of a barn, and the meandering line of a snow fence, but the viewer's mind fills in the details of what he did not paint. We know there's a roof of the barn—obviously covered in a blanket of snow—because of the placement of a crooked weathervane or lightning rod or a row of birds perched along the top. We know there's snow on the ground because of a tuft of weeds uncovered by the wind and the placement of the fence. But Dad didn't have to paint that in order for us to be certain that something is there.

Even after many years, Dad still loved doing his negative space paintings. In 1984, he said, "Those negative space paintings were the first images I painted that caught on, and at Saugatuck, Mich., a couple of weekends ago I sold 10 paintings at an opening and five were negative space—my original approach. Isn't that amazing it's held on for 26 years?"[15]

In 1977, Dad told Gaildene Hamilton, "My work has changed over the years... At first I was most interested in what I was painting, such as the texture of the wood. Maybe so much so that some of my early pieces were nearly black and white. Now I'm more aware of color which gives feeling to a picture."[16]

When he started in the 1960s, his early color palette—which, to the observer, looked more or less black or brown and white—consisted of three colors: black, yellow, and burnt sienna (a reddish brown). By the 1970s, he expanded to five main colors—mostly earth tones plus cerulean and ultramarine blue. That still sounds pretty limited, but he rarely used straight colors, softening them by adding a touch of cerulean blue to the browns, turning them grayer, or by adding some raw umber or sepia to his blues and greens to make them less gaudy. By the time he experimented with abstract imagery in the 1980s, he had ventured into a still wider color palette—though still comprising primarily earth tones and blues.

When he ventured into painting flowers such as hollyhocks, irises, and wildflowers, he had to buy some new colors: alizarin crimson, halo green, vermilion, rose madder, scarlet lake, Thalo yellow green, cadmium yellow—lots of new pinks and reds, vibrant greens.

I think he even surprised himself with the expanded color palette. In an interview in the Champaign-Urbana *Courier* back in 1969 or 1970, the reporter wrote, "He has an affection for the time-worn quality of the old, even in the seasons. You will notice that in none of these works has he painted the spring season, and only rarely the summer. 'Spring is beautiful, but I could never paint it,' he says. 'Its colors are too raw.'"

Yet by the time Dad died, his palette was vibrant and bright, sometimes almost garish. He once speculated to my brother-in-law, Doug, that maybe his cataracts caused him to paint with gaudier colors since he couldn't see as clearly.

Or maybe he simply wanted to more accurately paint the intensity of the beauty he saw.

If you've never driven through the Midwest at the height of spring or summer, the sheer vibrancy of the colors might surprise you—tropical paradises are no more green and thick and alive than Indiana in July. Lush and overgrown, the hundred shades of green and the bright blue skies and the purple and yellow flowers exude life.

As his color palette evolved, so did his view of the landscape. No longer merely shape and line and form, now it was an expression of abundant beauty. In 1992, Dad talked about how realism was less important to him than it used to be. "Now, I'm more into effect and color. As I use more color it's more artistic and less realistic. I get tired of painting grays. I still think grays are neat and will never get away from them completely, though."

I think Dad tried to resist the bright, pretty colors for the sake of form and design, maybe because it was easier to paint the green trees, whose branches are hidden by the leaves. Vibrant colors and sunny summery days are beautiful, but perhaps not as artistic.

But when you're surrounded by the cold, dark days of February—literally or figuratively—there is nothing more appealing than the colors of vibrant life.

On the other hand, Dad's negative-space paintings were speaking to me in new ways, now that he was no longer here. They showed me the beauty that can be found in the silence, and that Dad can still be present—even when he is not.

When I am looking at art by other artists, I find myself drawn to paintings that are full of energy, thrumming with life. Where I can see the gestures, where the colors are intensely saturated, where the strokes exude movement and life. I admit that those are not things that people say about Dad's paintings. And yet, when I look at those other pieces of art, I'm overly aware of the artist's role. I'm caught up in an individual's way of expressing.

Only recently have I become aware that it requires a truly masterful artist to create a work in which one can completely lose oneself. In which you enter the scene, almost as though you're actually there. In which you intuit the peaceful quiet, or hear the birds chattering, or feel the gentle breeze. When I look at Dad's paintings, I see nothing contrived, not one thing to make me aware of the hand of the artist in the scene. Nothing is overdone. I don't pay attention to brushstrokes or notice that perspective is off, which of course it never is.

All I see is exactly what Dad wanted me—and you—to see.
I don't see him. And yet I *feel* him in all of it.

KALEIDOSCOPE

14" x 22"

Description: Grid of 36 shallow
rectangles showing similar
landscapes—trees growing out
of a snowbank or standing
against a blue sky

In recent years, I've seen several early Rob O'Dells come up for auction, as Dad's patrons pass away and their children inherit art they don't have room for. The paintings are almost abstract in their simplicity. A loose shape of blue-gray sky with three or four simple, crooked, not-detailed trees. A sharp triangle of green hill, filling only about one-fourth of the page, with the peaked roof of a barn peeking over the hill. Graphic and plain, distilled to their essence, these paintings launched his career, snagged the attention of downtown Chicago galleries, and hooked his loyal clientele.

The biggest problem with them is that Dad painted on some non-archival watercolor paper or illustration board in his early years. I'm not sure if he just didn't know better, or if it was cheaper, but some of my favorite paintings of his keep growing yellower and yellower. They won't hold up forever. Luckily, he eventually began to work with higher-quality materials.

Over the years, Dad tried on some different styles and approaches, too, although his subject matter remained consistent. He went through a period in the early 1980s in which he experimented with the abstract. In an interview published in the *Indianapolis News* in 1982, he told Marion Garmel, "The more you paint, the more you're looking for the abstract." These works were so different from the work he was known for. He said, "Let's face it. After 14 years, I had to do something new. For a person to grow any, you're just going to have to experiment."[17]

Garmel described them better than I could: "The new works mark several departures. First are the pure abstracts, explosions of color in billowing blues and grays or browns and yellows to which is added an ink underpinning that often resembles the outlines of counties or states. This maplike understructure, which O'Dell admits he adds last, gives the work a solidity that many pure abstracts sometimes lack."

He started the abstracts with no plan or idea, adding several washes of color, building from transparent to almost opaque, then added the ink lines. "It's just fun to do. Pure color, line, and form."

Side note: Not only were the subject matter and approach different, but he got more daring with the titles, too, naming them things like *Aerial View* and *Spy Mission*. He was in his mid-40s, so perhaps it was his version of a midlife crisis.

The interview continued, explaining that Dad also did quite a few multiples, "intriguing studies of the same barn or tree or landscape done in such a way that there may be four or six or even 36 smaller pairings within one large frame. These can be particularly satisfying. They can also be instructive. *Decisions* includes three views of tree roots—possible ways of painting a subject—with the drawings that preceded them. Another, *Winter Dreams*, is like nine tiny traditional O'Dells framed together."

The article explains further: "But one is particularly dizzying. *Kaleidoscope* has 36 shallow rectangles stacked four across and eight deep, each containing parts of a similar landscape with trees growing out of snow or waving in blue skies. 'You might not want to have it over your sofa,' O'Dell admits, 'but you wouldn't mind passing it in the hall.'"

Dad goes on to admit, "By doing the abstracts I've loosened up my old work. It's not old any more, it's fresher."

I don't know for sure, but my memory is that he got a lukewarm response to these attempts. They were fun for him to create, because he got to try new techniques and play with color and form, not limited by real life. They were random runs of blues and browns and peachy colors, abstract lines connecting them.

But he didn't stick with those for long—because, after all, he liked real life, and loved to draw what he saw.

For many years, Dad went one night a week to the Indianapolis Art Center, an hour from home, for figure drawing classes, filling numerous sketchbooks with beautiful forms—even though he rarely included people anywhere in his scenes. But in that art show that prompted the interview, he included one painting of a nude pictured behind abstract strips of color that gave the appearance of looking through venetian blinds. He told the reviewer, "I'm always drawing them and I thought, well, I might include a half dozen in this show. But she's the only one who made it."

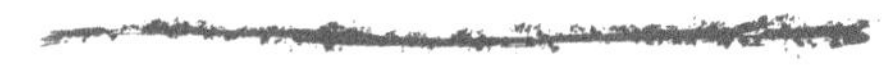

Dad did detailed studies of antique objects including a metal toy truck, an old milk jug, and a small stack of ears of field corn. He tried a handful of portraits—faces, but you never saw people walking or doing chores in the barns and fields. Just the evidence that they'd once been there—clothes hanging on a line, a built structure, an empty wagon in a field. He painted barns, covered bridges, silos, churches, grocery stores, abandoned schoolhouses, neglected homes, family cottages, mills, and even some lighthouses. Pickup trucks, wagons, tractors. Every variety of tree, irises, hollyhocks, wildflowers. Roads and gates, bridges, creeks, sunsets, silhouettes, fences, cornfields, and old metal signs. Once in a while he would paint a horse or some livestock, even bicycle races. He traveled to the southwest and painted Arizona cliff dwellings and canyons, Ireland's rolling hills and castles and towns, Maine boats and docks and rocks. In his last few years, he was fascinated by the foliage, trees, and birds in Florida.

Once in a while, Dad played with a technique he called "lost and found," in which he put a jumble of strokes and color on the page and then looked to see what he could find in the textures and shapes and colors laid down—often doors and burn barrels, junkyards full of abandoned boats and old signs. One time he even painted a fallen knight in armor alongside his horse. Or at least that's what my cousin Kathy and I decided it must have been when we found it after Dad's death.

Quite often, over dozens of years, Dad interspersed his work with "breakouts," in which he taped off an area to leave an unpainted border around the piece. The scene—a tree line, a creek, a road, or a section of grass in the foreground—would "break out" of the main rectangle on one or two sides, almost as if the image was bursting out of the contrived borders.

And, of course, he painted those damn decoys.

He never got tired of trying something new, but he always came back to the rural scenes he was known for. In an email to a distant relative in 2004 who sent some years-old samples of her work and asked for his opinion about whether she had enough talent to do this, Dad wrote, "What have you done lately? As an artist we have to work all the time to keep up on skills. I can tell the difference when I begin to paint again after a vacation. ... I don't think your age has anything to do with it. How much you want it has much more to do with it."

He definitely wanted this.
Maybe, just maybe, so do I.

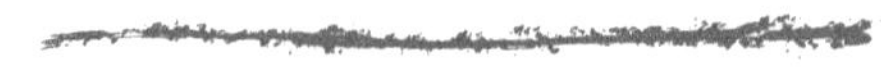

As much as many people loved him, not everyone was a fan. One reviewer in particular, Steve Mannheimer, posted a long review of a new art show in the *Indianapolis Star* in December 1989. It started out positive and then took a turn that sent Dad's self-esteem spiraling. The article, titled "O'Dell Watercolors Skillfully Evoke Sense of Lonely Melancholy," read:

> At his best, in works like *Open and Shut*, O'Dell shows a convincing ability to choreograph a formal minuet of shapes and spaces without sacrificing the emotional tone. His touch is deft. Watercolor is an ungenerous medium, tolerating little or no slop, and O'Dell keeps it clean. His images are uncluttered, pared to the essentials required to make his points and go on to the next idea.
>
> Now, that next idea is not going to be any different than the last. O'Dell consistently evokes the same sense of isolation and melancholy, even if he's depicting the red rock cliffs of the American Southwest.
>
> It is debatable whether or not such consistency is the sign of a profound, deep-seated personal vision or simply the artful handling of a well-honed formula, or both. ...
>
> O'Dell relies on this formula, the formulized response of his audience to a tried and true set of images guaranteed to evoke the measured response he seeks. This is no different than the majority of artists who pitch their projects at a clientele they understand. The results may not be great art, but it is first-rate cliché.

Ouch.

I suppose I know what the reporter meant. After all, how many times have I used the phrase *same ol' same ol'*? Plus, Dad never claimed to be some rogue, cutting-edge modern artist. He painted for the love of painting. And he painted what he did because his watercolor instructor at the American Academy of Art in Chicago, Irving Shapiro, told him to paint what he knew. Perhaps Dad chose his subject matter because he knew he could evoke the concepts the reviewers always mentioned—isolation, melancholy, yesteryear—by showing scenes that were frozen in time. He only rarely included people or animals, because he thought those signs of life had a tendency to date the piece. His scenes often carried a stamp of humanity's presence—the buildings, the fences, the man-made structures, the laundry on the clothesline. They left the impression that someone had just stepped inside for a moment—or maybe they left and weren't going to return.

He loved to win prizes, but he understood why he didn't always win. In *Montgomery Magazine* in 1992, Dad told a reporter, "A lot of the problem are the art magazines, showing what the latest thing is. My barns are passé. I get rejected a lot with my barns. Judges think art is only art if it's innovative, and my kind of art has been done. People haven't done it the way I do it, but it's been done. So I'm not worthy of a prize."

But if he hadn't believed what he did was truly art, he wouldn't have continued to paint, day after day, for 50 years.

I grew used to his incredible detail and finesse, the nuances, the moods and the feelings of his work. He had a distinctive style, and his subject matter was familiar. His technique was flawless, even if his work felt safe to me. I have always known instinctually that Dad saw beauty that others overlooked. And that he was much like the subject matter he surrounded himself with: Tried and true. Gentle. Content.

He told a reporter in 1994, "I really do have a short attention span. Six hours is the most I've ever spent on a painting. The average is four. If it's going to work, it's going to work."[18] Whenever someone asked, "Rob, how long did it take you to paint this?" he answered by smiling and saying, "Four hours and 30 years (of experience)". Eventually he got up to 40 and almost 50 years of experience. He had his technique down pat, after practicing almost daily all that time.

But art wasn't just his job, it was what he loved to do. That love never went away—but naturally it evolved and his focus varied.

Yet as I've contemplated my father's career and techniques, as I've studied the details in the paintings and the different phases of his career (in terms of subject matter, color palette, and tightness of his rendering), I see that there's a whole lot more behind them than Steve Mannheimer gave him credit for. I also see that there was a bit of a rebel in there. He pushed boundaries of composition. Took chances. Tried new things, pushed himself to get better and to grow. Experimented with techniques, went new places. Found beauty in the broken, not viewing any scene as cliché because he was simply representing that which was real. Dad painted what was true, not what was inherently pretty.

And he found ways to do each of those things that were uniquely, distinctly, and specifically his.

vignette

O'Dell said his craft has gotten easier for him in 30 years. "I'm not struggling to figure out how to get the texture of something. I'm in control now. I just have to figure out what I'm going to paint and how strong I want to paint it.

[When he doesn't produce a good painting], O'Dell comes back to the work in a couple of days and "fixes" it. Such a disciplined approach is the difference between an amateur and a professional, he feels.

—Glen Cumbrella, "Rob O'Dell's New Studio Fulfills Lifelong Dream," *Montgomery Magazine*, Crawfordsville, Indiana, July 1992

GATEWAY

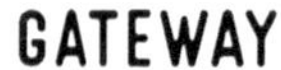

20″ x 28″

Description: Wooden gate
propped open beside a
dirt road filled with puddles
and tire tracks

The weekend after I completed that first acrylic painting, my brain churns, working out what I should have done differently, remembering how clunky my painting looked next to Dad's. Maybe the problem is the medium. Maybe I should try watercolor again. After all, I've spent the three years since Dad died surrounded by his work, sitting in his studio, driving the roads he drove—all the while thinking in my head how I would re-create these images in watercolor.

Watercolor is substantially different from oil paint because of its transparency. With oils, you can add layer upon layer to achieve a textured effect, or simply to cover up your mistakes. The paint is opaque and obscures what is below it, at least partially. You can add the whites and light colors at the very end, finishing touches to replicate light glinting off the surface.

Watercolor doesn't work the same way. For one thing, it is difficult to paint over anything because you can see through the paint. You have to almost overdo it to create depth or rich color with the pigment—people often add too much water, so the result is soft, light, literally watered-down, much like a memory compared to the actual moment. Another aspect of watercolor is that you have to work quickly while the paint is still wet. If one area dries and then you paint alongside that and try to blend it, you can ... somewhat ... but if you look closely you'll always see the harsh edge of that line. Watercolor requires careful planning, at least the way Dad did it. You have to leave the white of the paper showing through in any area that will be light, but you don't want to make it look as though you were painting around it.

The quick, responsive nature of watercolor appeals to me. I'm an instant-gratification type of woman. If it works, it works. If it doesn't, I can move on.

I spend an hour looking through photos on my computer, mostly architectural details from trips to Malta, Italy, New Orleans, San Francisco. That's what I love to photograph, but can I really draw those? They require finesse. Accuracy. Perspective.

I decide that on Monday morning, I will cut some small pieces of watercolor paper and try again, but these will not be finished pieces, just exercises to experiment with different techniques, see how the paint responds to water and salt, and so on.

I pull out a small piece of Arches cold press watercolor paper, wet Dad's big green sponge, and drizzle little bits of water onto the parched globs of paint still clinging to the white enamel palette. With the same sponge, I evenly spread water across the textured paper. The paper instantly curls and warps.

Crap. I forgot you have to tape it down.

So I grab the masking tape, which has been hanging on the elbow of his adjustable desk light for three years, and it shreds into tiny pieces when I try to pull it apart. Finally I locate an old roll of blue painter's tape, which is going to have to work.

Rookie mistakes. I'm not off to a very good start.

I draw my grids, rough in the outlines of the rusty, curvy wrought iron shapes in a window of murky blue glass. Tape the paper to the board, and decide that I should use Miskit to preserve the white of the paper. The wrought iron in the photo is painted white, with rust showing through, and the background is dark. Miskit is a liquid mask, so you paint it on and it prevents paint from reaching the paper in those areas. Once it dries fully, you use a rubber cement pickup to remove it. Easy-peasy.

I have to find three jars of Miskit before I find one that hasn't completely dried up. I select a brush and start painting. Cool. It's working. Crap, it's drying too fast. The brush is hard and clumpy now. I squint to read the tiny words on the bottle. It says you can clean the brush with soap and hot water, so I run to the sink, but the rubbery adhesive is stuck down in the center of the bristles.

I don't acknowledge, even to myself, that I just ruined one of Dad's good brushes. We have plenty more. I go back to the drawing board and finish covering the white areas with Miskit, and try again to clean the brush. I wonder what brush Dad used? I wonder how he kept it from drying and sticking? I'll Google it later.

In the meantime, I wipe water across the paper, mixing cobalt blue with a bunch of sepia to tone it down, and dab and brush the paint across the background. While the paint oh-so-slowly dries, I search for the hair dryer Dad used to use. Wonder what happened to that? I find one, probably not *the* one, but it will work. I completely dry the paint and grab the rubber cement pickup to remove the Miskit. It's working. Cool. But the stubborn adhesive doesn't really want to come up. I can get bits and pieces—like little grubby snot balls that I have to keep pulling off the corners of the eraser. Finally I get the hang of it, but it wasn't as easy as I expected.

I mix up a watery, warm gray (sepia with tons of water, and a teensy bit of cerulean blue) and start painting in the shadowy side of the wrought iron. I use raw umber to paint in the rust splotches. I remember reading in my notes from the workshop I attended 20 years earlier that once you've applied an overall wash, you can't use a sponge to rewet the paper or it will pick up some of the pigment, but you can apply another wash if you lay down water in only that area using a flat, wide brush. So I paint the background areas with water and add a dark, soft shadow reflected below and to the right of the iron curves.

Back and forth, I try different techniques. Rewetting an area and using a lot of water to smooth a harsh edge. Deepening the shadow. Painting with a tiny brush the details in an area of peeled paint. Huh. Not bad.

So I grab another sheet of paper and try something else. This time it's a stone staircase from Alcatraz, sort of rough and heavy and medieval looking with plants growing up the wall behind it. Again with the grid, but no masking fluid this time. I brush water on the background areas where there should be plants showing through the openings in the walls and apply a limited wash of greens, careful to maintain the edges of the gray stone rails. I even apply some salt to create the frilly texture of the flowers, and I get it right this time.

I decide to try using a small rectangle of mat board to apply paint for the stone texture, so I dip the edge of the cardboard into a puddle of cool gray paint and then swipe that down the textured paper. It works. Sort of. But I need a larger quantity of paint because it only covers a strip about a half inch long. Not to mention the mat board leaves a harsh edge every time I lift it up or set it down. I let it dry and then paint over it with a darker gray using very watery paint, and a darker gray yet to fill in the shadows. I use a scrubby bristly brush to apply green paint to

look like stems, stalks, leaves, trying to make it look like weeds
growing up from behind the steps.

Fail. How did Dad do that?

Maybe I should try a different subject this time.

On a new sheet of paper (taped down this time), I lay
down some green paint and then start painting in some darker,
triangular shapes, trying to mimic Dad's abstract approach to
representing the pattern created by a jumble of leaf shapes.

Another fail.

I walk over to one of Dad's hollyhock prints and study
the leaves. Oh, so the pattern isn't actually random. I need to
imagine that there are leaves climbing up the stalk and paint the
dark shadows around them, letting the lighter green wash in the
background show through. Better.

I add some rusty water stains on the railing. Some delicate,
dark stems of plants, trees, flowers—something abstract and
plantlike. Some dabs of yellow to replicate the flowers. I dab
on multiple greens, kind of loose, and eventually it looks like
a haphazard growth of plants and flowers. Nothing like the
original wall of climbing plants in the photo, but no one has to
know that because I kind of like this.

I need to go home to start supper, so I wash out the brushes
and leave, feeling better about myself. Maybe I do know
something. Maybe there is some potential here after all.

The next day, I answer a few emails and pretend I'm
working, then I go back to the drawing board. The two
watercolors yesterday were really meant to be experiments to
learn technique. This time I want to do a "real" painting.

I select a photo of a rooftop in either Malta or Italy. I can't
remember which. You can see the top of a black wrought iron
lamp, a rusty gutter, a discolored metal railing. Behind the rail
is a domed little guard booth of some sort, a mottled red color,
with a blue-gray metal roof, shadowed windows all around, tall

metal cross extending from on top. Behind that, patched stucco walls and a round window with a metal starburst of bars inside it.

I draw the grid again, using a ruler to keep the lines of the walls straight. This time I trust myself a little more and am pleasantly surprised with the results. Dad always said no one could paint well unless they could draw well, so I take my time and get it right.

No overall wash this time. Instead, I use cardboard to apply a haphazard texture to the walls. I add some watery paint to soften the harshness. I rough in the overall colors, then do a limited wash for the bottom edges showing the gutters. I start adding details, painting in the walls of the guard booth, carefully drawing the broken stone urns decorating the walls. As I paint the dark shadows of the windows, I keep them loose and leave some patches of white showing, which makes it look like reflections and shadows. I paint the little sprigs of grass growing in the corner of the rooftop, the discolored stucco where water has drained from the windows. I add more and more color and texture, layering the transparent tones, using brushes and cardboard and a sponge and even splattering fine sprays of paint to add texture. I paint in the delicate curve of black wrought iron, surprised at my control. Then again, I'm fortunate to be able to start learning with such top-of-the-line supplies and expensive brushes.

Sometimes I mess up, but I love the way the bars in the round window look—until I realized I forgot to leave light areas for the star-shaped metal bars in the center of them. I go back again and again, applying more black paint around them, adding water and blotting the area trying to remove the pigment from where it shouldn't be. In my excitement at adding the angled stripes of terra-cotta roof tile, I add the roofline on the right side and realize the round window is now off-center, so I blot and blot and blot and add some texture to try to camouflage it. I think the answer is simply to crop that area out when I mat it.

I keep adding color and texture to the walls, the rails. I notice the dome isn't symmetrical, so I add a dark edge on the right and make the booth a tad bit wider, but you can tell where I added on. Finally, I decide I'm done—at this point, I will only make it worse by trying to correct what needs to be fixed.

I prop it up on the wooden pew, and line the rail with my others. I put the garish acrylic in a drawer. I may be on to something here. Would Dad be proud? I think he might. Is this good enough to sell? No. (Not yet.) But there's something there. Something of him inside of me. I think I've provided evidence for my own theory that being an artist is as much about thinking like an artist as it is practicing art. My hands have rarely held a paintbrush, but I've ruminated for countless hours about how to create what I see, and I guess that has paid off.

I will never be the kind of talent Dad was. At this point, I'm nothing but an amateur, a cheap facsimile.

But if I make art because something inside of me won't stop asking to be let out, because I see like an artist, because my brain continually puzzles through process and technique, because my soul stirs when I see the purple shadows in the snow and the way light changes colors at different times of day and because my eyes trace lines and shapes and forms, re-creating them, working out how they all fit together—well, then, whatever I create is art. Even if the perspective is off (or, surprisingly, isn't!).

I start to ask myself a new question: How would I paint? I'm excited to find out.

DAYS FOR DREAMING

18″ x 21″

Description:
Flimsy, abandoned rope
hammock nestled between
two trees

I read somewhere that when you dream about a new house—finding new rooms, expanding, or going into a new place—it's because you're doing something new in your life. Stretching. Growing. Reaching out.

I've dreamed about finding a great big giant ballroom in my house. Just like that. I open a door and there it is, with all its shadowy echoes and dusty air and high ceilings and formal elegance, just waiting for someone to step into it.

In other dreams, I've found an additional guest wing while trying to navigate my way through unfamiliar halls to bathrooms I didn't know I had (mostly vaguely reminiscent of my grandparents' upstairs, although with a bunch of new rooms).

I've dreamed about my ideal writing space, one I didn't know I wanted until I woke from that dream. A second-floor, partially enclosed balcony nestled in the trees—with overstuffed wicker furniture and white brick and refreshing breezes and dappled sunlight in the soft breeze.

But lately, I've had numerous dreams about the studio.

In the typical confusion and/or suspension of reality in

dreams, I know that it's my dad's (now my) studio, but it doesn't look much like the real one. Throughout my lifetime, I've had similar dreams about all the places where I've spent large amounts of time: my grandparents' house (particularly their barely used, partially finished, scary-to-me-but-actually-quite-nice basement, where I always felt like I was exploring a place I shouldn't be), my parents' house, the yard between the house and the barn and my dad's old studio building, and apartments I've lived in.

So in this recent batch of dreams, I've been in this close-but-not-quite-accurate studio. In some, there's a big art gallery in front (similar to how Dad had it) and I feel like an imposter, sneaking through, wondering if someone will notice I'm where I shouldn't be. As I move through the building, I encounter my dad. He's never the "star" of the dream, just present in it with me. I'm aware that he's been gone for a few years—there's a moment of elated surprise when I realize he's finally back!— but otherwise the encounters themselves are fairly mundane.

He's usually building (or has recently built) something: A really cool chair, with a super-sanded, velvety-smooth walnut texture (but when I sit in it, it forces me to lean back at a weird angle, so it isn't really a success, even though Dad likes it). Shelves, tables, big wooden crates. In one, the ad agency where I interned in college was set up inside, and I try to find space for myself among the art directors' tables, longing to show them that I've grown up and now have what it takes.

In recent dreams, I find a cavernous room at the very back of this dream studio. Part of it, more or less one extended corner of it, is usable—like an urban, industrial, trendy/artsy workspace. High ceilings, lots of wood and lofty beams and open pipes and ducts—and in one section, always an area of discarded junk. Furniture, boxes, who knows what all is there. A treasure trove waiting to be explored. The TV show *Pickers* on steroids.

But the back corner is, well, broken. Big gaps in the brick are open to the outside, ragged edges standing open at the top, as if the roof was torn off in a storm. Sunlight filters in, wind blows through it. It feels as though the space wants to be this big perfect room but it's been broken down, destroyed by the elements. It's devastating to see the ruin where there should be beauty. I see the potential, what needs to be done, but I'm not sure I'm up for the task. It will cost more than I have, and I don't know if it's worth it.

In another of these dreams, the room expands into a whole building, similar to those abandoned brick warehouses in a city that, with enough money and vision, can be transformed into the ultimate co-working space or trendy wedding venue. In my dreams, there's so much space here. Room after room. Arched openings, courtyards, cavernous rooms. I keep going and discover more potential treasure, only to realize that I am not equipped to finish it. It's beyond my abilities, way beyond my finances, and in some places, simply too far gone to be repaired. One room has these gorgeous, artistic brass details in the corners, in the carved, luxurious crown molding—but mold had snuck in and was growing over all of it. I knew any potential buyers would be scared away if they knew. The building would become a lost cause, left to molder, dilapidated and failed. Over time, the losses would pile up, creating a permanent monument to unmet expectations—or, rather, to my inabilities to change things for the better.

After these dreams, I wake up feeling vaguely unsettled, but often don't remember the dreams until some event later in the day triggers an image from the night before. The memories are slippery and I can't quite grab hold of them.

I remember enough, though, and I think these dreams are telling me what I already know. That the possibilities are unlimited, that there is so much more available in this place, in this studio, than I can begin to comprehend. It's exciting, as well as overwhelming. It's never a lack of vision that stops me in my dreams, but a lack of resources.

Sometimes I daydream about actually getting to dwell in those places of my imagining, even with the brokenness, because it's rife with potential. There's something about the light in that place, the way most of the room is in darkness, like a dusty old attic—and yet the broken part is where the light comes in. There is mystery and possibility. (Not to mention the presence of my dad.)

When I imagine physically being in those spaces, I feel a bit homesick. I have a sense that there is such freedom to be found there, if I can just find a way to muster the energy and resources to do the hard work of transformation.

Even in the rooms I don't yet know are there.

KELLY GREEN

21″ x 29″

Description: Thicket of trees in late
spring with periwinkle and
yellow wildflowers sprinkled
across the forest floor

I am hard at work in the studio in December, five years after
losing Dad, when a woman pauses at the door. She is probably
in her 60s, thin, plain. Nondescript hair, no makeup. Her gray
sweatpants are a bit too long, ragged along the hem, and she wears
a hoodie zipped over a T-shirt. She carries a worn handbag. She
struggles to open the door (as most people do because the antique
doors open in the opposite direction from most). The woman
steps over the threshold into the studio, pausing right before the
three-inch step up into the main gallery space. She reminds me of
a kitten: Tense, alert, skittish. Ready to run.

"Hi! How can I help you?" I ask.

"Oh, I was just in town and I've never been in here."

I look away from the newsletter I'm revising on my
computer. I want people to come in, I really do—but it seems
I'm always in the middle of something and wish I hadn't been
interrupted. It's a weird thing to try to do my work in the
middle of a retail(ish) place. Nobody is ever quite sure what is
going on here.

I smile anyway. "Feel free to look around. We have a handful of originals left—the ones with the yellow tags—and quite a few prints. I'm a graphic designer and writer, so the photos on canvas are mine, as well as the books and things on that shelf." I point in the right direction and glance back at my computer.

"Are you Rob's daughter?"

I assume everyone already knows that I am, but maybe not. I introduce myself and ask her if she knew Dad. She walks slowly across the shining hardwood floor, moving closer to my desk.

"No, I never met him. But I heard all about him. We actually live …," and she goes on to tell me where their place is in comparison to Mom and Dad's old house.

"Oh, that's cool!" I say.

She continues, "But I never got to meet him in person."

I nod. "Take your time looking around. I'll just be here working."

I expect her to glance at the price tags and then quickly head out, like many people do. But she surprises me by walking farther into the gallery, past me, going straight to the rack of prints I'd indicated when she first came in.

"I could never afford his paintings, but I've always wanted one."

I'm never sure how to respond to that.

She goes on. "Then I saw your post on Facebook."

Oh! The marked-down prints. That's why she's here.

I pull out the two prints I'd advertised that were on sale for $30. The first is a hollyhock, 16" x 20", printed back in 1990—one of nearly two hundred still stacked in a drawer. The other is a larger print of a barn in snow (imagine that)—22" x 30"—a big barn on a hillside, lots of negative space. Color palette is simple: sepia and white. Both are classic Rob O'Dells, and both have been around for a long time. Maybe I'll earn a little extra cash as we head into Christmas—and clear out some space in my flat files.

I head back to my desk while she examines the two prints, then she sets them aside and starts flipping through the rest of the rack. I pull my attention away from email again to explain why some prints are $30 and others are a few hundred dollars. Basically, this: A giclée is a high-definition, archival-quality reproduction made from a super-high-quality scan, usually printed one at a time using a 12-color printer. The level of detail is phenomenal, and when you place one next to a more traditional type of print—conventional offset printing—it's clear why giclées cost more. Still, though, most are intimidated by the French word they have trouble pronouncing (*zhee-KLAY*). And by the higher prices they carry.

She pulls out a giclée print called *Kelly Green*. I confess, I feel a bit like an imposter when I tell people the name. I'm the one who named it—but in my defense, it's a very green painting, a gift from Dad after he helped me renovate my green-cabineted kitchen. Even though Dad hadn't given a name to the painting, that we're aware of, the title seemed just corny and punny enough to be appropriate. The 12" x 16" giclée print is $175.

She holds up another print—a Christmas card produced by a bank or university president. A sycamore tree in winter, a snowy creek, and a deep blue sky. "How much?" she asked.

I found it in a box one day, cut a mat for it, and shrink-wrapped it to have some lower-priced options for sale. "Twenty?"

"I'll take them both," she said, handing it to me along with the giclée. She pulled out a wad of cash and counted out the exact amount.

During this whole time, she really hadn't said much—at least nothing extra. Her voice was soft, almost timid. She shifted her purse from one shoulder to the other and pulled the hoodie tighter around her. She looked up whenever someone walked by the front windows. And yet she didn't move toward the door after she'd paid.

As I stand there next to her in the awkward silence, we both look up at the large original *Kelly Green* painting that hangs behind my desk. I like to work in the natural daylight, but on this typical gray winter day, I'd flipped on the lights. The floodlight over my desk shone directly on the painting, making it seem to glow. Framed, the painting measures about 32" x 40" and the paper is almost completely covered—foreground, subject, and background—with numerous shades of green.

Her print was half size, and still beautiful, but the original? Simply magnificent. One of his best.

"I love the one you picked," I said, nodding toward the original. "Dad helped me redo my kitchen and I had green cabinets, so when he saw how much I loved it, he gave it to me."

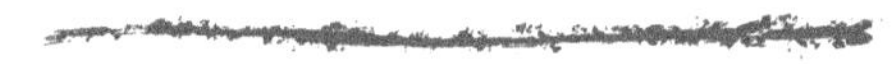

About a quarter mile behind my parents' house when I was growing up, there was a thicket, this little patch of dense and overgrown trees. Every spring, we'd climb on the three-wheeler or walk through the corn stubble left in the fields from the fall harvest, carrying a plastic grocery bag. We were not one of those families who goes mushroom hunting and comes home with hundreds. We were always lucky to find one or two. But that little patch was the perfect place to look, and we did it faithfully, once a year, on the first pretty day of spring.

That's what I think of whenever I look at the painting. In it, a few large trees, branches still winter-bare, stretch their arms in the fresh air as they wake up after a long winter's nap. Lush, rich, vibrant greens are bursting to life all around them. A few fallen, decaying branches angle across the foreground, tangles of weeds around them. Leaves are just starting to sprout on a few tree branches, and some ephemeral slender saplings are lined up in the background with their gangly teenage limbs. Around the fallen branches, dozens of vivid periwinkle wildflowers are scattered across the forest floor, interspersed with a sprinkling of tiny yellow blooms here and there. The sunlight falling across the white-barked sycamore tree is dappled and warm looking. The whole scene is green—the bright yellow-green of new life. Absolutely decadent in its abundance, especially with the vivid (but tiny) periwinkle and yellow flowers.

Off to the right, just past the sycamore tree, there is a clearing, an opening in the leaves. It's as if, once you've taken several steps into the woods from the field, you stopped to look back from where you came. The colors and scents of this magical and mystical place embrace you, but the bright light and blue skies of the real world are just there, within reach and yet miles away. You stop. Close your eyes. And breathe.

When I finally look away from the painting, I notice her face is brighter and she seems to stand a little taller.

"I never got to meet him, but of course I always knew who he was," she tells me again. "But it sounds like he was a really nice man."

"He was," I answer, as those darn tears make a surprise appearance again. "Of course I'm biased, but he was pretty awesome."

She gives me a sad smile. "Well, I best be going," she says, but we continue to stand there for a few long moments, both of us looking at the painting. A minute later, she catches my gaze and says, "Thank you so much!"

As she walks out, I think we both feel like we'd been given a gift.

People come into the studio looking for something. I don't know what, exactly, but it's about so much more than the art.

The art makes it possible. It gives us something to share and a common ground for conversation. But they want more than a painting to hang over the couch. They want a piece of the man who was so nice. The legend, the famous artist. Often, they don't know about much art. They're quick to say this, not wanting to be inauthentic. But there's something compelling them, still, long after his death, to claim a piece of him for themselves. Maybe it's because, in his work, Dad pays homage to the quiet, rural life. It's most definitely not flashy, but by honoring and revealing the beauty in this landscape, he affirms the people who live this life. Who choose this way. He lets them know that they are seen, that they have value, that they matter.

Now, and even when they are gone.

vignette

Any future O'Dell painters in the making? Kerry, age 3, is a bit young to criticize yet. On the kitchen bulletin board, however, is 6-year-old Kelly's magic marker drawing of a house. Color abounds, the little girl's dress is plaid, and cats appear under windows that open. AND, she signs her name just like her daddy with the long line: ------------------ Kelly O'Dell --------------------.

—Ann Hulett, "Sketches of Three Indiana Artists,"
Junior League of Indianapolis newsletter, November 1973

ONE ON ONE

24″ x 18″

Description:
Rusted basketball
hoop and faded backboard
mounted on a dead tree

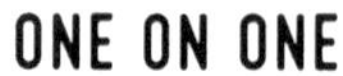

My dad was known for his distinctive signature—painted in a soft sepia (or white if the background was dark), usually along the bottom right-hand side of the painting. It starts with a long straight line, probably three inches wide, which becomes the top of the letter R. All the letters slant backward, soft and simple strokes made with a fine-point brush, open and unconnected. The O is flat and wide, and after the apostrophe the capital D has a pointed top, almost like a cursive old-fashioned S. The signature ends with another long straight line. He often waited to sign paintings until they were positioned in the mat, so that he could be sure his name ran parallel with the edge of it.

As Dad's art grew in popularity, people learned to look for the long straight line. Even Irving Shapiro, president of the American Academy of Art, who taught Dad how to paint, recognized Dad's mark. He wrote in a letter in 1975, "I don't know if I had ever told you that my wife and I were in San

Francisco some time ago and wandered into a gallery near
Fisherman's Wharf. One of the first things I saw, of course,
were watercolors that had your signature on them. It was a
good feeling."

I've only ever heard of one person with any complaints about
the way Dad signed his work. A letter Dad received in 1993 from
a stranger who "felt obliged" to write after seeing Dad's work in
a gallery, read, "Unfortunately, the first thing that caught my
eye on each of them was your signature. For that reason alone,
I didn't buy any. I felt that it would be a constant source of
annoyance for me to have a print that I liked very much on my
wall, when the first thing that I saw each time I looked at it was
something I didn't want to see at all." He closed by asking Dad
to send him a brochure of his other prints, because "Maybe I
will find that your signature doesn't distract me on your other
works." Dad kept the letter, so he must have found it amusing,
but I don't know if he ever sent a brochure.

Dad's name essentially became a brand: His name mattered.
Unlike some of Dad's interchangeable titles, this was specific
and distinct.

Months after Dad died, I started cleaning out a small
enclosed room in the back of the studio and unearthed an entire
box of old sketchbooks. The cardboard was dirty and warped,
and the stack of spiral-bound books was almost buried in bits of
insulation, cobwebs, and the various chunks of gritty debris that
had filtered down from the old brick walls. After pulling out
the shop vac, I paged through several of the books. I've looked at
Dad's sketches my whole life, so they were more or less what
I expected. Until they weren't.

I found a few pages with my name drawn multiple times
in different typestyles— numerous renderings of "Kelly" and
"Kelly O'Dell." I assumed my younger self had gotten hold of his
sketchbook at one time or another and drawn in it. Until a few

pages later, when I found a draft of a letter Dad composed to my grandfather, edited in Mom's handwriting. They were struggling with how to turn down the offer of a trip to Europe without offending her parents. One of the reasons they gave was that I was less than a year old and they weren't ready to leave me with someone else. (The other was that Dad wanted to be able to give that gift to his family with money he'd earned, not money that was given to them.)

That's when I realized this sketchbook was from 1968, so the sketches of my name couldn't have been done by me. Just as a girl might write the name of her future husband, trying out all the permutations of her soon-to-be-married name, Dad was in love with his baby girl.

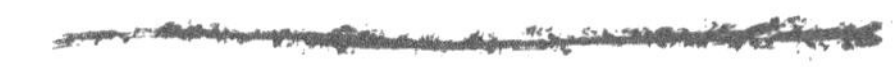

As a teen, I spent hours drawing his name, too, but it was in order to learn how to forge his signature. Dad wasn't always around, and sometimes Mom needed him to sign papers or endorse checks to go to the bank. So I went to work practicing until I could replicate the particular shape of his capital D, get just the right angle for the backward slope of the R, and end with his "signature" (get it?) long straight line. Don't worry; I didn't have any nefarious schemes in mind, and I had my parents' full consent. It was mainly a challenge to myself—could I pull it off?

Apparently the answer is yes, because on senior skip day, I was the only student not thought to be playing hooky. In the past, when I needed a note to excuse an absence, Dad always asked me to write it (because his handwriting was so hard to read), and then he would sign it. So while everyone else was at Turkey Run State Park, I was allegedly helping Dad deliver paintings to a gallery in Michigan for his latest art show.

I've been married for more than 30 years to Tim. I love him and love our life together, and I chose to take his name—so our kids would have the same name that we shared, and because keeping my maiden name wouldn't extend the family line of O'Dells, since all the O'Dell cousins were girls. I compromised by keeping O'Dell as my middle name. Even after all this time, I don't *feel* like a *Kelly Stanley*. That name seems ordinary, indistinct—nothing wrong with it, but it doesn't evoke the same deep connection I feel to the name O'Dell. Besides, *Kelly O'Dell* is clearly an Irish redhead. And the alliteration is nice. Whether drawn by him or me or someone else, the name connects me to a whole long line of O'Dells. (Full disclosure: Apparently when my great-grandfather went to school and they asked him his name—Odle—the teacher spelled it wrong and it stuck.) But the O'Dell name was mine, and it's who I was.

Letting go of that has gotten harder now that Mom and Dad are gone.

I've started introducing myself as Kelly O'Dell Stanley, and signing things "Kelly O Stanley" (because Dad called me Kelly O). When you grow up in a small town, giving your maiden name is a type of shorthand. When I say "O'Dell," people know I went to Southmont High School, and may even remember that I was in FFA. They know I'm from Ladoga. That my mom was the school nurse, my dad the artist.

It's like an anchor, a locator. It cuts through the small talk and gives me context.

It also highlights one more layer of my grief. Not only have I lost my parents, but I've lost the people who give me context. When the people who *literally* gave me my identity are no longer present, how am I supposed to have any idea at all who I am?

I don't know. Maybe the name *Untitled* is a better fit for me now.

But a little voice inside my head whispers, *No, that's the easy way out. You're strong enough to be something more than that.*

One of Dad's paintings, titled *Winter Stump*, depicted a weather-worn tree stump and dried leaves in the snow. Sure, he could have come up with a catchier title, but here's the thing about my dad: What you see is what you get. Pretentiousness is not part of his personality. The title tells you exactly what to expect—and unlike some modern art, you don't have to struggle to parse the meaning—yet there's always more than first meets the eye. Small branches shooting up from unlikely places. An abandoned wagon wheel inside the barn revealed by a small patch of light. A metal trash can practically buried in the weeds. It's the minute details that add depth and dimension, infuse a layer of reality. Because nothing is ever completely clean. Nothing is ever completely perfect.

But that doesn't mean it can't also be beautiful.

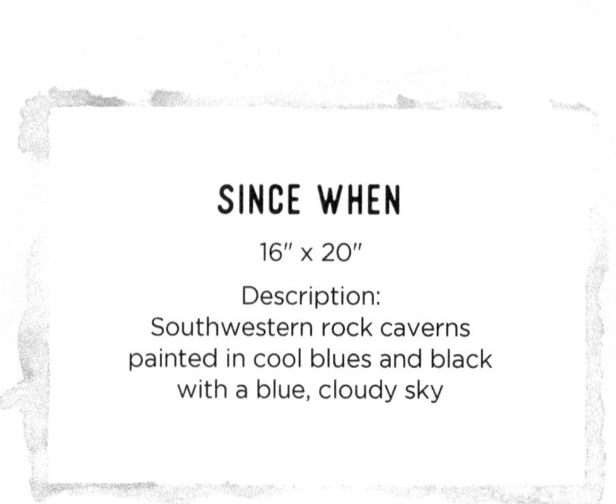

Five years after Dad died, I was preparing a sermon to share at church about the creative spark that drives an artist to create, and whether that might actually be the Holy Spirit. I planned to share what Dad said during the guided meditation during his cancer treatment, about how when he paints it's like a sanctuary to him. When my first book came out, churches invited me to speak to them about creativity and prayer, and I felt sick every time I had to stand in front of the room and talk. But there was no fear in this—people might question my faith or approach to prayer, but no one could argue that I don't know my dad. Quite a few church members owned Dad's paintings. On Zoom calls during the heart of the pandemic, we'd gather as a row of little rectangles on a screen, and inevitably I'd spot a large snowy barn hanging over a fireplace, or a small landscape or tree hanging on a wall, and smile.

I can pick them out from a mile away. (Seen one, seen 'em all.)

Some of the women were nurses who worked with Mom in the school system or the local volunteer medical clinic. At least one man was listed in my dad's old-fashioned Rolodex as a longtime customer and friend. Several were at the big sale after Dad died. We have pictures of them smiling as they hold their new paintings—before I joined that church or knew them, they knew him. They'd give me the benefit of the doubt because of who my parents were. They're rooting for me, not against me.

There is such comfort in the legacy they left for me.

A few days before I was going to speak, I was helping Kym, one of my dad's former workshop students and the maintenance person at the church, hang a display of Dad's paintings.

As Kym and I paused to talk about Dad, my eyes kept returning to a large painting of a lone, treeless sycamore against a stormy sky—the same painting I found in his flat files right after he died, as mentioned in the early pages of this book. Even though the painting (which we called *Untitled* for obvious reasons) tugged at my emotions, the only space in my house large enough to hang it was the upstairs hallway between the kids' rooms. It wasn't a place I spent much time in.

That day, I noticed something and interrupted her mid-sentence. I couldn't help it. "You know what? Dad never signed this." She turned to look where I was pointing. "I guess that makes sense. It was in his drawers, unframed, when he died. I just didn't realize he hadn't signed it."

Kym and I both stepped closer to get a better look.

The giant, bare sycamore tree, branches reaching toward the sky, is front and center. The sky is gloomy. Dark and watery, painted with sepia brown, it feels like storm clouds rolling in. The wooden gate, made by dragging cardboard strips dipped in paint across the paper, is nicely textured. Dad used his usual salt technique to create the intricate detail of the weeds, but there are only a couple of lines of barbed wire shown, not a whole fence.

"I never noticed it before, but there should be wires between the fence posts, and he didn't draw those in." A moment later: "Oh my gosh, and look—he didn't finish the tree branches, either!"

When Dad painted, he quickly laid in most of the areas of color and texture at the beginning, when the paint and paper were still wet. It had enough detail to feel complete, but it was really just a first layer. Typically, Dad would let the morning's painting dry and walk away to play golf or have lunch at the diner down the street, where they talked about important things like the weather (*colder than a witch's tit or hotter than a fresh f***** fox in a forest fire*) and who's farming whose fields. He'd walk across the street to the grocery store to get a Snickers or a banana (potassium helped with leg cramps) and then sit back down with his delicate brushes—or more often, a quill fountain pen with a very fine tip—and add a second or maybe third layer, ending with the finest details. The strands of wire that make up the fence, and the barbs along them. The nails sticking out of the wooden gate, and the shadows they cast. The knotholes in the tree, sometimes given texture with his thumbprint. And the delicate, tapered, fine branches at the tips of the larger limbs of the tree.

Realizing all that was missing took my breath away. Kym got it. She looked at me and said, "You should call this one *Unfinished*. Like his life."

Now I love that painting more than before, if that's even possible. It's so close—it's *so close* to having him here. So close to being all that it was intended to be. So close to being right, and whole, and perfect. In the end, I suppose the title is irrelevant. What matters the most is not what we're called but who we are.

But that tree, my love for my father?

Unfinished.

And yet, there it still stands. All alone.

TILL WE MEET AGAIN

14" x 22"

Description:
Old wooden wagon abandoned
in a field of wildflowers

When my oldest child, Katie, was 24, she invited me to go to Las Vegas with her for a few days. As a mom, I'd love to believe she just wanted to spend time with me, but I know better. She had a discount through her work, and she didn't have anyone else to go with her—plus, I'd probably pay for all our dinners.

Still, I booked a flight and was happy to go.

One day, we walked past several tattoo parlors. "Mom! Let's get matching tattoos!"

I already had one tiny one—a loose, hand-drawn dove meant to represent the Holy Spirit. The olive branch it carries signifies peace as well as the promises of God realized when Noah's dove came back from dry land to show it was safe to leave the ark. I was afraid to get anything permanently etched onto my body, but I hoped the Holy Spirit would always matter to me. My daughter Anna had scheduled that appointment for my 49th birthday and taken me to the tattoo parlor so I couldn't back out.

I love it. I haven't been sorry. But I wasn't sure I wanted another tattoo.

Katie, however, already had several, so another one wasn't

as big a deal for her. We started talking about what kind of tattoo we could get. A few weeks earlier, she and I had been sitting on the couch with Tim, watching TV. I can't remember the specifics, but it was one of those conversations in which Katie started a sentence like, "Do you remember—" but before she could finish, I'd answer something like, "No, not that time. What about—" Then she would say, "Yes, exactly."

Or I'd start, "Hey, Katie, have you—" and she'd say, "Yep." I'd reply, "Oh, okay, but what about—" and she'd interrupt me again. "I got it covered."

That day, Tim looked at us, exasperated and confounded by the kind of ESP we shared. Complete nonsense, as far as he (or anyone else) could tell. He proclaimed, "You're two peas in a frickin' pod."

He didn't mean it as a compliment.

So as soon as Katie and I started discussing tattoo possibilities, our very similar brains both latched upon the words "Two peas."

Still, though, I was 50 years old. My body is only going downhill from here. Did I really want ink to call attention to that eventual sagging and drooping and fading? What if this unknown artist messes up? The ink is permanent.

Hours later, I stepped into the ladies' room to escape the clanging machines for just a moment. Glancing at my Holy Spirit tattoo, I tossed up a little prayer, wondering if I should go through with this new tattoo or not.

Right away I knew this: If my daughter is not ashamed of the fact that we're so much alike, that's a good thing, right? Why *wouldn't* I do it? Every day, when she saw her wrist, whether she thought about it in these terms or not, she would be reminded that we were connected and know that I loved her.

Decision made. We were getting tattoos.

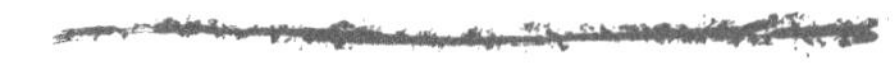

Katie was just 15 when Mom died. She struggled so much
after we lost Mom. Gran had been her person—maybe not her
pickle person, exactly, because Katie hates pickles, but the one
who believed in her no matter what. Gran drove Katie to weekly
voice lessons, took her shopping, bought her a guitar when she
wanted to learn. Gran always made her feel special.

On July 9, 2019, Katie gave birth to my first grandchild,
Sullivan Robert, and now I totally understand the bond Mom
had with Katie. I adore this little person. He's the smart one and
the adorable one and the funny one *and* the sweet one, just as
his cousins will be, but he was the first and in mere seconds he
absolutely captured my heart. Dad had died mid-day on July 9,
two years earlier. On that exact date, mere minutes from when
he left us, his great-grandson came into this world. I picture it
like the ending scene out of the movie "Big," almost as though
the old and the new passed each other, one coming into the
world and one going out. I've been told it's a Jewish tradition
to give every baby born into the family the name of someone
they recently lost, and though we're not Jewish, I love that Katie
named her baby Sullivan Robert. My son Bobby thinks Sully was
named after him, but since Bobby was named after his Bebop, I
guess it is somewhat true.

Once Sully was born, I couldn't help thinking about
generations. Legacies. Those who came before us, and those who
launched us into the world. Those who should have been there
that day, but weren't.

We're all connected, in a way I never understood before now.
It's not just genetics and bloodlines. It's this ethereal filament,
woven through time, connecting us in ways that our minds can't
fully grasp but that our hearts know.

Not long after Katie and I got our tattoos, I remembered something.

Before Katie was born, we thought long and hard about choosing grandparent names for my mom and dad. We wanted to incorporate their real names, so we came up with Gran Ann and Gran Bob. Katie couldn't say that, so their names became Gran and Bebop (or Beeb for short).

Our good friend Richard, who assigns nicknames for everyone he knows, couldn't remember "Bebop" and always called my dad "Peapod" instead. So now I think of my dad as well as my daughter whenever I see our "two peas in a pod" tattoos, which makes me love them even more.

vignette

His noted barns come in all sizes and seasons—with snow, with sun, with Coca-Cola signs, with old cars, with fences, with pumps.

—Ann Hulett, "Sketches of Three Indiana Artists,"
Junior League of Indianapolis newsletter, November 1973

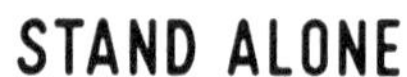

STAND ALONE

14″ x 22″

Description: Sycamore tree
in winter with dark,
gloomy sky

It's April 2023, and I'm talking on the phone to a man from Michigan who emailed me through Dad's website about buying one of the eight remaining originals that we have for sale. It popped into my inbox last night. "I'm wondering if this original is still available. If so, would you be open to an offer of $550? It's a cool work by your dad. I met him years ago at the Joyce Petter Gallery. I also met your mother one time as well. Such a down-to-earth couple. I also enjoyed watching one of your Dad's workshops as well. It was interesting to witness his techniques. Look forward to hearing from you."

The painting consists of a sycamore tree in the upper-right quadrant, reaching beyond the edge of the paper. There's some snow, but it's the kind of snow we see in the Midwest in late winter, snow that's been sitting for a while and drifting around the clumps of brown grasses and weeds, settling in the hollows. A barbed wire fence and a gate span the width of the scene, partly lost in the sepia shadows and grasses. The sky is a deep, steely blue-gray, so the sycamore's light bark and snowy branches pop against the background. The horizon is defined by sepia shapes, dark, soft impressions of a tree line in the distance. Nondescript and vague.

I like it but not enough to keep it for myself. It was originally $1,000, but I'd reduced the price to $800 and now it was $600. The guy asks if I'll take $550. Oh, what the heck. Dad always gave people 20% off if they were repeat buyers anyway.

I'll pretend it wasn't already marked down.

The painting has been hanging on the wall across from where I sit at my desk in the studio, so I've looked at it a lot—and it's a good one—but I wouldn't mind a little bit of incoming cash. Originally we called this one—surprise, surprise—*Untitled*, but when I loaded the paintings onto Dad's online store, I decided to assign them names found on lists of paintings he took to galleries over the years. He wouldn't mind.

I'm not sure if *Stand Alone* is a declaration of power and strength or simply the heart of a lonely daughter. But it seems to fit, either way.

The guy on the phone is a talker, but I don't really mind. He tells me about his collection—sounds like he has quite a few paintings. Some he bought from galleries, but he has an eBay alert set for Dad's name so he is notified whenever a new one shows up. As he describes several of his paintings, I recognize them. I've saved the photos from various auction sites so we can have a record of more of his work. I'm nodding and saying, "Mmm hmm," into the phone, when I recognize the next painting he describes. "It has a brown wintery gate, with tufts of grass and a broken fence and a sign hanging on the gate that says ..."

"No hunting without permission," I finish for him.

He kind of falters, but then keeps going. "I bought it on eBay and they were asking too much. I don't know who kept bidding against me, but I ended up paying $455."

"Yep, they were. It was me," I say.

"What do you mean?"

"I'm the one who was bidding against you. I loved that painting." I don't want him to feel bad, so I add, "I bid up to $450, so that's why you got it for $455. I loved it, but that's okay. I'm just glad someone has it who appreciates it."

Part of me wishes he'd offer to sell it to me.

He goes on, "I just got it back from the framers. It looks really great. I'll send you pictures of all my paintings."

Part of me feels a rush of relief that he didn't offer to sell it to me after all. Where would I put it? The only open space on my walls is the hole where *Stand Alone* no longer hangs (or, ahem, *stands*). Maybe now I can move in one of the paintings stacked in back, painted by an artist other than Dad.

FALLBACK ROAD

22" x 28"

Description: Downed tree across a
lane; woods and trees all around are
vibrant oranges and browns, full of
late-day shadows

In December 2023, I decide to hold an open house to try to
sell more of Dad's prints and the remaining few originals (three
of which are decoys—just sayin').

A week before, a woman had come into the studio, excited
to actually catch me there. She and her husband were selling
their farmhouse and moving into a modern condo, and she
needed all-new art. She kept returning to the one called *Barn
Formation*, which is a grid of nearly identical barns against a
white background. Dad clearly made a barn-shaped template,
which he traced to get the shapes the same, but each barn had
different darks and lights, interesting shapes and shadows. I
described it earlier as an Andy Warhol, but with barns instead
of Marilyn. Dad painted it in the early '80s, when he was in his
abstract and experimental phase. You can date it by the brown
velvet mat and the sticker on the back from the company that
framed the pieces displayed at the Carmel, Indiana, gallery.

No one has seemed interested in it, and it's not one of my
favorites, although I enjoy looking for the differences in each
barn. This woman's husband is a farmer, so she thinks he'll like

the barns, even though he's not normally a fan of more abstract or contemporary art.

I wrap it in brown paper for her, since it's misting rain outside, and carry it and another framed print to her car. When I come back inside and see the empty space on the wall, I am surprised to feel bereft.

At that moment, my criteria for which paintings to keep changes. I ask: Will it make me sad to see it walk out the door? If so, I will keep it.

Lesson learned, a little too late.

As I continue to prepare for the small open house, I make a price tag for a painting I bought for myself a couple of years ago in an online estate auction. I like it, but I don't think it will make me sad to live without it. There are others I'd rather put on my walls instead. When it sells, I'm genuinely happy for the buyer—and for myself because I made a little bit of profit.

The day arrives, and the crowds are sparse—maybe 20 people total over the course of a whole Saturday—but by the end of the sale, I've sold several prints and three more originals, bringing the count down to five paintings left from the 212 we started with.

One man who bought a hollyhock print lowered his voice and said, "I was supposed to come in here and get a tour of the studio from your dad. He said I could. I had to coordinate with some friends, and before we could get it figured out, your dad was gone."

"Oh, I'm sorry to hear that!"

He continued. "I always wanted to ask him, did he have to feel *inspired* to do a painting? Did he wake up and ask himself if he felt like painting that day?"

I told him how Dad painted most mornings, whether he felt like it or not. He'd flip through his drawers of photos, and pull one out, and paint 'til noon—and then spend the rest of the day doing whatever else he felt like doing.

"Thank you," he said. "I was just always curious about how that worked."

I smiled at him as he walked out. He was sweet.

I took my time closing up. I counted up the sales, mobile-deposited the checks, put away the cash box, and turned off the lights. As I was driving home, out of nowhere, tears came with a vengeance.

Dammit. I don't want to be the person people go to with questions about Dad. I don't want to be the expert on his life.

I just want Dad.

The "missing" doesn't hit me as strongly or as often anymore. But *dammit*.

ONE OF A KIND

18″ x 18″

Description: Close-up of tree trunk
with several sets of initials
carved into the bark and
long shadows striping the trunk

I have hundreds of Dad's digital files on my computer. He took pictures periodically to have a record of what he painted. I don't think he did it throughout his whole career—or if so, I haven't seen them, probably because many of the early ones were on slides, and I haven't pulled out the slide projector since I started this project. I'm making a catalog of sorts for our family—but to do that, I must weed out the duplicates, figure out which images are the highest resolution, adjust warped perspectives, brighten darker shots, print them, and place them in albums.

I begin by viewing the images as icons on my screen. Every few months I Google "Rob O'Dell" and download photos of paintings sold through online art auction sites since I last checked, dropping them all into a big folder on my computer. So many.

I start sorting. I make several folders: barns, fences and gates, roads, landscapes, trees, creeks, Southwest, Maine, Ireland, Florida, flowers, experimental. It's a good start. But still too many to make sense of. I mean, how do you, at a glance,

differentiate among 30 different brown barns in white snow?
Or 42 vertical hollyhock paintings? They all look so similar,
with similar colors, but each one is a tiny bit different. And
sometimes I have multiple photos of the same image taken at
different times, so I have to sort through the duplicates to find
the best-quality option.

I make subfolders within folders. Barns: *winter, summer, fall,
close-up, silhouettes/sunsets*. Within *winter barns*, there are still
dozens and dozens of images. So I sort again into subfolders:
barns with snow, barns with skies (as opposed to white negative-
space backgrounds), *vertical images, horizontal ones, multiple barns
in scene*.

Within the folder *barns with snow* (*no skies/normal horizontal
orientation/single barns*), I then start looking for ones with silos.
But wait—these two barns are almost identical but one silo has a
rounded top while the other is flat. Okay, those are different.

In the *creeks* category, I realize that the body of water in two
photos is shaped exactly the same, but one scene is winter and
one is fall. Same composition, down to the fallen tree branch
lying vertically across the foreground. But one is yellow and
brown and one is rendered in shades of green. I bet I have the
photo and sketches somewhere.

For some of the paintings, I have five or six different digital
images. I compare file sizes to see which is the largest and
therefore highest resolution. But in thumbnail form I notice that
the colors are drastically different. In one, the barn is reddish-
brown, in one it's almost black. I arbitrarily adjust the color
balance based on how I think it probably looked. I adjust the
levels in Photoshop so the background is pure white. Lighten
the barns slightly to show more detail. And in the process, I
notice that the files have very different names. In one, *RODELL3*.
In another, *winter-barn*. In a third, *Odell-watercolor-snowy-
winter*. Sometimes I can't tell if the filename is a painting title

or descriptor. (For instance, did he call it *Winter Barn*? *Snowy Winter*? *Friday Flurries*? Or did the auction company simply describe what it looked like to them?)

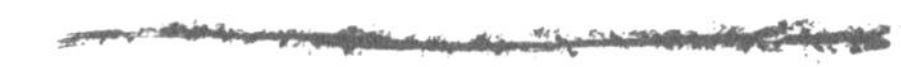

Whenever Dad needed to submit images for a juried art show, gallery opening, newspaper article, or upcoming show invitation, he would show up at my house around 10:30 in the morning, carrying a manila file on which he had written "Kelly O" in pencil in his messy cursive.

Usually, the SD card from his 35 mm camera was taped inside with masking tape so he wouldn't lose it. We'd sit in front of the computer while I opened the images and found the paintings he wanted to send. Sometimes they were photos taken through glass, often from an extreme angle to try to minimize the glare and reflections. No matter how he tried, though, inevitably the images were skewed by perspective—wider at the top and narrower at the bottom, or some such thing. I'd crop and color correct them in Photoshop, save them with the requested filenames, and write the accompanying email.

I was Dad's own personal assistant. (The smart one, don't you know?) We worked well together, each of us knowing just what our roles were. I let Dad do the fine art, and I stuck with the peripheral stuff.

And then we'd head out to Little Mexico for lunch, where he always got the Speedy Gonzalez or Lunch Combo #3. The waiters all stopped by the table to joke with him, and Irma, the owner, always gave him a big hug when he left.

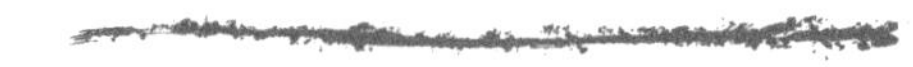

All that to say, the digital photos I have are all different sizes and quality, depending on how someone had requested we save it and what version of Photoshop I was using at the time. Recently I learned how to manipulate the files to correct the distortion when the images weren't photographed straight on. I ordered a bunch of photo albums, planning to have one for barns, one for trees, one for flowers, and so on. Maybe within that system I will try to roughly group them by the decade in which they were likely created.

On top of that, I have postcards and printed invitations from dozens and dozens—probably hundreds—of art show openings, and black-and-white, grainy reproductions of award-winning paintings featured in Hoosier Salon exhibitions across the years. Some newspaper photos. All different sizes, so I also ordered some books of full-page plastic pockets to help protect the photos from further deterioration.

Finally, I pull out the small metal boxes in which Dad stored his photos. I sort the prints into piles, organized by subject matter. I notice some of them are also in the digital files on my computer. Sheesh. This is going to be complicated.

Later that afternoon, feeling rather organized and pleased with myself, I take my usual seat at Kerry and Doug's kitchen island while Kerry pours me a glass of our favorite cabernet and Doug preps food for that night's dinner.

"Guess what I've been doing? I've gathered all the digital files of Dad's paintings, plus all the ones I can find online, and I'm sorting them and getting rid of all the duplicates. I've ordered photo albums and I'm going to have them all printed and organized by subject matter and season. We won't have a copy of everything he painted, but at least we'll have the last several years."

My brother-in-law, Doug, laughed. "Do you know how ridiculous he would think that is?" Kerry agreed with him.

I laughed, but I've spent some time thinking about it. Deep down I don't think Dad would think it was ridiculous at all. He was the first to gently make fun of himself, but he was serious about his work, and I think he would love that I was trying to preserve it. That I thought it worthy of such effort.

Then again, maybe he *would* have thought I was ridiculous, and would have told me, "Kelly O, you've got more important things to do."

And yet. When I moved into the studio, I felt that Dad's legacy had been entrusted to me. I got the artistic gene, after all, and I spend my days surrounded by his art, by his things. I am writing about Dad, thinking about Dad, preserving whatever legacy there might be. I feel a strong sense of obligation to do this, in order to be true to my feelings about Dad and his talent.

I hate thinking of all this beautiful work—piles of sketches and boxes of reference photos, hundreds of pictures of his paintings—decomposing in some damp storage area until they're no longer salvageable. They're way more valuable than that, and not just because they belonged to my father.

Do I think Dad was the most important artist of the century, or anything like that? No. Do I think he's a household name? While his work is part of collections across the globe, no, the "art world" as a whole does not know him. Do I want to build a shrine, a monument, elevating Dad to sainthood status? As he would constantly say about anything and everything, "N-O-double Z-X-N-T!" In other words, *No way, José.* (He also said that a lot.)

BUT.

Dad knew that what he did mattered. Maybe he felt a responsibility to capture and record what he saw; perhaps he simply liked to paint. I don't know with absolute certainty, and

I'm relatively sure he would never have used these words to describe it, but I think he inherently understood that art has the power to connect us, and that his work was more than simply a job. Perhaps a calling, a sacred duty. A privilege, for sure.

Maybe I'm the only one who cares about preserving and recording his body of work. I'm okay with that. Even if it's just for me, it feels right to do what I'm doing. As I undertake this sacred responsibility, I'm beginning to see that sometimes I can honor him best by building upon what he started, and other times by finding my own way. Building my own legacy—whatever that may end up looking like.

vignette

Critics have said that what makes O'Dell paintings good is what he leaves out of them. "My negative areas or white space is what sets my paintings apart."

—Cheryl D. Peck, "O'Dell Paints Scenes of Disappearing World," *Herald & Review*, Decatur, Illinois, August 2, 1971

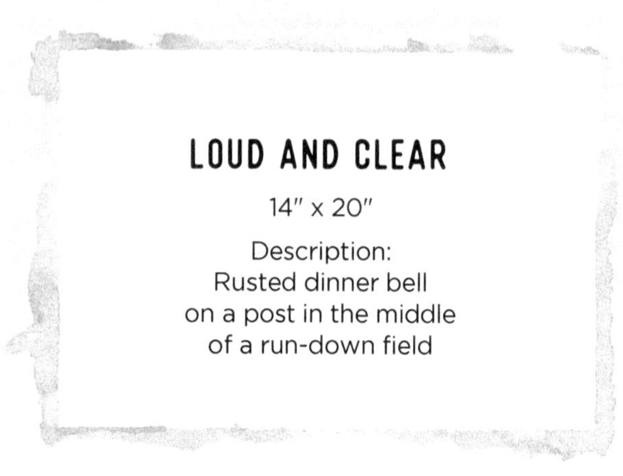

My friends keep asking me, "Do you feel like you're channeling your dad when you paint? I bet it makes you feel so close to him!"

I hate the disappointment in their faces when I respond. "No, not really."

Writing is where I have always felt most creative. I'm consumed by language.

All day, I think. I contemplate. I compose words, sentences, phrases, finessing and smoothing them in my mind as I drive or have conversations with friends, wearing them smooth like river stones until they're right. I decided long ago that I have flexibility with my schedule, and even when I'm crazy busy with work, people matter to me, so I try to adapt to their schedules to have time for them. Because I want to have lunch with people I enjoy several times a week. I want to be part of a book club, an active member of a church. I've started writing groups, and accountability groups, and creativity groups, all in an attempt to give people a safe place to be, to be encouraged, to create. And selfishly, because it helps me grow. Reminds me I'm not the center of everything. And gives me new things to think about.

On top of that, I speak to groups about prayer or faith or writing. I read words while I eat my meals, two or three books each week. I dictate words into my voice app, jot them in notebooks and on scraps of paper, type them by the thousands. I make lists of words, ideas, concepts. My whole life seems to be about words. My life is filled with observing, processing, wondering, and waiting.

But when I paint, there is nothing.

Which is much better than it sounds. Because my brain rarely turns off. As I try to sleep, as I drive to the studio, as I watch TV, as I listen to a preacher, my brain churns constantly.

But when there's a paintbrush in my hand, thoughts cease.

I guess maybe I see why Dad liked it so much. It's peaceful there in the silence.

Only whispers and instinctive response. Watercolor is reactive. Timing is everything. You don't have time to think too long about any move or you've already ruined it. When you paint with watercolors, you have to operate on instinct. Sure, maybe over years you've honed that instinct into a learned response, but you can't stop the process in the middle and Google it and watch a YouTube tutorial to see what to do next, or it will be too late.

Which is the reason why I have so many failed paintings. Why I can look at what I've done and pick it apart, noticing the lines where two wet areas (even of the same color) don't blend right, because I let one section get too dry, or I had too much water in my brush. Why I notice the harsh lines where things should have blended—and would have, had I known to keep the paper wet.

There's something about that kind of instinct that is simply beautiful.

I have a dog, a black goldendoodle. She's more poodle than golden retriever. And man, can she run. She kicks it up into high gear with her head up and her legs moving so fast and she leans into the corners as she makes circles around the yard, faster and faster. Every time I watch her, I think, *This*. This is what it looks like to do what you were born to do. To delight in it and find joy in the action. No thinking required.

When Dad told me that he goes to a place of sanctuary when he paints, that he inhabits the spaces and moments he paints, I didn't really understand, although I thought it was a beautiful sentiment.

But now I get it. I have glimpsed it myself. When Dad painted, he was acting largely on instinct. It was solitary work—mostly—but it wasn't lonely, because he was fully engaged in the moment. It wasn't about him. It was the universe, the paint, the water, the pigment, the moment, the light, the color, the emotion. He merged, seamlessly, with the elements and the world he was creating, and because it was what he was born to do, we all shake our heads in wonder and joy when we witness what he made.

I don't have the craft down pat. Not even close. I am unlearned and unpracticed, and in spite of my head knowledge about art, I am a novice.

But something in me lights up in those moments when I am painting, when there is nothing else there.

Nothing, and yet everything.

vignette

Art has a way of moving and stretching us. Of making us consider our experiences in a new light. Stanley utilizes her first-hand knowledge of the artistic process to shine new truth on what it means to commune with God and the full spectrum of ways we can see His answers manifest in our lives, if our eyes are open.

—Sarah Kovak, author of *In Capable Arms*, in her endorsement of my first book,
Praying Upside Down

OFFSPRING

30" x 22"

Description: Close-up of three weathered tree stumps with several slender saplings growing from them. Awarded Best of Show (outstanding work, any medium, in the entire exhibit) in the 48th Annual Hoosier Salon, 1982.

"So, has any of your dad's artistic talent rubbed off on you?"

I was standing near my dad during a gallery opening for one of his one-man shows. The pale hardwood floor glinted in the strong spotlights illuminating his artwork. Dad's paintings of rural Midwestern landscapes hung on the bright white walls. People filled the space, heads tilted to view one painting after another while they sipped their wine and waited to meet him. Mom, who would have preferred to be at home reading a book in her fleece robe rather than talking to strangers, avoided the limelight at these events. Kerry usually stayed close to her, but I liked to be with Dad. I'd leave his side only to grab another cream cheese and turkey-filled pinwheel or to look for the little red dots that meant a painting had sold, silently tallying up the total to whisper to Dad in between conversations.

As admirers stood in line to talk to Dad, these kind men and women talked to preteen me, inevitably asking if I was an artist. Dad would pause his other conversation, touch my arm, and smile.

"Yes, and she got my red hair, too."

I was always so proud to belong to him, to have so much of him inside me. But I knew I'd finally succeeded on my own merits when I was in my late twenties. Dad went to an advertising association event with me, and someone said to him, "Hi. So you're Kelly Stanley's father?"

They probably had no idea why I laughed out loud. For that moment, at least, Dad was defined by his relationship to me instead of the other way around.

But really, I think we were both defined by our relationship to each other.

We were a pretty good team.

I grew up standing beside Dad at art shows, listening to him brag on me to his fans, learning from watching him. Then, as an adult, I used my skills to promote his work. Later, our worlds overlapped in a new way when I asked for permission to use some of his artwork to illustrate the concepts in my book. A customer and friend of Dad's (a prolific and well-known author, the keynote speaker for the first writing conference I attended) kindly read this unknown writer's work and offered a generous endorsement of my first book. People who didn't even know Dad began to see me as an artist and expert. And then I got to hear Dad's wonder after he read that book, opening the door to conversations we'd never had before.

I got to hold his hand when we crossed streets, first because he was keeping me safe, and later because it comforted him.

I got to witness the way he walked to the studio in the backyard after breakfast because he couldn't wait to paint again. And watch him load his golf clubs when he didn't feel like painting—or when it was just too pretty a day not to be outside. When he didn't have things he had to do, he often chose to spend it with Kerry, or me, or our kids.

I crafted my own career path as a self-employed graphic designer, following a similar path to his—working from home with my kids watching *Rugrats* or *Barney* in the background, holding the baby while typing emails to clients with one hand. The money hasn't always been steady, and I am often distracted and too busy, but I've tried to be physically present for my family. I wanted my kids to see what it looks like to not have to choose career *or* family, but to have both.

I was sensitive to his criticism about my art, but I also saw him proudly display the stained glass I made for him and the brochures I designed for him and heard that he often bragged to his friends about how successful I was and how much I charged per hour. He appreciated my tech help and was sincerely interested in my comments and suggestions when we discussed his latest work. I watched him accept awards and he watched me do the same, in a different industry.

I also had the chance to listen to him discuss his art mistakes, see how he went back and cropped or painted over a weak area, lifted the paint or added a fence, or found a way to make the mistake beautiful. And when that didn't work, I saw him put his paintings in a drawer so he could try again another day—or use the back of the page when he ran low on watercolor paper.

I walked across the driveway to see him when he had dinner at Kerry's, our proximity meaning he could visit us both at the same time, no favoritism implied—although Kerry was more of a cook, like our mom. We drank red wine and talked, always having something more to talk about—or not, but either way, feeling comfortable enough to simply relax together. I heard in detail all of his health complaints, the small and annoying ones, and yet when it got really bad, his complaints seemed to decrease. I got to hear how his pain level was always the same— "it really hurts, probably a four or five," and "not bad, probably just a four or five" (another version of the same ol'?)—and exchange smiles with my sister across his hospital bed as one of us reached for the next dose of medicine.

I was able to fill his water glass and hold his straw, set my alarm to give him his meds through the night, and lie there while he slept, silently crying for him. But I also sat beside him, rubbing his arm, his hand gripping mine, as we talked about the things he dreamed, knowing he was comforted simply by my presence.

I knew that generosity was one of his defining marks—finding ways to praise the oncologist who gave him the bad news, the aide who helped bathe him, and the nurses and therapists who came in—always, even in his pain, commenting on something good that they did. Then at the end, Kerry and I had the opportunity to practice the generosity he taught and offer back to him all the love he so freely gave us.

I saw the way he opened his arms to our friends who wanted to have a dad like him. And I witnessed the loyalty of his own friends, the character of the men he chose to let into his life, and the tears shed by some of these big, strong, masculine men as they said goodbye. And now I get to talk to them about how amazing my dad was as I sit in his studio building trying to find my own way.

When I meet someone for the first time who's lived in this community for a long time, if I say, "You probably knew my dad," I don't have to worry if their stories will be good or bad. I am proud of the way he was admired and loved, and I can try to offer the people in my own life some of what he instilled in me.

It wasn't always the case, but I even love my red hair. And now that I'm in my mid-50s, I see my oft-bemoaned legs and freckles in a kinder light, feeling thankful for the strong muscles and sturdy body I inherited from him.

I watched what it meant to be an engaged and loving grandparent as Dad made that funny little smiling face that

I can't describe or imitate, the one that always made our kids laugh. I was there when they climbed on him, sat on his lap, begged to go for rides on the ATV, played Kings in the Corner, or got him to take them for a drive when they got their driving permits.

I watched the way Dad loved Mom in her last days, the way he would hold her hand to steady her as they walked together. The way that, even when the toxins in her brain turned her mean, he'd wait until she was sleeping and walk by and kiss the top of her head when no one was looking. And Kerry and I loved Dad in his last days, even better and more intentionally than we had our whole lives, holding his hand until he was no longer able to hold ours back.

And now, even though they are no longer here with us, I still get to be the person he and Mom made me to be. I don't have to be just like them.

But I can be, if I choose to be. I can let as much of them shine through me as I want.

SIGNS OF SPRING

20″ x 14″

Description: Cluster of vivid,
spring-green trees with
purple flowers blooming
beneath them

I push the button to close the top on my car, a little shiny silver Mazda Miata, which people often mistake for the convertible Mom bought Dad, a Saturn Sky. A man I know from the Laughing Cow Diner, three or four doors down from the studio, is still laughing from his friend's parting comment as they make their way to their cars.

"You know if you close that it won't rain, right?" He shuts the car door he'd just opened and waits on the sidewalk in front of Dad's studio.

My studio.

"I think about your dad all the time," he says. He leans toward the picture windows, peering inside. "You still have his paintings?"

I unlock the door, wrestling with the old-fashioned lock, and flip on the gallery lights.

"He was such a good friend," he comments, picking up various prints from the rack and examining each painting on the wall. "I loved coming in here and talking with him. Especially after your mom got sick. I used to come pray with him all the time."

I try not to look surprised. I don't know why I am. This man is a retired pastor. Just because Dad didn't talk about faith doesn't mean he didn't have it.

Huh. Always something new to learn.

I turn on the lights in the workroom as he examines one particular study Dad painted. It hung in the living room at Mom and Dad's for as long as I can remember. It's a cluster of vignettes from wartime advertising signs, Dad's commercial art background showing in his careful rendering of the sign typography: *Buy More Liberty Bonds*; *Call for Philip Morris: America's Finest 15¢ Cigarette*; *When It Rains, It Pours*; and *Enlist: On which side of the window are YOU?* The different typestyles and slogans are held together by an Old West–style post office building made of whitewashed siding with "General Merchandise" painted on the front, with an antique delivery truck parked in front.

In between the stylized fonts from the old signs, Dad handwrote some sayings from that era. I'm not sure I ever took the time to decipher his handwriting to see what he wrote. It was only right in front of me my entire life.

Apparently Dad's art has not always been the center of my universe.

One of the quotes reads, "In the United States there is more space where nobody is than where anybody is. This is what makes America what it is."

And another: "The world will little note nor long remember what we say here; but it can never forget what they did here."

I pull myself back to the conversation. "I'm sure you know Dad was trained as a commercial artist in Chicago. I think that's why he loved old signs so much."

He nodded. "We talked about Decatur a lot. I grew up over in Quincy. I used to ride with him when he took paintings over to the gallery in Decatur."

"I didn't know that," I said, surprised again. "I love being in here because so many people come in and talk to me about Dad."

"I'm sure there are lots of stories you don't know."

There are. So many. And each one gives me a new part of Dad to hold on to. Each story makes him come alive for me again. Each one makes me feel a little less lost—and makes me miss him just a little bit more. I thought there would be fewer and fewer glimpses as time goes by. This past week was the six-year anniversary of Dad's death, and the 12th anniversary of Mom's, and it seems nearly every time I come to the studio lately, another new person comes in to talk about him.

I love being in the heart of this small town where not much happens but people constantly come and go outside my plate glass windows. And I love it even more when they pause in front of the doors, then lean close to the windows to look past the reflections and see if I'm here before they make their way inside.

Most days I don't turn on the lights, preferring the natural light let in by the wall of windows. Sinking into my chair in front of my computer, I listen to the roar of the industrial furnace ticking on. I breathe. I straighten the paintings on the wall, most likely vibrated out of alignment by the tractors and grain trucks constantly barreling through town. I knock away a cobweb or two, maybe rearrange the display of Dad's prints and my own products and books in the front windows. I usually come in with words and ideas bursting forth, needing to be preserved, my brain filled with descriptions and phrases inspired by the landscapes I observed on my way to the studio. I used to think the 15-minute drive to Ladoga was so long, and now I find it's not long enough for all that I have inside me.

I feel full. Overflowing. But not stressed.

Settled.

I don't make it here every day anymore, although I don't love it any less. It seems my days are filled with other things besides work. I've stopped rushing from place to place; I don't do 40- or 50-hour weeks anymore. I let myself sleep until eight and then I read a book while drinking three cups of coffee with frothed milk in my quiet house. I Facetime my grandkids, or meet my daughter in Indy for a Target trip, or put together a charcuterie tray for friends who are coming to drink wine later. I volunteer to lead a book club for my church. I host a group of women every other week (a group that includes Kerry), a community in which we share our lives, tell stories, find understanding. We've all faced loss, and we all wrestle with our faith, and we have found like-minded souls in each other. I write—sometimes at home, more often at the studio , and sometimes from the crowded quarters of an airplane seat as I travel to see the grandkids. I've hosted some "open studio" days where people gather to work on whatever art or craft they want to bring, and we just spend time creating together. I started a writing group for local writers. I still work, though not nearly as much as before. And I squeeze in some time between tasks by standing at Dad's painting table, exploring.

Being in this place has changed me. It's become my sanctuary. A place of remembrance, but even more so, a place of hope.

And *this* is the stuff you can't make up: As I typed the previous paragraph, my phone rang. When my friend Jeannine, whom I've barely seen in years, got married recently, I sent her one of Dad's framed hollyhock prints as a gift. When I answered my phone, she was laughing and crying.

"Oh my goodness, Kelly. I can't ... You did something for me that I don't think you realized. This little, poor, brown girl from Montgomery County always knew of the legend Rob O'Dell and always wanted one of his paintings. I never dreamed I'd have one."

I couldn't get in a single word, but couldn't stop smiling.

"I knew who your dad was before I knew you. You just have no idea. I waited a day and a half to call you because I didn't want to cry. You are such a source of goodness in this community, you and your sister. I just … I have no words. Kelly, I don't think … I don't think you could have any idea what this means to me. You can't know."

Oh, Jeannine. I'm crying too.

But I promise you this: I *do* know. I absolutely do.

VIEW THROUGH

21″ x 14″

Description: Barn nestled in lush
green grasses, seen through a small
window framed within another barn's
door and dark shadowed interior

I lean forward, blowing the dust off the trays of watercolors and brushes that cover the credenza next to ~~Dad's~~ my painting table. I pick up the folded piece of paper that reads "Please do not touch" and drop it into the trash.

I fish it out of the trash can and place it carefully back on top. Then throw it away a final time, and leave it there.

Six and a half years. That's how long this stuff has been sitting here, mostly untouched. I've picked up a pencil now and again, experimented with some brushes, tried my hand with the fountain pens Dad used for fine detail. I've opened the drawers and flipped through Dad's stacks of reference photos, pulling out one here and there to try to paint.

I threw away some partially empty tubes of watercolor (after carefully documenting the area with more photos). Over the years, with the lids haphazardly screwed on, many of the tubes dried into solid little concrete-hard twists. I could only bear to get rid of a few. What if there is something I need to know about why he had seven tubes of sap green and four of alizarin crimson? What if I'll never be able to paint like Dad because I'm using the wrong color?

Kerry told me the other day that the studio is mine; I can change things. It felt like permission I didn't know I was waiting for.

I know she's right, so I pull everything out of the drawers, clear off the enamel trays, and reorganize, throwing away the ruined brushes, lining up the drawing pencils in one place, tossing a few more dried-up tubes of watercolor, and storing implements that I don't know how to use. Yet. I will learn.

I *am* learning. I've been driving an hour to Indy every week to take watercolor classes—from a woman with a style very different from Dad's. I enjoy her classes, but my favorite paintings are the ones I do on my own, standing at this table in my studio, using the brand of paints my teacher recommends and a type of brush he didn't have, finding a happy medium between what she's taught me and what I know from my years of proximity to Dad.

A few weeks after I cleaned out Dad's table, Tim and I started talking about downsizing—selling our home and moving into the studio. Kerry and Doug had cleaned out their house and moved to a townhome in Indianapolis, so the Compound had lost some of its luster. Once I make a decision, I tend to move fast—so six weeks later, the construction was underway and our house had a *For Sale* sign in the yard. Previously, I'd made tiny changes in the studio such as moving furniture around a nd painting the walls, but nothing major. Now, though, the changes would be bigger, bolder. It won't look like it did when Dad lived here.

The gallery in front will remain mostly the same—I moved the framing supplies back up front and the walls are even more full than before with the paintings I moved from home. When Dad lived here, he installed kitchen cabinets, a shower, and a stackable washer and dryer, but we are improving from there. I've made vision boards, chosen colors, and ordered a few pieces of furniture. We're adding a more efficient and less clunky heating system (no more metal boxes hanging from the ceiling), having hardwoods installed to match the floor in the front room, and adding a granite countertop and larger bathroom vanity.

I've donated numerous boxes of random items to Goodwill. Tim and I have hauled off loads of trash and given away metal tables, easels, and even an empty wasp's nest still attached to a branch that Dad had tucked in the rafters in back. I've also tackled the small stuff, like going through Mom's and Dad's Rolodexes. I did my due diligence, reverently reading each card in turn, then pulled out a handful of cards to keep (the jumble of all our addresses and numbers through the years, the golf buddies Dad called when he needed to fill out a foursome) and threw the rest away.

I've organized—but kept—most of the scraps of mat board because they will be useful to me. I've used some of the watercolor paper for my own painting experiments, but after seeing the difference while using the cheaper stuff for class, I realize what a treasure trove I have, so I'm holding on to the expensive paper until I'm a bit more accomplished.

A "Rob O'Dell Original Watercolors" sign still hangs in the front window, but now I have a separate area full of *my* paintings. I've even sold a few, because, as my instructor says, our goal as artists shouldn't be to create a huge collection of paintings for ourselves, but to share them with others. (She and Dad would agree about this.)

I know that Dad would still have suggestions (and likely criticisms) about my paintings, but I'm conceding that, as my friends tell me, perhaps the apple really didn't fall far from the tree. Dad wasn't perfect, either. Every painting wasn't great, or else we wouldn't have needed to discuss whether a painting was a "good one."

Sometimes *ordinary* is good enough. It allows room to imagine something more. Something better. It gives you room to breathe and find yourself, on the way to becoming extraordinary.

I feel certain Dad would be proud to meet the newest Artist in Ladoga, Indiana.

EPILOGUE

It's a clear summer day in late June of 2024, just one month shy of seven years since Dad died. I'm gathering the last of our things from our house in Crawfordsville. It feels different without furniture and rugs absorbing the sounds, but it makes it easy to admire the structure that originally drew me in. I still love the upgrades we made, the colors, the patterned kitchen tile. It still feels peaceful, but it's no longer ours, and that's okay with me.

In the dining room, I pull down the winter creek painting that hung over the piano, which we moved a few weeks ago. It was the cover image for one of Dad's brochures—at least two versions ago—so it's been in this same spot since he gave it to me at least 14 years ago. He did so many in this style, but this is still one of my favorites.

My eyes always go straight to the lower-right side of the painting, to the smooth, snowy expanse of the creek bed draped with blue-purple shadows. I want to wrap myself in that color, pull a cloak of it tight around me. So peaceful. On the left bank of the creek stands a stately sycamore tree, its white bark in stark contrast to the deep blue sky and sepia expanse of trees behind it. A few individual trees, not much more than crooked lines, are lifted out of the dark brown background. Sunlight reflects off the bark and casts harsh shadows across the trunk. In the foreground, a pile of downed branches and rocks is loosely suggested, a sapling growing out of it. Details abound—clumps of grass on the banks, splatters of weeds poking through the snow, a fallen branch extending over the creek. Along the left bank, the dark blue water shimmers along the undulating edges of the ice, but on the right side, the surface is frozen smooth. You could walk on it, if you wanted to disturb the unmarred white drifts. As the creek moves into the distance, it is softened by a magical mist that seems to go on and on, without end.

I lean the painting near the back door while I gather the remaining art. The house is now empty; we sign the papers this afternoon and officially close this chapter. I carry the paintings to my vehicle. The winter creek is last, and I place it face down on top of the pile. As I do, I notice Dad's handwriting on the back, his name written above the painting title.

And in the title, I hear Dad's voice and I see his life—and mine. It is a benediction, a blessing, clear and simple, understated and true. It's *What Comes Naturally*.

END NOTES

1. Kathy Becker, "An alumnus shares his art," *Herald & Review*, Decatur, Illinois, April 19, 1985
2. Gaildene Hamilton, "A Rustic Magic Flows From the Hands of Rob O'Dell," *Journal-Review*, Crawfordsville, Indiana, April 23, 1970
3. Ann Hulett, "Sketches of Three Indiana Artists," Junior League of Indianapolis newsletter, November 1973
4. Psalm 27:4-5, *NLT*
5. Gaildene Hamilton, Year's Trial Becomes Successful Venture," *Montgomery Magazine*, Crawfordsville, Indiana, February 1977
6. Israel Houghton, "Moving Forward"
7. Herb Slodounik, "Back Home in Indiana with Rob O'Dell," *Sunday Herald & Review*, Decatur, Illinois, April 7, 1974
8. Kathy Becker, "An alumnus shares his art," *Herald & Review*, Decatur, Illinois, April 19, 1985
9. Jim Vorel, "Park works for artist," *Herald & Review*, Decatur, Illinois, September 21, 2013
10. Gaildene Hamilton, "Year's Trial Becomes Successful Venture," *Montgomery Magazine*, Crawfordsville, Indiana, February 1977
11. Herb Slodounik, "Back Home in Indiana with Rob O'Dell," *Sunday Herald & Review*, Decatur, Illinois, April 7, 1974
12. Jim Vorel, "Retrospective shows the farmer in O'Dell: Artist finds inspiration in Central Illinois," *Herald & Review*, Decatur, Illinois, February 4, 2011
13. Brochure for The Midwest Landscape show at Krannert Graduate School of Management, Purdue University, 1981
14. Jim Vorel, "Retrospective shows the farmer in O'Dell: Artist finds inspiration in Central Illinois," *Herald & Review*, Decatur, Illinois, February 4, 2011
15. "Art," *Journal and Courier*, Lafayette, Indiana, September 18, 1994
16. Gaildene Hamilton, "Year's Trial Becomes Successful Venture," *Montgomery Magazine*, Crawfordsville, Indiana, February 1977
17. Marion Garmel, "O'Dell Develops Love For Abstract," *Indianapolis News*, April 10, 1982
18. "Art," *Journal and Courier*, Lafayette, Indiana, September 18, 1994

ACKNOWLEDGMENTS

Memoir is tricky to write because our minds are fallible, so like most writers of memoir, I've had to recreate conversations and fill in gaps in my memories. I have done my best to be factual and accurate—and even if some details or descriptions may not be exact, the emotions, stories, and tone of the conversations are as true to my memory as I could make them. All of the articles and brochures I've quoted were found in boxes throughout the studio, but many of the clippings were saved without the publication name, article title, or date. Any errors, mistakes, or omissions are mine alone, and some names have been changed for privacy.

I owe a debt of gratitude to the writers who interviewed Dad and reviewed his shows, because I learned things through them that I had not known. Thanks to friends and family and visitors to the studio who talked to me about Dad, and to those who encouraged me to put these stories on paper—including Lisa Wheeler, an early reader and dear friend. Thanks also to Cheri Clark for her careful proofreading.

I never would have completed this book without the Wayward Writers. Steve Charles, Maria Reynolds-Weir, and Gwynn Wills, you have made this book so much better than it ever could have been without you. Your insights and kindness and passion for the craft of writing inspire me in so many ways, and my life is so much richer with you in it.

Thanks to my husband, Tim, for his patience with me and all of my scheduled writers groups and events that get in the way of us not being able to find a thing to watch on TV.

Finally, I want to thank the other pretty/smart one for simply being herself. Kerry, I have to say, I never imagined you would someday become my best friend. (Or that, once in a while, we'd actually hug.) I hate that we no longer share a driveway, but I'm grateful that we have each other.

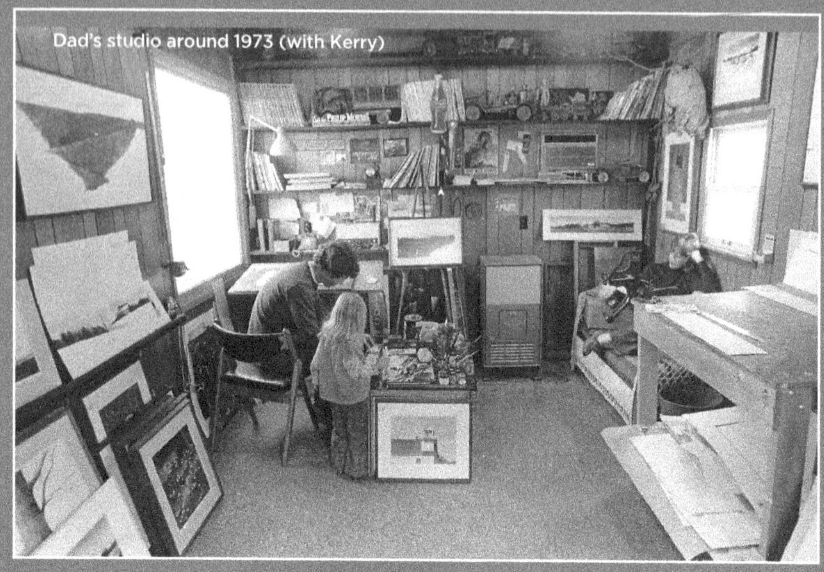

Dad's studio around 1973 (with Kerry)

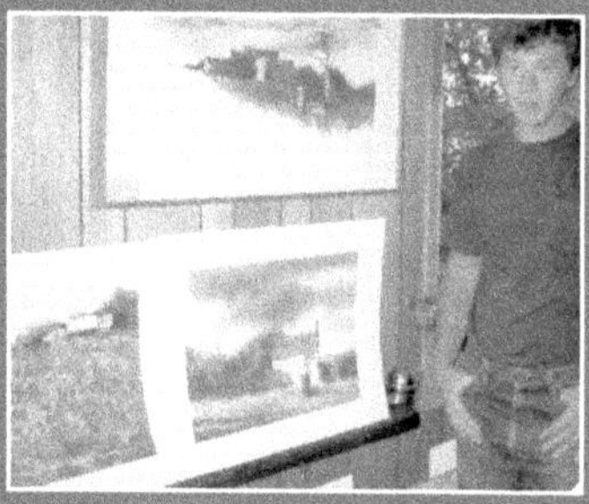
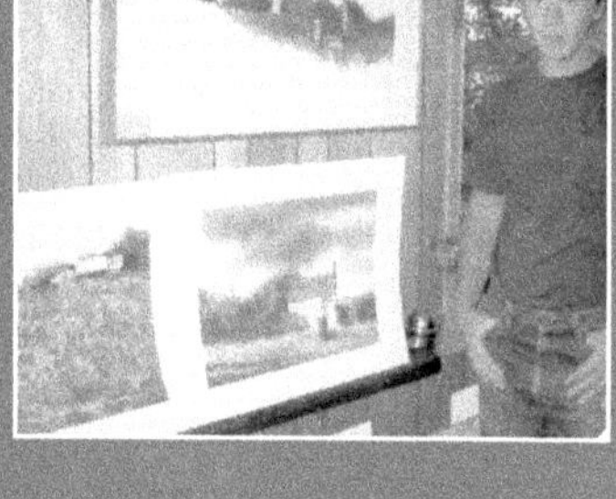

Early '70s

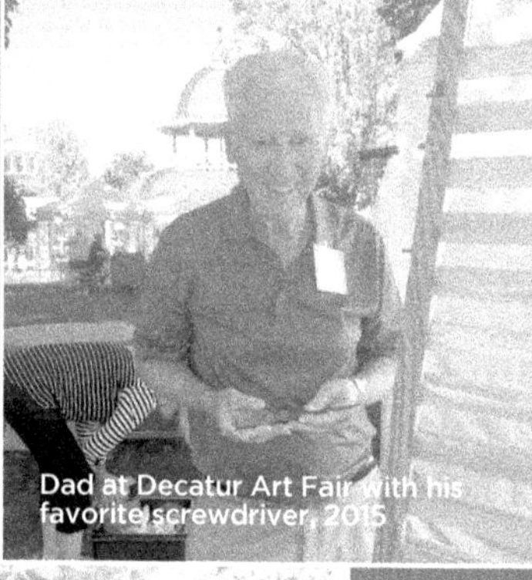

Dad at Decatur Art Fair with his favorite screwdriver, 2015

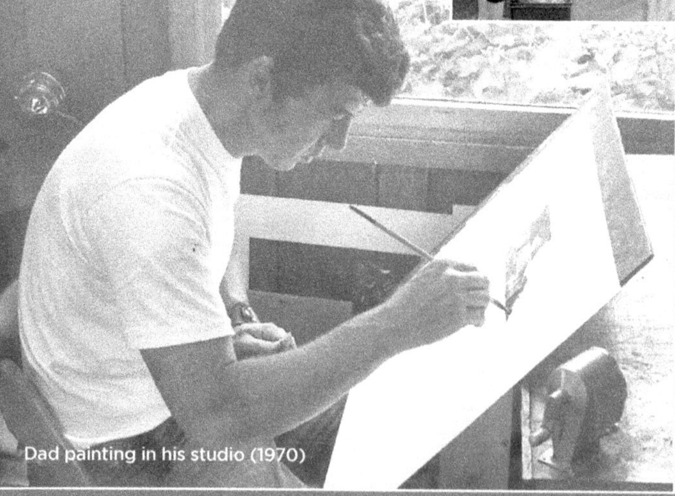

Dad painting in his studio (1970)

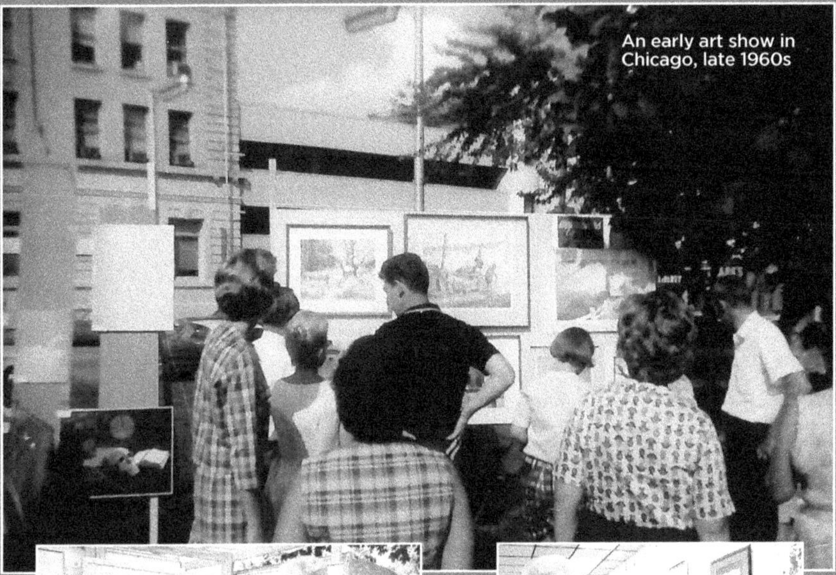

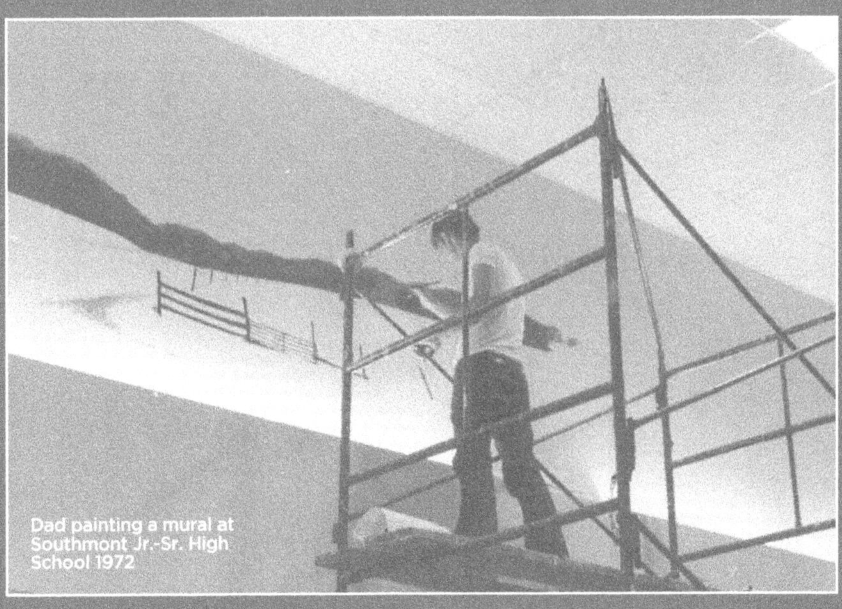

An early art show in
Chicago, late 1960s
1999 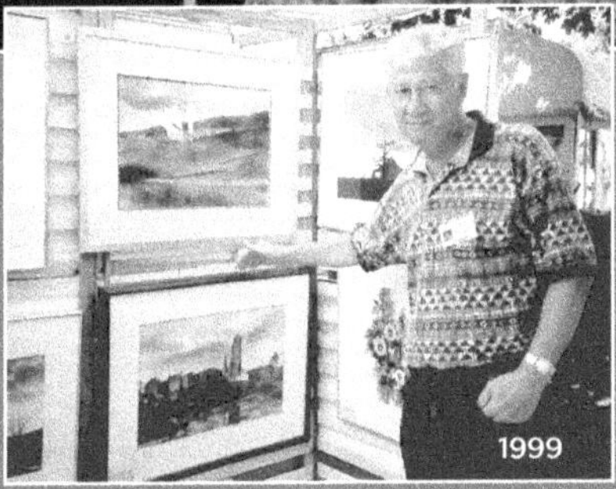
2016 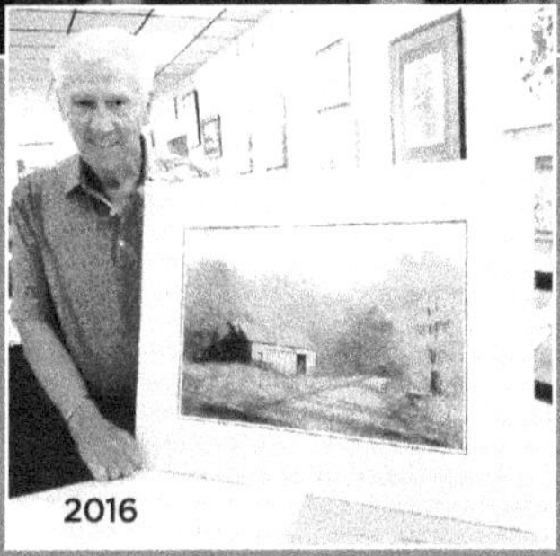
Dad painting a mural at
Southmont Jr.-Sr. High
School 1972

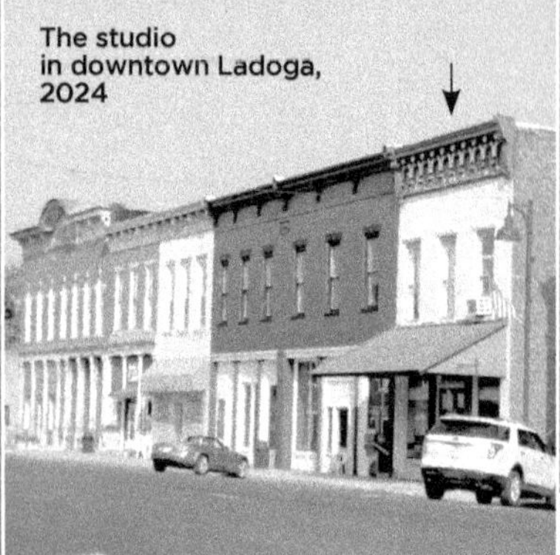

The studio
in downtown Ladoga,
2024

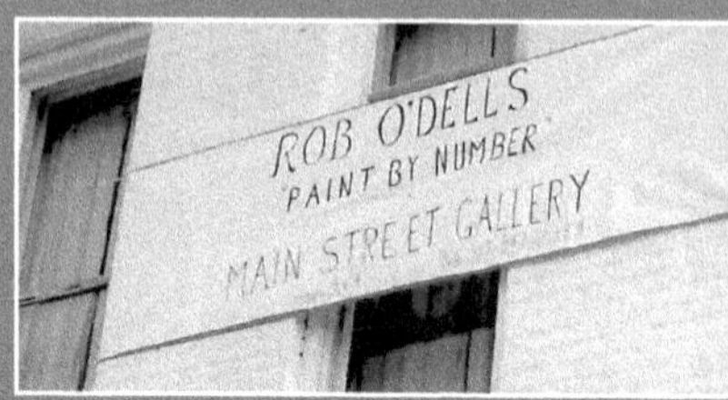

Hand-lettered banner
while Dad was renovating
the studio in Ladoga, 1990

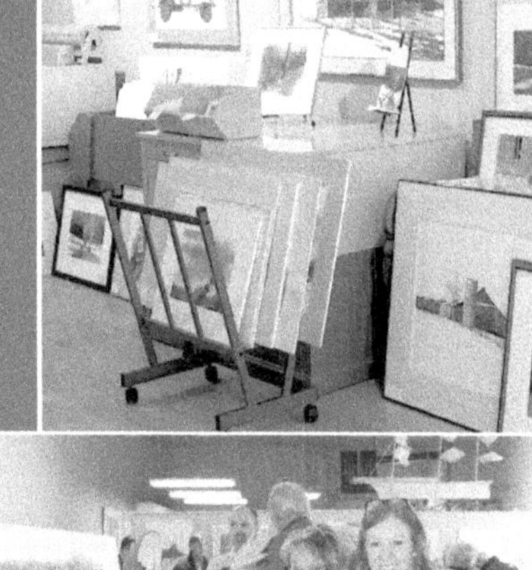

Before the sale, 2017

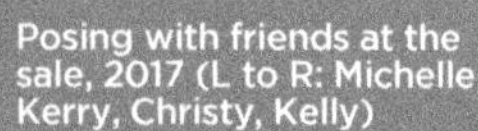

Posing with friends at the
sale, 2017 (L to R: Michelle,
Kerry, Christy, Kelly)

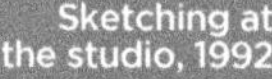

Sketching at
the studio, 1992

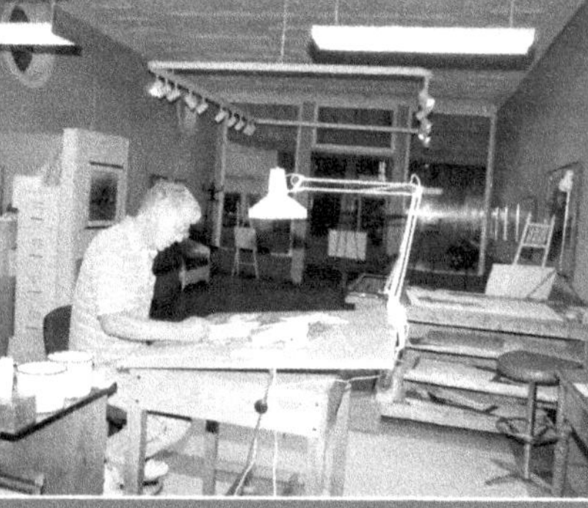

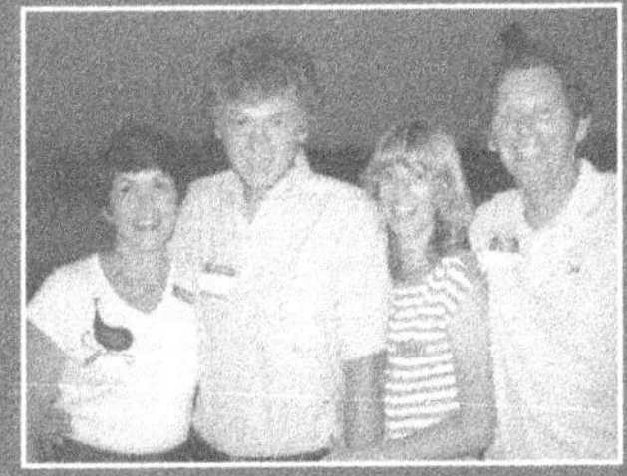

Left: Jeannine, Dad, Mom, and Jim in the early '80s. Jeannine is the one who mailed the card to "The Artist, Ladoga, Indiana."

Below: Dad at an art show near St. Louis, near the same time.

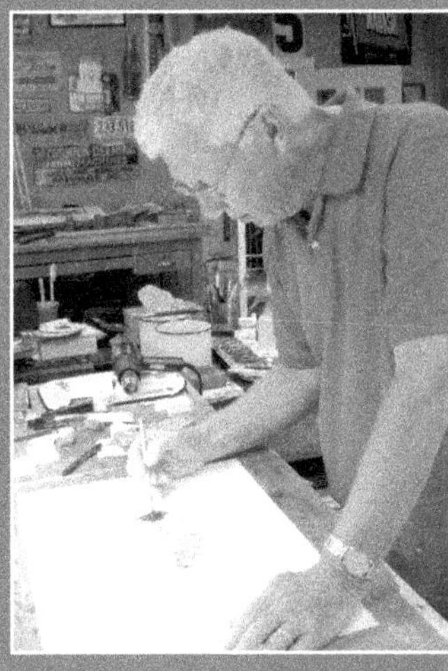

Painting in his studio, approx. 2010

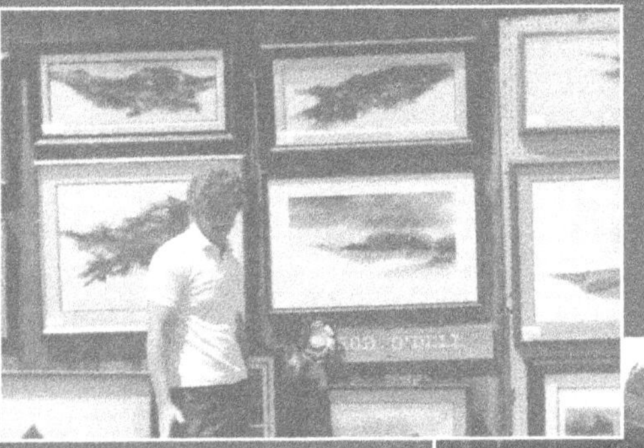

Dad doing a demonstration for Reilly and Anna, 2006

Dad and Rita in Florida, 2017

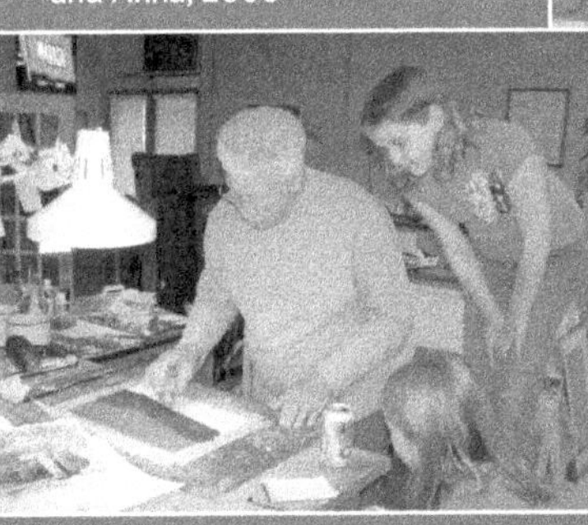

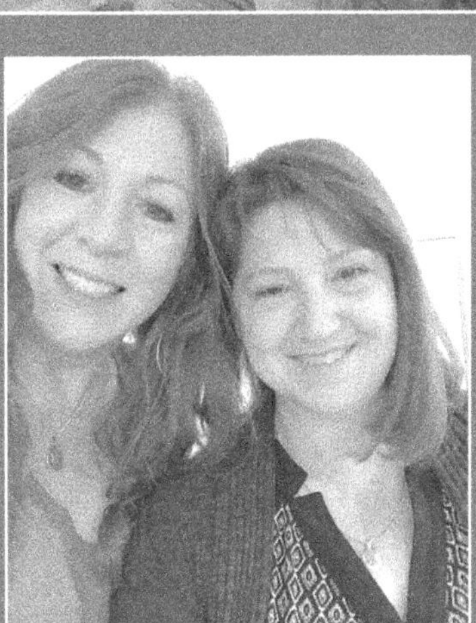

Terry (Dad's younger brother and Kathy's dad) with my dad, early '80s

The KAO Club (L to R: Kelly, Kathy)

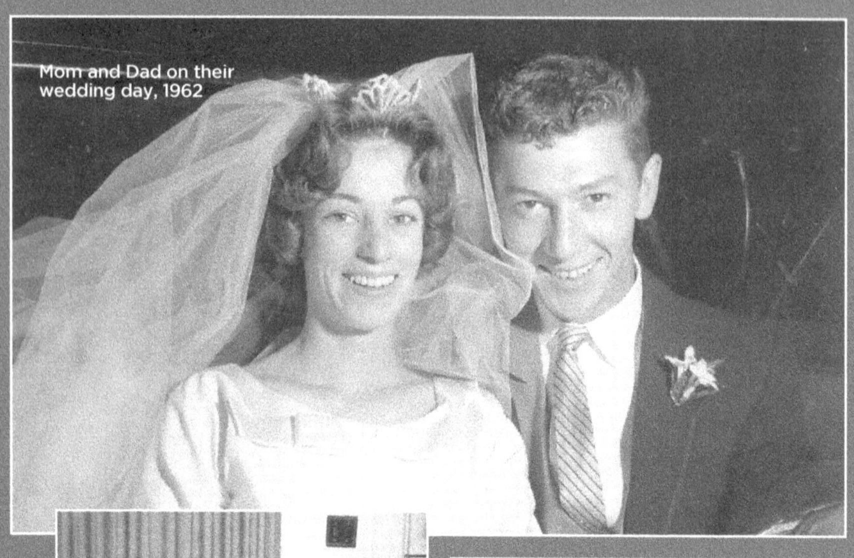

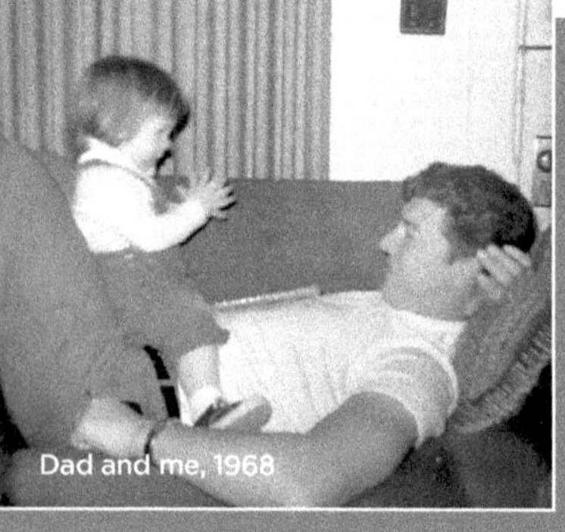

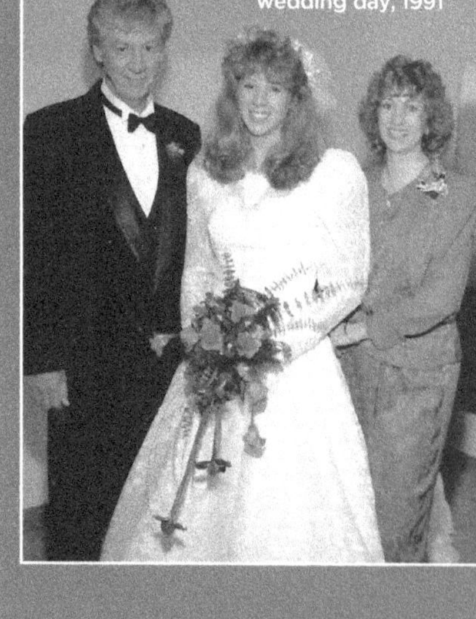

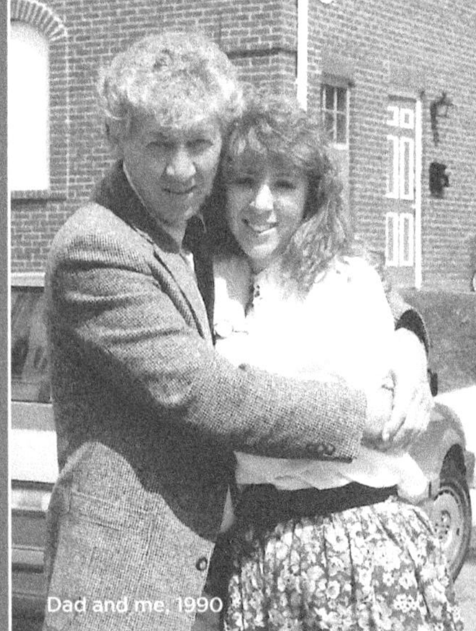

Dad and me, 1970

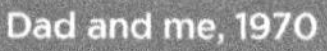

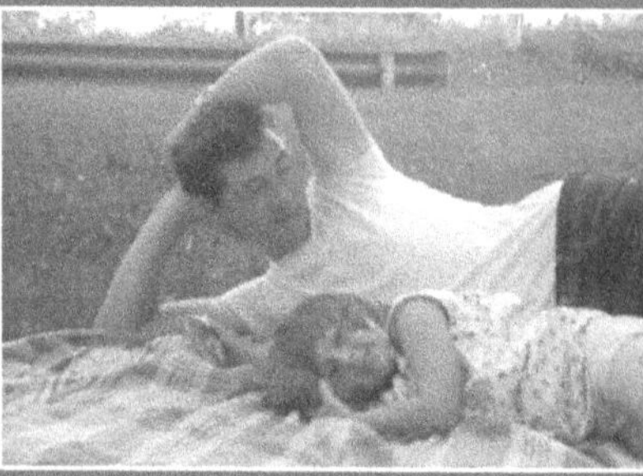

The whole family, 2003
(Front row, L to R: Reilly, Mom, Dad, Bobby, Anna,
Katie. Back row: Luke, Doug, Kerry, Kelly, Tim)

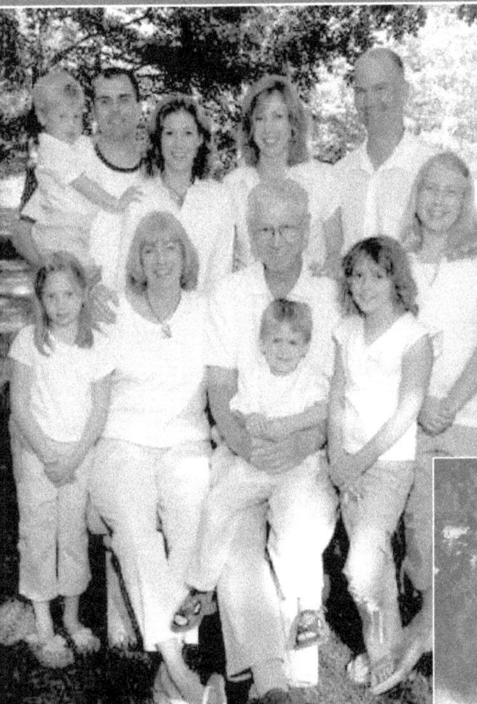

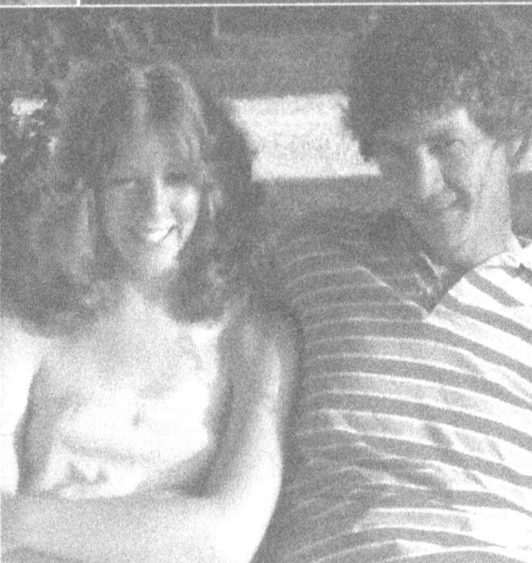

Above: Kerry, Rob, Ann,
and Kelly, 2010

Below: Kelly and Rob, 1982

Below: Christmas 2010 (Back row, L to R:
Katie, Bobby, Kelly, Tim, Ann, Rob. Front:
Anna, Reilly, Luke, Kerry, and Doug)

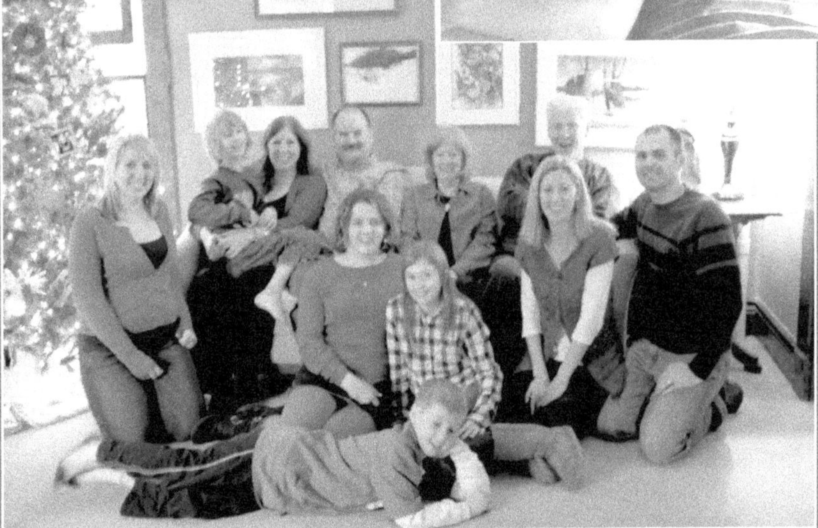

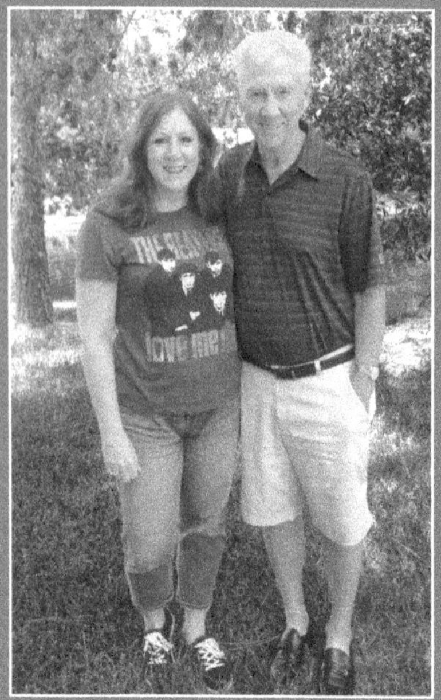

Dad and me after his cancer
treatment in 2014

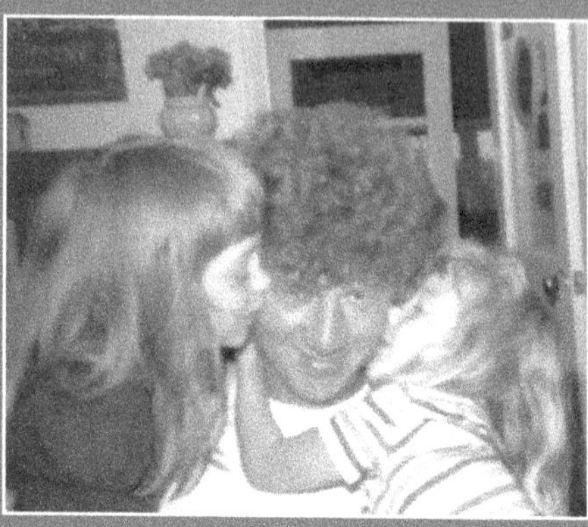

Mom and Dad with Kerry,
Doug, Reilly, and Luke, 2009

Trying to be just like my dad, 1970

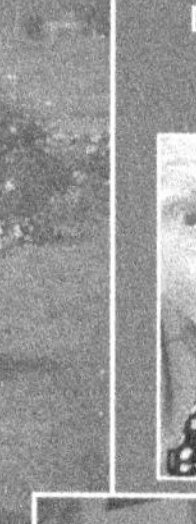

Dad and
Reilly

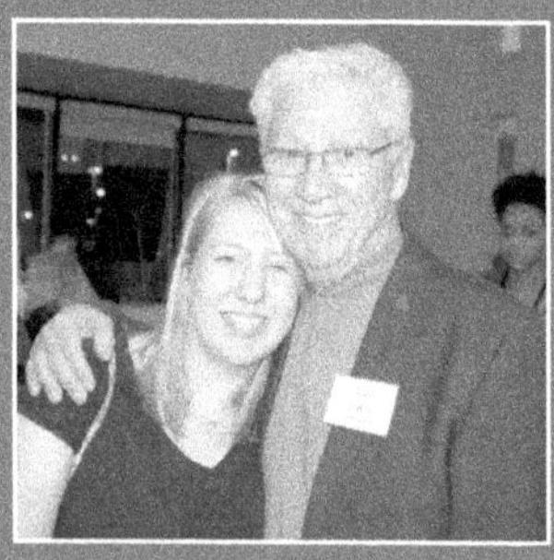

Dad and
Katie at a
retrospective
show in
Decatur, 2010

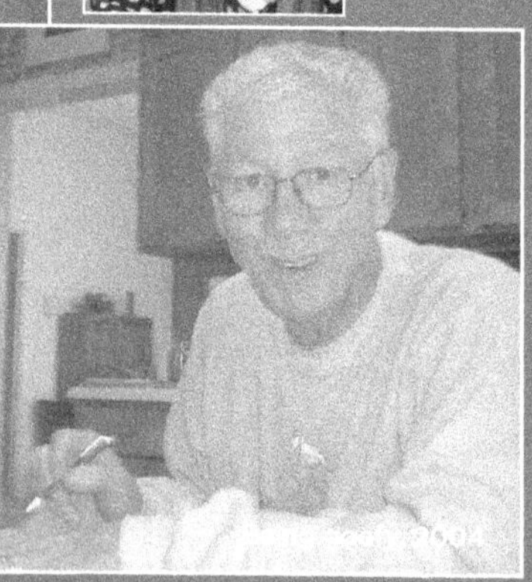

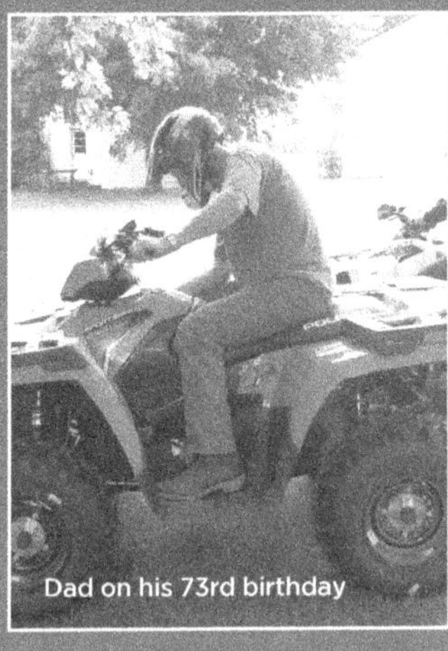

Dad on his 73rd birthday

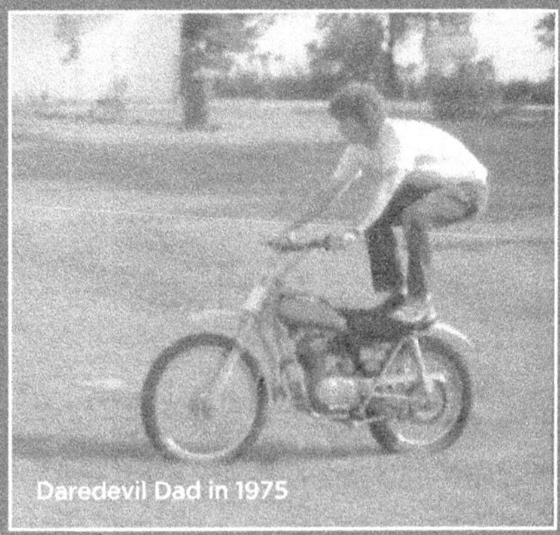

Daredevil Dad in 1975

Dad with Anna and
Reilly, 1998

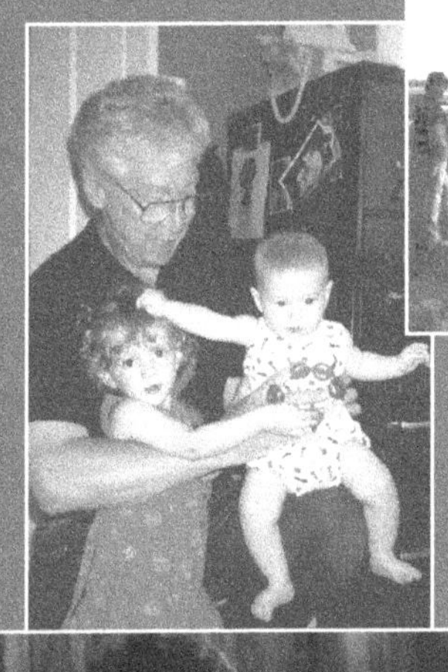

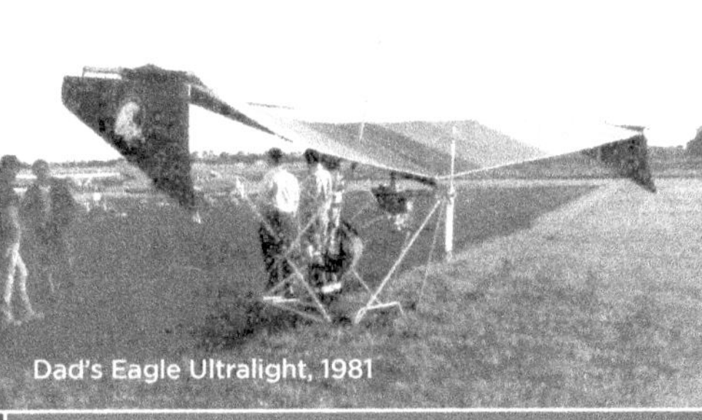

Dad's Eagle Ultralight, 1981

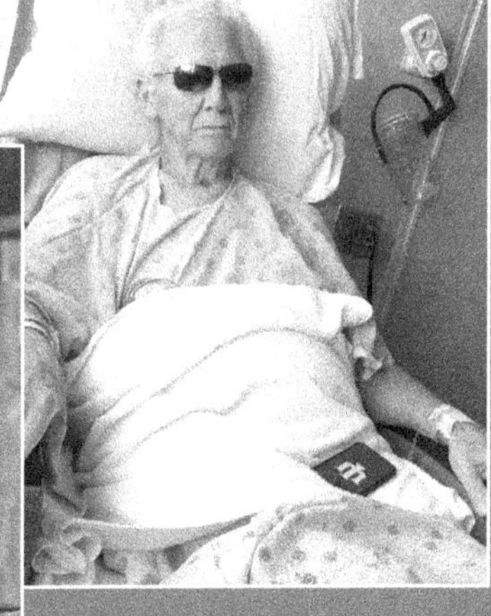

Wearing sunglasses
in the hospital,
June 2017

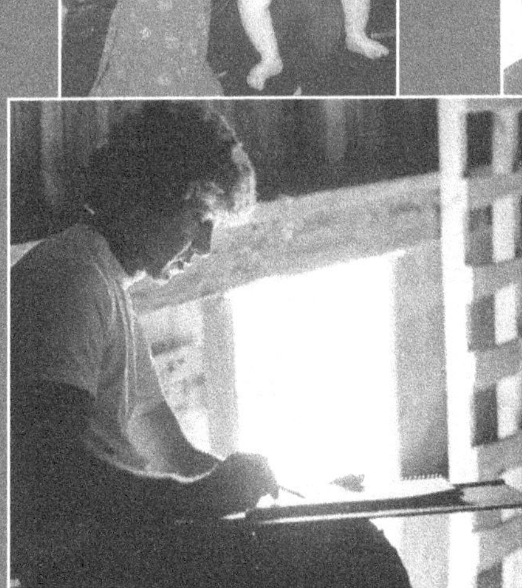

Sketching, 1976

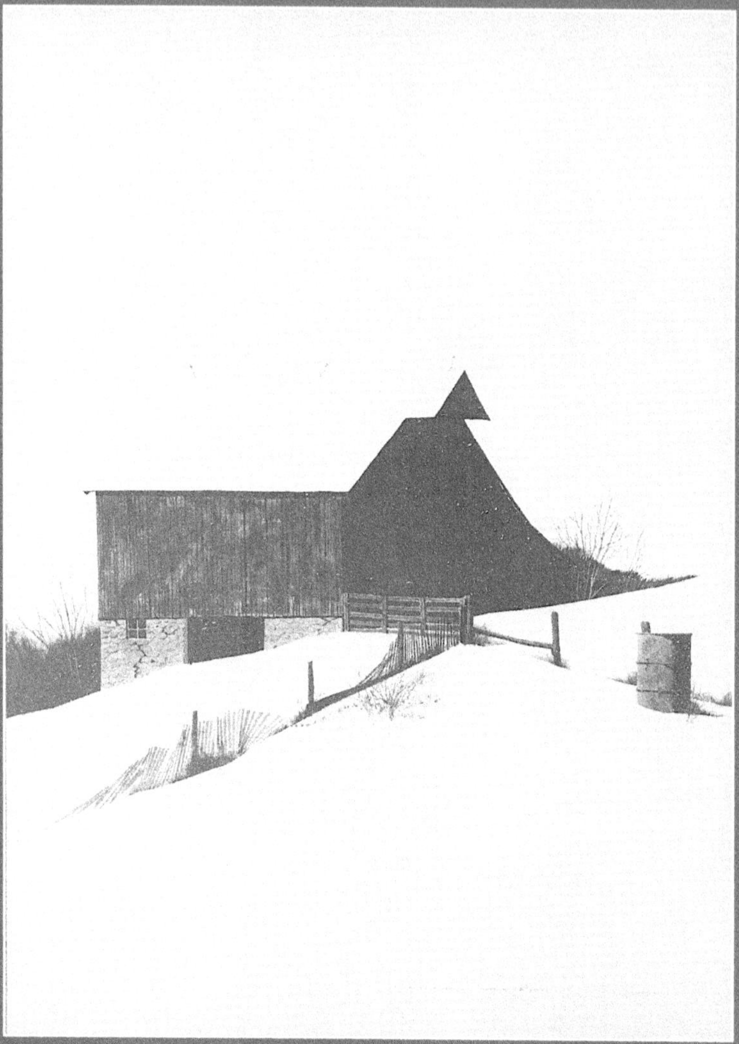

Sugar Tree Farm

Winter Gate

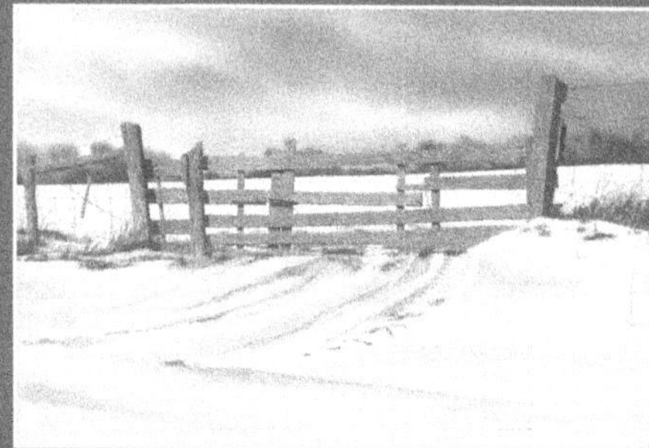

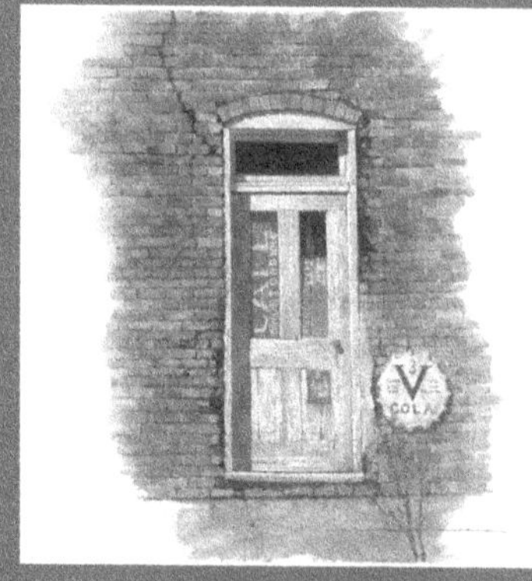

V Cola